Volume I

ANCIENT MIRRORS of WOMANHOOD

Our Goddess and Heroine Heritage

The original Sibylline Books were the sacred records of the statements of the ancient Sibyl priestesses who foretold the future, and passed judgement by ancient Goddess law. Although the Sibylline Books were supposedly destroyed in the early Christian period, the wisdom and holy decrees that were written in them still live with us today.

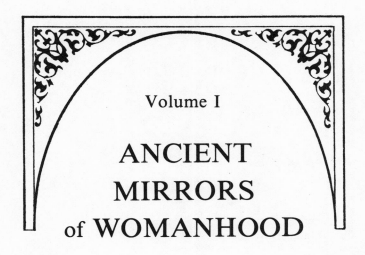

Volume I

ANCIENT
MIRRORS
of WOMANHOOD

Our Goddess and Heroine Heritage

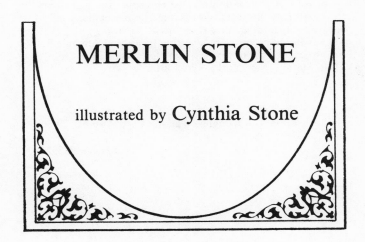

MERLIN STONE

illustrated by Cynthia Stone

NEW SIBYLLINE BOOKS

First Printing November 1979/9979
Second Printing February 1980/9980

Library of Congress Catalog Card Number 79-90027

ISBN 0-9603352-0-X

*Typeset in Times Roman and Palatino
by Janet Blair, Waterfall Graphics, New York City*

TABLE OF CONTENTS

TABLE OF CONTENTS

TABLE OF CONTENTS

Volume II of ANCIENT MIRRORS of WOMAN—
HOOD includes our Goddess and Heroine Heritage
from: the Native Americans of North America, Scandinavia, Egypt, India, Japan, Sumer, Greece, The
Aegean and the full bibliography for both volumes.

preface

Nothing would be more interesting in connection with the WOMAN'S BIBLE *than a comparative study of the accounts of creation held by people of different races and faiths.*

CLARA COLBY—COMMENTS ON GENESIS
THE WOMAN'S BIBLE 1895

There has been an ever growing consciousness of the advantages of being able to personally identify with positive images and role models, in developing the self-esteem that encourages the fulfillment of individual potential. This consciousness has made us increasingly aware of the general lack of strong and positive images of women, in the literature and traditions, both sacred and secular, of our own society. In reaction to these realizations, some of us have been searching in the obscure records of the last few centuries, reclaiming the histories of important women who have been all but ignored. Others have been developing fantasies of the future, inventing new images of woman, in the hope that they will be there for the women of today and tomorrow. These efforts and contributions are of immense value to the building of a body of positive female role models, but is this truly all that is available to us, as we search for role models and inspiring images of womanhood?

The hopeful request quoted above, made by Clara Colby, editor of the nineteenth century *Woman's Tribune,* was written as women were initially confronting and challenging the gender biases, and roles of women, in the Hebrew Scripture (the Old Testament), and the New Testament—and the negative effects that various aspects of these religious scriptures have had upon women. With just a slight knowledge of Mexican, Scandinavian, and Algonquin beliefs, Clara Colby observed that images of womanhood seemed to be somewhat different in the religious lore of non-Judeo-Christian cultures, and thus suggested that a further exploration of this lore might produce some valuable insight and information.

Yet many women of today suspect, or even firmly believe, that a study of the religious accounts "of different races and faiths" would probably only result in finding that womanhood has always been perceived and portrayed as secondary to manhood. Statements, some even by well educated feminists, often convey the idea that if actual accounts from societies that regarded woman as powerful, as supreme creator, or as important culture heroine, ever did exist, such information is now buried in the dust of prehistory—a Goddess name here or there all that is left to ponder.

The gradual formation of these attitudes has been accomplished in various ways. One has been to confine grade school and high school studies primarily to what has existed in relatively recent, generally Caucasian, male-oriented societies. Another has been through reassurances by university teachers, and texts, that if some cultures had viewed woman as supreme deity, or that an accompanying female clergy had deeply influenced moral and social structure, indication of this occurs only in the scantiest (and therefore inconclusive) of references. A more subtle factor at work has been the rejection of all things 'religious' or 'spiritual', by many who might agree with the need for finding positive images of woman, but would prefer not to discover them in other than secular sources—thus ignoring the power and influence that contemporary male-oriented religions have upon even the most atheistic or agnostic of women today. Though stemming from an almost antithetical set of values, the above attitude manifests itself in a manner that is almost identical to that of the orthodox or devout Catholic, Jew, Protestant, or Muslim, who chooses to ignore any information that might bring long held religious beliefs into question. An even further buttressing of these attitudes has been provided by the few scholars who were aware of a wider body of knowledge on the subject of Goddess reverence, and/or female

2

clergy, in a particular period or area, but continually referred to this material as 'mythology'—thereby relegating it to a topic closer to fairy tale or fantasy, than the religious beliefs of a particular society. These factors, along with several others, have combined to quite efficiently smother the fires of motivation to search. After all, it is pointless to look for something that one has been taught to believe does not exist, is sinful, or is not especially pertinent or meaningful to 'real' life.

Just casually scanning this first volume of *ANCIENT MIRRORS of WOMANHOOD—Our Goddess and Heroine Heritage,* the reader cannot help but observe that assurances of non-existence, or very minimal existence, of information about woman as deity, as clergy, or as important culture heroine, were simply not true. Though widely scattered in brief, often fragmentary, references, a large body of detailed information about woman as deity, often as supreme, omnipotent deity, has long existed in the written literature of many cultures, and in the oral traditions of many others. Perhaps, in our contemporary quest for role models and positive images, the accounts of woman as Goddess, or as culture heroine, that reveal portraits of woman as strong, determined, wise, courageous, powerful, adventurous, and able to surmount difficult obstacles to achieve set goals, may be of even greater interest and value for women of today. Yet nearly all of the information included in these two volumes has been completely ignored in our educations, and in popular literary themes, while in the few, usually obscure, texts that do include any information, it is most often covered in the most cursory of references.

Gathering the material presented in these volumes has required many years of patient gleaning of fragments of information, from an enormous number of archaeological and ethnological studies, and literature as diverse as the Prose Edda to the Shan Hai Ching. Thus each of the fourteen sections in these two volumes is the result of lengthy research, and correlation of information, about images of woman as Goddess and culture heroine, as they have been known in various cultures. It is these generally unfamiliar images, these proud portraits of womanhood, discovered and brought together as a body of information, that comprise *ANCIENT MIRRORS of WOMANHOOD—Our Goddess and Heroine Heritage.*

For those like myself, who suspected the existence of this material (although to be honest, I never expected to discover so much), these volumes will affirm those suspicions—and I hope bring joy at the reclamation of these treasures of our woman heritage, that belong to all women. For those who believed that such images had perhaps once existed, but had been lost to us forever, I hope that these volumes will bring the satisfaction of having long lost possessions returned. For any who had been convinced that images of woman, such as the ones included here, could only have existed in contemporary feminist fantasy, it is my hope that the spiritual wisdom, inherent in many of the accounts, will be of help in coping with the rearrangements of basic realities that such readers might need to make.

Writing this preface as the final pages, before this manuscript is sent off to be printed, I admit to feelings similar to those of waiting to watch loved ones open presents for which they had yearned—but never really expected. Although it has taken some eighty-five years to finally fulfill the hopeful request of Clara Colby, I type these last lines with thoughts of those courageous and perceptive women, who dared to confront Judaic and Christian thought, as it negatively affected the lives of women—the twenty three who were responsible for *The Woman's Bible*—and dedicate this book to their memory.

introduction

he ancient Akkadians wrote that the Goddess known as Mami pinched off fourteen pieces of clay, and making seven of them into women, making seven of them into men, She placed life upon the earth. The Dahomeans said that the Goddess known as Mawu built the mountains and the valleys, put the sun in the sky, and placed life upon the earth that She had made. Chinese texts record that the Goddess known as Nu Kwa patched the earth and the heavens, when they had been shattered, and thus restored harmony and balance to the universe. Mexican records reveal that the Goddess known as Coatlicue lived high upon a mountain, in a misty cloud, and there She gave birth to the moon, the sun, and all other deities. Hesiod wrote that the Goddess known as Gaia gave birth to heaven, and mating with heaven, She brought forth the other deities. Sumerian texts tell us that the Goddess known as Nammu was called upon as the mother who gave birth to heaven and earth, and that She supervised the creation of all life by Her daughter Ninmah. Australians explain, that it is to the Goddess known as Kunapipi, that our spirit returns upon death, thus remaining with Her until the

5

next rebirth. Indian records state that if the Goddess known as Devi were to close Her eyes even for a second, the entire universe would disappear. In Egyptian hieroglyphics, it was written that the Goddess known as Au Sept was the oldest of the old, She from whom all becoming came forth. Navajo people know that Changing Woman is sacred Nature, in all that She unfolds.

These are just a few of the images of woman as deity, primal force of existence, as they have been known in various cultures. Can it be completely coincidental that the multitude of accounts of female as deity have been classified as 'mythology', rather than as sacred and religious scripture? It seems that there are few people, in contemporary western societies, who are able or willing to perceive the creation stories and accounts of deities, that were written on the clay tablets or papyri of ancient cultures, as truly 'religious' concepts, and even fewer who are willing to regard the beliefs of the tribes of Dahomey in Africa, the Toba of Argentina, or the Chinese of ancient Chi' province, as anything more than interesting mythology, or intellectual curiosities.

Writers, with psychological concerns, often approach the spiritual beliefs of other cultures with scholarly interest, believing that they can discover patterns, observe universal archetypes, or analyze the underlying meaning of symbols—all the while referring to the accounts as curious, intriguing, creative—but nonetheless, mythology. Yet the accounts of deities of other cultures, separated from western religious thought by chronology, geography, or levels of technological development, are obviously much more than mythology, as we generally comprehend the term. They reveal spiritual contemplations, and religious concepts, that developed within various cultures, just as the stories in Hebrew Scripture developed within early Hebrew society, The New Testament within early Christian society, and the Koran within early Islamic society. Some claim that it is a 'primitive' quality, an 'irrationality', in the events and images, that define an account as myth, yet how many of the people who make these claims or definitions would refer to the Genesis account of creation, the account of the opening up of the Red Sea, or Jesus walking upon the water and feeding five thousand people with five loaves of bread and two fish—as mythology?

The reader might ask, 'What is wrong with referring to these accounts of other cultures as mythology, since Webster's Unabridged Dictionary defines myth as "A story of great but unknown age which originally embodied a belief regarding some fact or phenomenon of experience . . . " and as " . . . an ancient legend of a god, a hero, the origin of a race . . .", while mythology is simply defined as "The science which treats of myths . . . "

My reply would be that Webster (1913) goes on to define mythology as " . . . the collective myths which describe the gods of a *heathen* people . . . " while at the same time defining the word theology as "The science of God or of religion; the science which treats of the existence, character and attributes of God, his laws and government, the doctrines *we* are to believe, and the duties *we* are to practice . . . " I might add that the more contemporary American Heritage Dictionary defines myth as " . . . a traditional story presenting supernatural beings, ancestors or heroes that serve as primordial types in a *primitive* view of the world", and offers as a second definition, " . . . *any fictitious or imaginary* story, person or thing.", while it defines theology as "The study of the nature of God and *religious truth."* (My italics)

Aside from the so called generic usage of the male terms— gods, ancestors and heroes—and the differentiation implicit in the uses of upper and lower case G/g's for God/god, the inclusion of the words "heathen" and "primitive" make it quite clear that mythology is to be regarded as the accounts of *others,* while theology is to be viewed as "the doctrines we are to believe", and "religious truth". Nowhere, in these definitions of mythology, does the word religion even appear.

Though heathen literally means from the heath, as pagan is derived from the Latin *paganus,* a country person—both heathen and pagan are defined by Webster as *other* than Christian, Jew, or Mohammedan. It is in this way that the distinction between how we are to perceive the religious beliefs of those whose sacred accounts are classified as mythology, and those whose are to be considered as religious truth, is semantically structured, far from church, temple, or mosque. One might be tempted to ask if these three major religions have qualified as non-heathen simply because they happen to be in the small minority of faiths that revere no female deities within their beliefs, each having made overt efforts to suppress earlier Goddess reverence—and to wonder if, when so called primitive people of today are converted to Christianity, their acceptance of the New Testament then classifies that scripture as mythology?

Surely, in the midst of this semantic ethnocentricity, it is time to question these divisions, between what is to be regarded as mythology, and what are to be considered as sacred accounts and beliefs. We must begin to be conscious of the cultural blinders, the cultural static, that keep so many of us from acknowledging that the spiritual and religious beliefs of others, past and present, were or are as valid and integral a body of "religious truth" in their lives, as Hebrew Scripture, the New Testament, and the Koran, are to Jews, Christians, and Muslims.

For the many who have rejected all religious beliefs and literature, the semantic boundary lines between myth and religious accounts are perhaps not so clearly defined, but readers who may regard *all* religious literature as myth—and as such not worthy of serious interest, or careful examination—may be embracing yet another form of tunnel vision, one that is aware of little else but that which is directly in front of it.

In reading the following accounts, that are included in these volumes, I ask that all readers attempt to approach the evidence of the religious beliefs of all cultures with as open a mind as possible. They provide a body of information that allows us to broaden our knowledge and comprehension of the vast diversity of human thoughts and ideas about origins and existence, and, of especial importance to us today, about the diversity of roles and images of woman, as perceived within many cultures—information that has for the most part been ignored in general literature and education.

The task of collecting information about each image of woman included in these volumes— as Goddess or as heroine—is one in which I have now been involved for almost fifteen years. It has certainly been a long lasting task, but seldom an uninteresting one. Searching for the evidence of reverence for deity as female, and for accounts of legendary heroines, from nearly every area of the world, from people of every racial group, has been a treasure hunt with all the excitement, suspense, and pleasure, that such a term implies. Each clue, each lead to another source, each discovery of a specific fact, each additional fragment of knowledge about deified or heroic images of women, has been an ever refueling energy source, that has never run dry throughout my many years of research.

How could any woman, raised and living in a male-dominated, male-oriented society, fail to remain fascinated, while continually discovering gems of woman heritage such as: an account of a High Priestess of the Moon Goddess Jezanna from the Mashona people of Zimbabwe, explaining how she alone revised an important religious ritual; Chou and Han period texts of the Goddess in China, that describe Her role in structuring the harmony and patterns of the universe; an account of a welcoming ritual into the society of womanhood among the Cuna people of Panama—for young women reaching menarche; Egyptian records that describe the Goddess Maat as the very essence of the rhythm and order of the universe; Tantric Indian texts that explain Shakti Goddess power as that which causes all action to occur; a poem of the poetess Avvaiyar to her woman lover, written in the Tamil language in the city of Madura in the first century B.C. of India; or the text of an ancient ritual that included a temple gift offering of a vulva carved of the precious stone, lapis lazuli, for the Goddess Ishtar in Semitic Mesopotamia.

As I continued my research, the joy of finding accounts of images of woman as creator of the universe, provider and teacher of law, possessor and prophet of ultimate wisdom, initiator or inventor of important cultural developments, or as courageous warrior—continually enticed me to carry on with the search—ever on the edge of new discoveries of images of womanhood, that were far different from those generally familiar in our society. There was a gift for every woman, of every racial background, of every age, of every temperament, a proud heritage, precious mirrors of womanhood that I was gradually accumulating in the chest in which I stored my ever more numerous notes—until the day that this treasure would be shared with all women.

Many people of today, even many with university educations, think of Goddess reverence as having existed only in prehistoric periods (some doubting its existence at all). Yet archaeological evidence attests to the fact that at the initial period of the development of writing (the Jemdet Nasr period of Sumer—about 3200 B.C.), and for at least *thirty five centuries* after that development, that first brought us into the period of written history—the Goddess was not only revered, but honoured in *written* tablets and papyri. Written prayers, written descriptions of rituals, written titles and epithets, and religious scripture (generally referred to as epic legends), have been excavated from their long hidden burial places, to provide more than ample witness to Goddess reverence in *historical* periods. Although archaeological evidence almost certainly assures us that Goddess worship existed for many millenia prior to these historical periods, the erroneous belief, that worship of the Goddess existed *only* in prehistoric periods, must be laid to rest, in light of the mass of actual written evidence. We may want to question the possibility of racial bias, as well as gender bias, in the initiation and maintenance of the idea that the study of Ancient History should begin with Homer and Classical Greece, when writing had been developed, and in use, for over *two thousand years* before that time. Perhaps, as with the perceptual division between myth and sacred scripture, the human mind is capable of intellectually absorbing factual knowledge— while at the same time avoiding full comprehension of that knowledge for various emotional reasons.

After about eight years of research on deified and heroic images of women, I began to write about what I had found, and was soon working on an introduction to point out the similarities, the differences, the influences and transitions within the context of historical data, and the effects of migrations and invasions, upon Goddess reverence. It was this 'introduction' that eventually became a volume in itself, originally published as *The Paradise Papers—The Story of the Suppression of Women's Rites* in London, later published as *When God Was A Woman* in the U.S. But I had already collected a vast amount of material, evidence of Goddess worship, and heroic accounts of legendary mortal women, from nearly every area of the world. This was the material that *When God Was A Woman* had initially been based upon, but only a very small portion of it had been included in the actual text (which rather organically developed into an historical analysis of the suppression of Goddess reverence in the Near and Middle East— the areas in which Judaism, Christianity and Islam first emerged).

After *When God Was A Woman* had been published, I returned to the problem of how to present all else that I had found—most of it discovered in fragmented and piecemeal bits of information. This problem of a mode of presentation was more challenging to me than all the years of research had so far been. How to best present each piece of evidence, each fact that pertained to a specific Goddess or heroine name—in a way that would share the overwhelming sense of a long hidden heritage—as well as the enormous number of specific details? In writing the introduction that eventually became a book, I had drawn upon methods learned during many years of writing college term papers and theses, replete with quotations and references. But how to structure such a mass of fragmented, diverse, and generally unfamiliar, bits of documentation, gleaned from such an enormous number of disparate sources? There were prayers and parts of prayers, rituals and parts of rituals, legends and parts of legends, titles, epithets, symbols, inscriptions—that had each been gleaned from: translations of cuneiform tablets; translations of papyri and carved inscriptions; ethnological and anthropological studies that included accounts of spiritual beliefs; and translations of the early literature of Mexico, Scandinavia, China, Ireland, Iran, Wales, Japan, India, Greece and Rome. In addition to this written information, there were my personal observations of sacred artifacts that I had studied at the museums of the U.S., Europe, and the Near and Middle East; as well as my personal observations of ancient temple sites. Each provided evidence of images of womanhood, that ranged all the way from the creation of the entire universe and all life—to the winning of a horse race, and giving birth to twins at the finish line.

Over my many years of research (which has never really stopped), I had begun to observe that most European and Euro-American presentations, of the religious beliefs of other cultures, were done as if the writers were describing a banana—still in its skin. Crescent, deep yellow tinged with green or brown, somewhat hard to the touch—perhaps useful as a prop for a still life painting, or brightening up a fruit bowl—but not truly known because it had not yet been peeled, and its inner fruit experienced by tasting and eating it. Yet it seemed that at the very moment one actually tasted, chewed, and swallowed, a piece of the banana, no longer was it considered possible for that person to describe the banana— objectively. Objectivity, emotional distance from subject matter, may be a viable method or approach for the study of certain subjects, but ignoring the spiritual or religious qualities of the *core* of religious beliefs—a deity—though it may be regarded as good scholarship, insures that at best, the subject will only be partially understood. Such objectivity, carefully avoiding the subjective aspect of the *sanctity* of the subject discussed, when the facts discussed were about religious beliefs, resulted in descriptions that may best be likened to the scholar having used a telescope or microscope with an inverted lens—one that viewed the subject as smaller than it actually was. It was also clear, after years of reading many texts on the spiritual beliefs of other cultures, that the initial choice of a topic, as a subject for examination and discussion, as well as what each scholar chose to include—and to exclude—were purely subjective decisions, thus negating the possibility of totally objective studies, even as they began.

It was with these observations in mind, that I began to reject the idea of a strictly academic presentation of the information that I had found. Having read several carefully footnoted studies of Egyptian beliefs, in which the Goddess as Isis or Hathor, was not even mentioned; and studies of Greek beliefs, in which Artemis and Hera were mentioned in two or three brief references, while entire chapters were devoted to Zeus and Apollo, it was obvious that to footnote biased emphasis of specific material—did not make it any less biased. Thus I openly admit to my own bias in choosing to study only female images, a form of bias that few male scholars have even considered, as they chose what was of interest to them, and wrote volumes with titles such as Gods and Heroes, or Man and His Gods.

It was also clear to me, that if I was going to present this material at all, I was going to do so with respect—the respect of seriously considering the religious ideas of others as more than intellectual curiosities. I was dealing with images and information about deities that people had prayed to, honoured, held as sacred. Could I do less than to try to regard and present these beliefs, and the evidence of them, with a feeling of respect and sanctity—the very qualities that had been carefully discarded, in the efforts to comply with the requirements of at least a superficial semblance of scholarly objectivity? I was determined to peel the banana and taste it—preferring an honest admission of subjectivity to a pretense of what passes for academic objectivity, when writing about the religious beliefs of others.

As a result of this inner debate with my years of academic education and conditioning, I began to consider the facts about each image of Goddess and heroine with what some might regard as a difficult, perhaps even impossible, point of view, for a person of western Caucasian background. Somewhat like actors, whose current roles begin to seep into their offstage lives, I spent long hours of every day considering the facts that I had gathered on each specific image of woman, as I imagined one who had actually lived in the culture that had held that specific woman image as sacred or heroic, might consider or describe it. I better understood why my mother had so often referred to me as a daydreamer, as I spent my days with my thoughts and feelings more in Buto, Erech, or Hattusas, or among the Buhera Ba Rowzi, the Kiowa, or the Chibcha, than in any current reality. Half consciously, I found myself writing the account of Sun Sister, of the Inuit (Eskimo) people, on a day that my room was chilled by a heavy midwinter snowfall; the story of Australian Lia, when the summer temperatures sizzled in the high 90's. Mother Nature seemed to be cooperating, for it rained incessantly during the week I wrote of the Zulu Rain Goddess, Mbaba Mwana Waresa.

Thoughts came to mind of the time I had glued the pieces of my grandmother's favourite serving dish back together again, when it had broken many years after she had died. As with my grandmother's dish, I could not bring myself to throw away the shattered pieces of an object that I had known and admired on her abundant table as a child, and as with the dish, I would not allow myself to add any extra pieces, though I confess to using a small tube of glue. Though truly saddened by its damaged condition, the reconstructed presence of the serving dish still provided me with nostalgic thoughts of a woman most dear to me, my emotional response to the repaired dish perhaps even heightened, by the consciousness that it would never be completely whole again—as I would never again be able to sit as a child at my grandmother's table. A visual reminder of the passage of time, in which joy and sorrow flow together. It was in much this same way, that I spent two years in piecing together the multitude of broken fragments of Goddess and heroine images, that are our heritage as women—with loving care, respect, and a deep concern for the integrity of using only what was truly a part of it.

Though somewhat hesitant about confessing to the following, throughout the process of organizing and writing of each of the many images of Goddess or heroine, I sensed, almost heard, the voices of women reciting the information that I had collected, read, and repeatedly reread, on the pages of my notebooks. Even as I typed, my mind was often filled with images of sitting around a

13

campfire or on the bank of a lake or river, of being in an ancient temple or inside a communal tribal shelter—as if listening to the recitations of a story teller, hearing the pace, the pauses, the phrasing of each account, as if it were being told aloud. If I over romanticized such situations, I offer my apologies to any who may object, but I explain these experiences to any who may be puzzled by the form of writing that evolved. Years of having studied the translations of the ancient tablets of the Sumerians, Hittites, Babylonians, Ugaritans, and others, most surely affected my perceptions of how such information may have been initially orally conveyed. Added to this were the years of listening to parables told at various churches and temples, along with having long been intrigued by hearing a good yarn being spun along various waterfronts, or in the Irish pubs of London. Such was the strange potpourri underlying my feelings about story telling, as they evolved through years of telling bedtime tales to my daughters, and as they synthesized to pass along all that I had discovered about our heritage as women. Now, somewhat uncertain about just whose voice or voices told each account, I assure the reader that the events, actions, and conclusions, of each account, are as I found them. If I may again resort to an analogy with food, it seemed that with some of the primarily narrative accounts, it was as if water was being restored to the contents of packages of dehydrated soups. Having had the chance to compare the translations of many actual ancient tablets, to the brief summarized accounts of those same tablets in other texts, I was aware that as with the sanctity—the drama, the poetry, and the suspense, had also often been removed. It is my hope that having restored the 'water' to 'dehydrated' summaries, when there were no tablets available with which to compare them, has made it possible to relate each account in a form that is more in keeping with what is known about the traditions of oral recitation within so many cultures. If there are cultures who repeat their legends, of sacred and heroic figures, in as perfunctory and terse a manner as most of the summaries of anthropologists, historians, and ethnologists, I offer my apologies for assuming that all cultures would describe accounts of their own heritage with more respect and care.

I imagine there will be some who view my intentions and experiences, thus this form of presenting factual information, as not quite valid—just as Sir Arthur Evans' reconstruction of the temple of Knossos on Crete has been viewed as unacceptable by some archaeologists, who would have preferred that Evans had left the fragments of Knossian walls and pillars lying where he found them. It may offer some insight, into the nature of the academically critical mind, to realize that no archaelogist has ever suggested that Evans' removal of the piles of earth, that had for so long hidden the buried ruins—might in itself be tampering with the realities of the past. At any rate, chancing the criticisms, rather than produce a dictionary or encyclopedic volume of fragmented and dehydrated details, I too chose to reconstruct.

Now that I am better able to view this multitude of Goddess and heroine images, as other than hundreds of pages of fragmented pieces of information, I believe that the rich and diverse images of womanhood that they reveal, emerge above and beyond any of the weaknesses that may confess to my reassembling and restoration of the many broken and shrunken pieces. My hesitations, that these images of woman might be thought of as other than those of the many varied cultures included, fade away, as I am better able to grasp the immensity, the uniqueness, the ingenuity, of all that each culture has created. And viewing the study as a whole, it seems obvious that no one culture, certainly no one person, could have conceived of all that is included.

When all fourteen sections were completed, I realized that once again, as with the introduction that became a book, the amount of material had far exceeded my expectations. It was at this point that I made the decision to divide the mansuscript into two volumes—with thoughts of avoiding overwhelming readers with a tidal wave of fifteeen years of research, and to ease the problems of printing. But it is my deepest hope, that all who read this first volume, will be fully aware that each and every section, in both volumes, is equally as important to the true and complete realization of the immense richness of our heritage as women. The accounts of woman images, of each racial background, each culture, each section grouping, are each but a part of the whole. To read and become familiar with only a part, or a half, is to settle for a partial understanding—and therefore an inaccurate idea—of all that is our rightful inheritance. Each arc of colour may be lovely to behold, but it is the full spectrum of our woman rainbow that glows with the brightest promise of better things to come.

ANCIENT MIRRORS of WOMANHOOD

Once familiar with all the accounts of Goddess reverence, and legends of heroines, from so many cultures, the reader soon becomes aware that no simple archetype, or duality of archetypal aspects (e.g. Good Mother vs. Terrible Mother—as in Erich Neumann), or simple stereotype, or duality of stereotypes (e.g. madonna vs. whore), could possibly encompass all the images and perceptions of woman, as they have actually been known. It is in the rich diversity, the almost astonishing multitude of various traits and aspects—many often attributed to the same deity—that the consciousness of what images of woman have been, and what images of woman can be—emerges most clearly. I believe that it is this diversity, and the acknowledgement and celebration of it, that offers the firmest foundation for our growing strength—as we move ahead in our consciousness of ourselves as women, and of our potential as human beings on this planet. The dishonest canvas rips, the dishonest carved marble cracks apart—as we are each better able to declare ourselves as the unique, multi-faceted beings we each are—leaving behind all false or simplistic portraits, that were said to symbolize *all* womanhood.

Symbols such as the moon, the sun, the various stars and planets, volcanoes, caves, springs, rivers, lakes, ocean, lioness, serpent, heifer, mare, whale, heron, raven, vulture, dove, fig tree, laurel, corn, marigolds, meteorites, obsidian, Earth Mother, Sea Goddess, Queen of Heaven, the force of existence, the flow of existence, traits that appear to mesh, traits that appear to conflict— are each a part of the full and wondrous treasure. Images of the creator of the universe, the creator of life, the one who takes in death, the one in whom our twin spirits unite until we are reborn, provider of law and cosmic pattern, provider of herbs and healing, the one who is compassionate, the one who is wrathful, the essence of wisdom, the guiding holy spirit, Liberty, Victory, Justice, Destiny, Lady Luck and Mother Nature—all have been known in the form of woman. As anthropomorphic huntress, judge, warrior, tribal ancestress, inventor of writing, protector of animals, prophetess, inventor of fire, guardian of the celestial chamber of grain, teacher of carpentry and masonry, scribe of the tree of life— and as the more transcendental, metaphysical, female principle, that brought existence into being, and continues to cause all to occur—each known concept attests to images of womanhood that refute generalized archetypes, stereotypes, and simplistic dualities.

16

INTRODUCTION

There are accounts: of mothers mating with their sons, such as in Bachue, Fire Woman and Inanna; of daughters both helping and defying their fathers, such as in Mella and Golden Lotus; of rituals for the Goddess including lesbian relationships, such as in the Mysteries for the Greek Goddess Gynacea and the Roman Bona Dea; of the Goddess choosing a mortal male for a mate and living happily ever after, such as in Mbaba Mwana Waresa; of the women of an entire tribe leaving the males to set up a community of their own, such as in Lia; of the worship of both Mother and Daughter as the sacred pair, such as in Lato and Artemis, Demeter and Persephone, Mahuea and Hina; of reverence for the Mother, two daughters and a grand daughter, such as in the Sun Goddess of Arinna. However one attempts to construct a mold, it will not fit them all.

Along with the pride of regained heritage, in becoming familiar with these many accounts of images of womanhood, we may also gain some insight into the various efforts made to suppress and alter these images, even to erase the very memory of them, by various male-worshipping groups. In the earliest periods there are the Sumerian transitions, from the most ancient Creator Goddess Nammu to the less powerful Inanna, and the loss of power by the Goddess Ereshkigal, through the trickery and violence of the male deity Nergal. Kuan Yin, whose image may be derived from the pre-Buddhism Creator Goddess Nu Kwa, is described as having once been a male boddhisatva, who decided to return to earth as Kuan Yin. The Arabian Goddess Attar, associated with the Semitic Ishtar and the Egyptian Hathor, is described in later South Arabian inscriptions as a male deity. The effects of early Judaism are noticeable in the accounts of the Goddess of the Semites as Asherah and Ashtart; Ashtart (Ashtoreth) used as a name of a demon in the Middle Ages, though the gender was also changed to male. Early Christians made the Goddess Bridget into a Catholic saint, but doused Her eternal flame at Kildare; while later Christians burned the holy books of the Mayans, but appropriated the Tepeyac shrine of the Goddess Coatlicue and dedicated it to the Virgin Mary as the Lady of Guadalupe. Long after St. Patrick destroyed the sacred cairn of the Cailleach Bheur in County Covan, missionaries in Hawaii encouraged converts to defy the Goddess Pele, by throwing stones into the crater that was sacred to Her.

17

Thus as we become familiar with images of womanhood that were once held as sacred, we also come to realize how various male worshipping groups degraded, and/or erased, their existence. For those who question just what effects these images might have had upon the status and perceptions of womanhood in the societies that had revered these images, we might in turn ask why the male-oriented religions were so anxious to hide or deny them by these various means—and why the once almost universal existence of female clergy, that accompanied Goddess reverence, is a precept that today draws ridicule and dissent from so many.

Perhaps it was some of the symbolism associated with ancient Goddess reverence, as various elements of nature, and at times the enactment of ritual in a natural environment, that led to the labelling of ancient Goddess reverence as a "nature cult." Along with the demeaning implications of the word cult, as compared to the term religion, when applied to any body of spiritual beliefs, it may also be time to challenge the type of thought process that automatically assumed that a nature cult revealed a lower level of spiritual development, than that inherent in the major religious institutions of today. Faced with the all too real threats of poisonous pollution of land, sea, and air, and the complete extinction of many species of life on earth, perhaps even our own, we might do well to examine the rituals, parables, and symbolism, of spiritual beliefs that included regarding various aspects of nature as sacred— thus inviolable. Along with a reclamation of our heritage as women, we may gain from the spiritual wisdom inherent in many of the accounts. One cannot help but wonder, if polluting the environment was to be regarded as blasphemous to our deepest religious beliefs, and if our religious values were truly in focus with natural life and existence, such beliefs and attitudes might help to ensure the very survival of life upon this planet. As I explained, there are great diversities in both images and practices of Goddess reverence, as it has been known in various cultures. Yet a careful consideration, of some of the links between Goddess reverence and the sanctity of nature, may provide us with a useful understanding of why the even now familiar title, Mother Nature, has survived in societies that claim to reject Goddess reverence, and preach against so called "nature religions".

Upon the prompting of an editor several years ago, I had briefly considered the idea of dividing the evidence about Goddess reverence by specific types of symbolism, e.g. moon, sun, sea, agriculture, healing, warrior, serpent, bird, etc. I soon realized that such divisions inherently negated the actual multi-faceted dimensionality of many of the female deities, as they had been described and revered, by those of their own culture. Would I place the Egyptian Goddess Isis under stars (for Sirius), heifer, law, agriculture or magic? Would I place the Goddess Hina of the Polynesians under fire, water, moon, caves or agriculture; the Mexican Goddess Coatlicue under creator, volcano or serpent? In thinking about this, I became ever more convinced that my initial intention, of dividing the sections by cultural source, was the only way to retain the full integrity of the image of each Goddess and heroine.

As women, we are many, more than half the people of the world. We come from many diverse backgrounds, and many varied racial and cultural roots, even as we are each unique within our own racial or ethnic groupings. To strive for a sameness or classification of image, might mean to aim at a categorization that could smother and obliterate our precious differences. Perhaps just the knowledge that womanhood has been held as sacred, and/or heroic, among the Athapascans and the Anatolians, among the Chinese and the Chibcha, among the Irish and the Iroquois, among the Japanese and the Jicarilla, among the Egyptians and the Eskimoes, among the Mashona and the Mexicans, among the Semites and the Scandinavians, among the Zulu and the Zuni—helps us to begin to comprehend the enormity of what we have seldom been encouraged to know, about the diverse images of woman, as perceived by the human mind. (It may, in fact, be helpful to keep a world atlas or a globe near at hand while reading, to better understand some of the geographical connections).

A few years ago, I wrote and spoke at some length about the distortion of our perception of the events of the past, that is caused by our referring to all periods that occurred before the rise of Christianity as B.C. (Before Christ) or B.C.E. (Before the Common Era). At that time, I explained that such an arbitrary division of the passage of time not only forces us to count backwards, when discussing any period before two thousand years ago, but inherently encourages the idea of our separation from the series of events that led to society as we know it today, e.g. the development of agriculture, architecture, ceramics, textile making, metallurgy, wheeled vehicles, and methods of writing. By implying that those many millenia of cultural development (i.e. before One B.C.) were not in *our* era, we automatically place many millenia of Goddess reverence in those same B.C. periods, that seem to waft away into a vast emptiness of time that is not quite real—time that seems to move in reverse rather than towards today.

In reaction to this distortion of chronological perception, I suggested if we were to simply add the eight thousand years, that began in what we refer to as 8000 B.C. (a central date in the period of initial agricultural development), to the years that we then counted as 1977, we would arrive at the more logical date of that year as 9977 A.D.A. (After the Development of Agriculture). It is with apologies to those who *do* understand this temporal distortion, that I have reverted to B.C. ◄──────► A.D. dating in these volumes. Given the choice of double dating all given dates, or confusing readers who have not read or heard my full arguments about this, I once again submit to this distortion of chronological perception, with some misgivings, and hope that my more enlightened readers will forgive this inconsistency.

As with *When God Was A Woman,* it was clear that to attempt to include specific footnotes to the sources of each of the enormous number of fragments of unfamiliar information, such documentation would have taken nearly as many pages as the text itself. For those truly interested in doing further research on this subject, and I hope that these books will motivate at least a few readers in that direction (being all too aware that there is still much more evidence to be gathered), some primary sources are included in the introductory sections and in the accounts, and a full bibliography is included in the second volume.

*   *   *

In considering the much more recent past, I want to acknowledge my appreciation to the many scholars whose work I have studied, and to those who have personally helped in this long project. My gratitude to Myrna, Alice, Batya, Fran, Z., Nancy, Ruth, Jean, Lenny, Charlene, Gloria, Judith, Marion, Linda, Buffy,

Tracy, Susan, Elisa, Kay, Rory, Joan, Donna, Jill, Barbara, Roma, Carmen, Ursula and Yolanda. I especially express my appreciation to my two daughters, who first motivated me to present this information, precisely because they are daughters and deserved to know of their proud heritage as they grew into womanhood. In turn, I was rewarded, not only with their unflagging encouragement over the many years, but with Jenny's illustration for the section on Egypt (Volume II), and with Cynthia's patient and knowing lines of hand and pen, that over the years began to flow with the ever-developing ability to create visual images of women that were non-sexist, non-racist and non-agist. This combined text and illustrations of mother and daughters was a dream we first had some ten years ago, and as with all other goals and hopes for these volumes, we hope that the positive woman energies of our working together on this will be shared by all women.

Just as Cynthia's and Jenny's contributions are important to me, it is my hope that the information about Goddess and heroine images, provided in these books, will motivate many women to absorb them into our culture, by using them as themes for drama, dance, poetry, fiction, song, painting, sculpture, and in any other form that will speak of our long hidden heritage as women—regained. Thus we offer this work not only as hopefully enjoyable and worthwhile reading, but as reference books to which the reader may repeatedly return for inspiration in the years ahead.

The knowledge of these images of womanhood, and old/new ways of perceiving ourselves as women of this world, is our inheritance, our legacy of pride and self-esteem. Whether atheist or minister, scholar or carpenter, avowed feminist or fence-sitter, nine or ninety—we can all grow stronger on these treasures of our world-wide heritage that have been kept from us for far too long.

a gentle omnipotence

The way of Mother Nature, ever moving, ever changing, ever beginning, ever ending, flowing calmly along, or rushing quickly by, yet never ceasing to flow—as the cycles of life continuously occur—is the essence of the image of the Goddess, as She was known among the ancient peoples of China.

Perhaps the best way to begin to understand the image and nature of the Goddess within the culture of China is to become familiar with a world view that appears in many early Chinese texts, a recording of mythic memories of a period long before—that of The Era of The Great Purity. In the *Chuang Tzu,* written in the third century B.C., the time of the Great Purity is described as the epoch in which people knew their mothers but not their fathers (29:1). Other texts speak of this period as a time when all people lived in a state of innocence, being genuine and simple, spontaneous and direct in their conduct. They were in harmony with the seasons and with the ways of nature; animals and humans did no harm to one another. The Chinese texts then explain that this paradise was destroyed by mining minerals in the mountains, felling trees to build houses, hunting, fishing, and even by learning to make and control fire. The period of the obliteration of this perfect life, and the loss of touch with the patterns of nature, was referred to as— The Great Cosmic Struggle. Nature had been defied and this was

23

said to be the original cause of human discord and problems. Thus we may observe in very early Chinese thought, the very problems most of us regard as those of our own time—the struggle to preserve natural life on the planet as modern technology threatens to destroy it.

In an effort to better comprehend this ancient past of which the texts speak, let us take a look at human development in China, and the view of nature—the guiding essence of The Era of The Great Purity—and how it came to be associated with the female principle. The lands that we now know as China have been inhabited for at least 500,000 years. This is the time generally assigned to the scanty skeletal remains of about twenty-five pre-homo sapiens, described as Pithecanthropus Pekinensis, more commonly known as Peking Man—discovered some thirty miles southwest of Peking.

The development of full homo sapiens is attested to by the Ordos culture of the Upper Paleolithic period of about 25,000 B.C., a culture that developed along the Hwang Ho (Yellow River) between the provinces of Shensi and Shansi. The cave at Choukoutien near Peking, where pre-homo sapiens have been found, was also used by full homo sapiens whose skeletal remains reveal the beginnings of specifically Mongolian racial characteristics. By about 4000 B.C. small settlements were being made throughout the provinces of Kansu, Shensi, Shansi and Honan. Cultures such as the Yang Shao and Ts'i Kia P'ing are especially noticeable, their sites revealing ceramic work of well developed quality and design. Despite our pleasure in the esthetic and cultural achievements of these early peoples, we must also admit that it seems that The Era of The Great Purity had ended, or at least that the time of The Great Cosmic Struggle had certainly begun.

What of the spiritual beliefs of these ancient people of China? A form of hieroglyphic writing, that seems to have developed some time in the beginning of the second millenium B.C., is known to us from articles of bone, shell and bronze. Many scholars suggest that bamboo may also have been used as a material for writing, and although there is no actual evidence of this, the absence of it may well be the result of the natural deterioration of such a material. But on the more permanent writing surface of bone, a phrase written at Anyang in Honan Province tells the reader to "pray to Grandmother Yi for rain." This fragment of writing, using the term grandmother to designate a female being who was powerful enough to affect the weather, leads us to the probable origins of belief in the

Goddess—as Divine Ancestress. The worship of ancestors, a religious practice known throughout the world, is well attested in China. In a society such as that described in the Chuang Tzu—where people knew only their mothers and not their fathers—ancestor worship may well have been ancestress worship.

In the existent texts of the Chou period (about 1000 B.C.) and the later Han period, it was written that Nu Kwa created all people, thus revealing Her nature as the original parent or most ancient ancestress. But according to these texts, it was not only as the Mother of all people that Nu Kwa was revered. She was also described as the one who established harmony and the patterns of the universe, arranging the order of the seasons, and setting the stars and planets upon the proper paths. It is this more complex and omnipotent view of The Mother, not only as She who first gave birth to people, the Creator of human life, but also as She who arranged the workings of the universe, the patterns of nature—that reveals that the image of the most ancient ancestress was that of Nature Herself—the harmonious essence that was defied in The Great Cosmic Struggle.

Are the few accounts of the Goddess, the earlier ones of Nu Kwa and Hsi Ho, and the later ones of Kuan Yin and Tien Hou, all that remain of these ancient beliefs? I think not. A careful reading of the most basic book of Taoism, the *Tao Teh Ching,* believed to have been written at about 600 B.C. by Lao Tzu (which literally means Ancient Teacher), may be the mirror in which, to some extent, we are able to observe reflections of ideas and beliefs that may once have been the theological/philosophical core of ancient Goddess reverence in China. In the *Tao Teh Ching,* we do not find prayers to a concept of Goddess that is external to, or separated from, earth and ourselves, but rather the understanding of Nature as the maternal spiritual essence that is inherent in all that exists and occurs. It is a concept of Goddess that is also to be found in the texts of India, concerning the Goddess as Shakti or Devi, and in the texts of E-gypt, concerning the Goddess as Maat. It is this gentle omnipotence of She who is the essence of the patterns of the universe, all that is actually implied when we speak of Mother Nature, that appears to be the core of the wisdom and the way of the Tao Teh Ching.

Perhaps one of the most significant aspects of this understanding of Mother Nature is the light that it throws upon the concept of the female principle, *yin.* Contemporary interpretations by western writers often translate or define *yin* as that which is totally passive, unmoving, waiting to be acted upon by the male principle, *yang*. But the female principle of the *Tao Teh Ching*, as well as the accounts of the ancient Goddess, suggest that yin did not originally imply passivity, but rather a specific form of activity, as compared to that of the more aggressive yang. The wisdom of the activity of the water flowing around a great boulder, rather than repeatedly crashing against it, is the wisdom of Mother Nature— the female principle of following the strategy, that to some may seem passive, yet in the long run is most likely to assure a reaching of the destination. Thus the scriptures of the Goddess religion are to be read in the observation of the organic processes of Mother Nature. The concept of the Goddess is not that of a static being, but an omnipotence that is manifested in all of Mother Nature's constant workings.

Nu Kwa arranges the patterns of universal activities. She is Nature in action. The later image of the Goddess as Kuan Yin, though not imbued with attributes as all encompassing as those associated with the image of Nu Kwa, still retains the idea of gentle but consistent, determined action, that which succeeds in eventually overcoming each obstacle. Even in the story of the mortal heroine Gum Lin, we may observe the importance of the studying the natural way and pattern of each being. In this case, by knowing the natural patterns of the dragon, Gum Lin and the dragon's daughter are able to devise a plan of strategy that avoids direct confrontation—but achieves their ultimate goal.

The emphasis in these accounts of Goddess reverence among the ancient people of China is not on a passive acceptance of all that happens as the will of Nature, but on the advantages of studying the ways of Nature very carefully. It is this observation of all that Nature does, and how She does it, that seems to be the true study of the wisdom of the Mother Goddess. Continually ramming into a boulder that is in one's path simply leaves the body hurt and bruised, though it may wear the boulder down a bit. Flowing along as the river flows, rushing past on one side when the boulder blocks the other, making new paths when there are none available, gathering more speed and power as the volume of the waters increases—the student of Goddess wisdom understands the importance of an ever continuing observation of the way that all proceeds. Learning from the ways of Nature, She who has mothered all, we may learn how best to reach our goals, and perhaps to realize that the erosion caused by our constant rushing past the side of the boulder—will eventually wear it down to the size of a tiny pebble.

NU KWA

Reverence for the Goddess as Nu Kwa (Nu Kua) comes to us from the people of the northern provinces of China today known as Hopei and Shansi, the area once known as Chi'. The most detailed accounts of Nu Kwa's creation of all people, and Her repair of the universe, are from texts of the Han period (about 200 B.C.-200 A.D.). They appear in the writings known as the *Lieh Tzu*, the *Feng Su T'ung Yi*, the *Shan Hai Ching*, all from the Han period. There are less detailed remnants concerning the nature of the Goddess Nu Kwa that appear in the literature of the Chou period (starting at about 1000 B.C.), but according to Chinese tradition the story of Nu Kwa repairing the universe dates to about 2500 B.C., the time spoken of as the period of The Great Cosmic Struggle. The emphasis on the harmony and rightness of nature's patterns, in the legends of Nu Kwa, offers an interesting comparison to that same emphasis that is the core of the *Tao Teh Ching*. Visual images of Nu Kwa, with the tail of a fish, provide interesting parallels to Atargatis and Nina (see Semitic and Sumerian Sections).

To the valleys of the wide flowing Hwang Ho, came the Goddess Nu Kwa and there from the rich golden earth, She fashioned the race of golden people, carefully working the features of each with Her skillful fingers. But so arduous was Her task that She soon tired of making these individual creations and began to pull a string through the mud. In this way She made the others, though not as carefully formed, as She had made those of the golden earth, the ancestors of the Chinese people.

From the Kun Lun mountains, sweet western paradise whose summits reach the heights of heaven, Nu Kwa sent the great winds and the life giving waters, making the earth good for planting, pouring the excess waters into the Chihli Po Hai Bay—and then She filled it with fish so that all might eat to satisfaction.

But there came a time when all the universe was in great chaos; fires raged and waters brought floods. At this time, the pillar of the north, the pillar of the south, the pillar of the east, and the pillar of the west—all of these were destroyed. The nine provinces of the earth separated from each other and even heaven and earth were no longer suited to each other, for they had blown so far apart. Everything was wrong. Animals ate the people. Vultures seized and killed the elderly and weak.

Then Great Mother Nu Kwa saw what had happened and came to repair the damage, using coloured stones to patch the heavens. Seeing the ruins of the pillars, those which had supported the four corners of heaven, She took the legs of the great turtle and used them as columns, placing them firmly at the four compass points of the world. With Her mighty arms She smothered the blazing fires and when the burning reeds had turned to ash, She piled the ashes high enough so that the wild flooding waters came to repose where they are today. When all was once again in place— only then was Mother Nu Kwa satisfied to rest.

It was then that She looked upon all that She had done. It was a time of perfect harmony when all flowed in its course, each at its own pace. The stars followed their correct paths in the heavens. The rain came only when the rain should come. Each season followed the one before—in rightful order. Mother Nu Kwa had repaired the pattern for all that occurred in the universe, so that the crops were plentiful, the people were no longer the meal of the wild animal, vultures did not prey among the weak and old, nor were serpents harmful to them either.

Life was spent in nights of peace, undisturbed by anxious dream, and waking time was carefree and untroubled. It was the time of Mother Nu Kwa, She who established the patterns of existence, the order and rhythm of the universe, the sacred way of harmony and balance.

KUAN YIN

The Goddess Kuan Yin (Kwan Yin) is still revered in China today, but it may well be that Kuan Yin is a relatively recent reflection of the more ancient Nu Kwa. Both *Nu* and *Yin* mean woman, while the word *K'uai* means earth, and although the connection is not certain, both names may refer to a concept of the Goddess as Earth or Nature. Some of the accounts of Kuan Yin, still told today, describe Her as having originally been a male who had reached the state of Buddha being, but who then decided to return to earth as a Boddhisatva, a spiritual teacher—taking the form of Kuan Yin. This idea, that the Goddess was once a Buddhist devotee, can of course

28

only have developed after the birth of the first Buddha, Gautama Siddartha (about 560 B.C.), and may reflect the influence of one set of beliefs upon the other, the newer concepts of Buddhism superimposed upon beliefs about the ancient Goddess. Images of Kuan Yin, riding upon a dolphin, may be related to the fish tailed images of Nu Kwa.

Holy Mother of Compassion who achieved ultimate enlightenment, yet chose to return to us when we called in times of trouble, though we are grown, to Her we turn in our moments of deepest need, and She heeds our childlike calls for help—the Merciful Mother, Most Holy Kuan Yin.

In the blazing pit of fire I called and She came to take me to the cool of the river waters. When thieves overturned my wagon and left me beaten in the mud, I called and She carried me to my home, there healing and soothing my wounded body. When cruel ones threw me from the rocky cliff, I called and She came and in Her arms I gently floated down to earth unharmed. When the scorpion and the tiger hissed their anger at me in the jungle, I called and so loud did She shout that they ran in fear, and I escaped to the safety of my village. When my beloved child lay lifeless upon her mat, I called and She came and sprinkled the water of life from Her sacred willow branch, until the child breathed again and rose in health. Truly She is the Merciful Mother, Most Holy Kuan Yin.

There once was a time when She came to live as the youngest daughter among three, watching Her elder sisters: marry a lusting warrior, marry a greedy merchant. At Her refusal to take a husband, asking only to be able to enter the temple of women, did Her father not arrange that the women of the temple should treat Her with cruelty—so that She would change Her mind and accept the bonds of marriage, as he wanted Her to do?

Difficult was Her life at The Temple of the White Bird, for those who feared Her father's wrath assigned to Her the most arduous of tasks, but when She worked while the others slept peacefully upon their mats: the serpent came and helped Her fetch the water; the tiger appeared and gathered the wood for the fire; the birds flew busily about collecting the vegetables from the garden; the spirit of the fire rose up and helped to cook the food; the peacock even used its elegant feathery tail to sweep the kitchen floor.

When news of these miracles reached the house of Her father, so angry was he that his plan had not worked, did he not then set fire to the shrine, willing to burn each and every woman who lived peacefully within, just to revenge the thwarting of his will? And when Kuan Yin came and smothered the fire with Her own hands, hands that did not burn nor blister, did he not then order that Her head be severed from Her body?

Was the astonishment of the headsman not great when he tried to follow the orders of Her father, only to find that his sword broke itself in two, rather than harm Her holy body? But was not the headsman's fear of Her father even greater than his fear of the message that his sword conveyed, for it is said that he then murdered Her with his own hands about Her throat—and tied Her lifeless body to the back of a tiger, setting it loose in the jungle.

Was it dark in the Land of the Dead when Her precious soul descended and did Her young girl heart feel fear? Yet we know, that even in the house of death, She sang sacred chants of goodness and mercy, relieving the suffering and pain of the souls that dwelled therein, until they kneeled about the hem of Her robe in gratitude and respect. This so infuriated the King of the Dead, he who delighted only in punishment and torture, that he could not bear Her perfect presence near him—and thus banished Her from his kingdom of death.

Once again alive on earth, compassion and mercy triumphant over cruelty, Her soul rejoined Her body. So it was that She made Her way to the island in the Northeastern Sea where She now lives in peace, but never has She forgotten us as there She chants and meditates for our well being, still listening for our cries when troubles overtake us, always coming to our rescue when we call upon Her name—Merciful Mother, Most Holy Kuan Yin.

HSI HO

These scanty references to the Goddess as Hsi Ho appear in the *Shan Hai Ching* and the *Huai Nan Tzu,* both texts of the Han period. In these writings, Hsi Ho is said to live beyond the southeastern waters, in an area referred to as the Sweet Waters, *Kan Shui.* Even more minimal remnants of information about the nature of Hsi Ho appear in the earlier Chou texts. The Fu Sang tree is generally thought to be a mulberry. Three hundred li is about one hundred miles. It may be completely coincidental, but it is interesting to realize that the concept of there being ten suns also appears in the beliefs of the Native American Shasta tribes of California.

Mother of the ten suns,
She who creates the heavenly bodies,
She who creates the calendar
of the ten days of the week—
She causes all to happen
by Her celestial design.

Each morning we may look upon
the Valley of Light,
watching Her bathe one of the suns,
the one that She has chosen for that day,
in the sweet waters of the Kan Yuan Gulf
and then watch Her place the sun
in the branches of the Fu Sang Tree
where it sits among the multitude of tiny leaves,
raised three hundred li into the sky,
until it starts upon its way
across the wide heavens
finally coming to rest
on western Yen Tzu Mountain,
only to return to Her again—
as each of us shall do
after our journey upon the earth.

TIEN HOU

This is a story that can still be heard around the area of the island of Meichow Tao, located off the central coastline of China. It is an account that appears to be about a young woman who might be considered to be a mortal heroine, rather than a Goddess figure, yet the mystical aspects of Her supernatural abilities and powers, and the manner in which they are used, transcend Her mortality. The evidence of shrines and statues of Tien Hou suggests that the image of Tien Hou was a long held religious image that, as with many other ancient Chinese beliefs, was later embroidered upon to explain the origin of Her existence.

On the ragged coastline of the province Fukien, on the easternmost end of Meichow Bay, sits the island of Meichow Tao, homeland of the maiden Tien Hou—She who is known as Protector of the Sea. Those who live along these coastal waters remember this young woman who lived in days so long ago, and often tell of the joyous day that she was born—to a mother who had given birth to four sons, and had prayed fervently, during the many months of her fifth child growing within her, that she might have a daughter.

While the four brothers of Tien Hou went off in the fishing boats, the daughter kept her mother company, delighted when they gathered shellfish on the beach, or wove baskets that they would trade for yards of cloth or bowls of clay. Sometimes sitting quietly together in their home, the mother told the daughter tales of the sea, tales that she in turn had heard from her husband and her sons. When still a growing child, Tien Hou was satisfied enough to listen to the stories of men's adventures on the wide sea, but as young womanhood arrived, her desire to experience for herself grew greater—until she began to wish that she might do something as important and exciting as the deeds of the men in her mother's stories.

A day arrived when Tien Hou's father and her brothers had been gone for half a moon, promising before they left to return with baskets full of fish. Tien Hou sat upon her mat, sorting the lengths of reed, when suddenly she felt a great pain in her head, gasped for breath as if there was not enough air in the small hut to fill her lungs, and slumped flat upon the ground—her eyes closed, her throat emitting the hoarse dry whispers of a dread fever coma.

Desperate with worry, the mother bathed the daughter's brow with cool well water, stroked her soft golden arms with mother tenderness, pleaded with Tien Hou only to hear her voice, to fight whatever strangeness had claimed her—to waken to let her mother know that all was as well, as it had been but moments earlier. Tien Hou felt her mother's tears and kisses upon her fevered body and finally revived, repeating as she woke, 'I should have stayed just a moment longer. I should have stayed just a moment longer.'

Little was said of this incident until the arrival of the fishing boats, and the father and the brothers return to the island—telling the strange story of how their boat had floundered in the waters, as violent storm and thunderous cresting waves had washed them from the deck. Each explained that somehow Tien Hou had come to pull them from the waters, flying down from the heavens as if she had the wings of a great bird. But once the father and three of the sons had been placed safely in the boat, Tien Hou had disappeared, and the fourth son had succumbed to the sea, unable to fight the raging waters without the help of Tien Hou.

'It was for this reason', Tien Hou explained, 'that I did not want to wake, yet I heard the frantic worry in my mother's voice and felt I could not stay any longer.' So puzzling was Tien Hou's account, so puzzling were the others, that little more was spoken among the members of the family, who mourned the loss of one of their own in silent confusion.

Only when the coma was repeated, only when the mind of Tien Hou once again seemed to leave her body, and when this time no one called to wake her, so that she breathed with life but did not wake, did the family remember aloud the miracle that Tien Hou had done. Trusting that she might again be flying over the wide sea, rescuing those in trouble, they cared for her body in its daytime and night time sleep.

Alive, yet not alive, Tien Hou lay upon her mat, tenderly cared for by her mother, while all about the islands of Nanjih and Haitan, even as far as Penghu Tao, those who fished began to tell stories of a young woman who flew from the skies—to pull them from furious waters, to push a boat of murderous pirates far away from their own, or even to hold a ship together, one that had been torn on jagged ocean rocks, long enough for all to swim to shore.

Grateful for the many lives that had been saved, families began to build shrines to honour the courageous Tien Hou. Even after life completely slipped from her small young body, still the people of the sea told of new miraculous rescues by the young one with the long black braids, who flew to their sides just when they thought life would soon be gone. Carving statues, now adorning the simple Tien Hou in robes of royalty, placing a stately crown upon Her head, they called upon Her as Queen and Protector of the Sea, as they kneeled before Her statues to pray for the lives of those who daily faced the dangers of the sea, and for the protection of the daring and compassionate Tien Hou.

MOTHER NATURE (TAO)

Tao is not generally regarded as a Goddess name but rather as a term most often translated as The Way or The Path. The reasons that I have included this adaptation of a few excerpts from the *Tao Teh Ching* in this volume is the continual suggestion, in the *Tao Teh Ching,* that the ways in which one may better understand Tao is to understand and follow the ways of Mother Nature—as well as the fact that the values, applauded in the book of the Tao, are those which are repeatedly referred to as feminine and maternal. This emphasis upon following the ways of Nature, and the image of Nature as Mother, suggests that this treasure of wisdom, in which philosophy and religion are inextricably entwined, may well be a most enlightening text in our efforts to better understand the true nature of ancient Chinese beliefs about the Goddess. Though I had long speculated about this possibility, as my knowledge of Goddess reverence grew, my decision to include this piece in this volume was encouraged by a recent reading of Ellen Chen's paper *Tao as The Great Mother and the Influence of Motherly Love in the Shaping of Chinese Philosophy.* Ms. Chen bases her reclamation of Tao as Goddess religion on her careful examination of the *Tao Teh Ching, Chuang Tzu,* and other early Chinese writings, in the original Chinese.

Nature, since it has mothered all, may be regarded as Mother Nature. Only those who understand Mother Nature, understand Her many children. If we choose to avoid mistakes and desire to have a wise guide throughout life, we should study the wisdom of Mother Nature's ways.

There is no way to truly describe Nature, for to describe Her completely, we would have to create a perfect duplicate—and this no one but Nature could do. We might try to explain Nature by saying that She is the ultimate source of all that exists, all that comes and goes, all that begins and all that ends, all that is and all that is not—but to describe Mother Nature as the ultimate source of all is only to use a few of Her sounds.

Mother Nature contains all natures, yet no matter how many natures come into being, Her supply is without end. We may learn from Mother Nature, as She reveals the way in simple lessons: those who try to reach beyond their reach by standing on their tiptoes, soon lose their balance; those who stretch their legs too far apart to try to walk more quickly, soon find they cannot walk at all; those who brag about themselves too much, soon find themselves more ignored than others; those who push their views most heavily upon others, soon find that fewer people will agree with them; when people claim credit for what they have not done, they soon find that they do not even receive the credit they have earned; the more one is filled with arrogance and pride, the further the fall when humiliated; the longest journey beings with the first step; the tallest tree starts as a small seed; the highest tower starts with the first brick.

Learning from the ways of Mother Nature, one continually discovers how best to proceed.

GUM LIN AND LOY YI LUNG

The tale of Gum Lin is another that is still remembered in China. Although its central theme is that of hardship and drought, certainly real enough problems in the life of people in some parts of China, it is also the legendary memory of a young woman who was so concerned about the people of her village that she would not be swayed from her goal of helping them, even when tempted by personal comforts and riches. The portrayal of the mortal Gum Lin is all the more interesting, as it is interwoven with the somewhat supernatural image of another young woman, Loy Yi Lung, the daughter of the dragon. As the story proceeds, it is clear that only by the cooperative efforts of the two young women can the difficulties of the people be overcome. The interpretations of this legend, and its possible underlying morals or messages, may be numerous, but the sense of self-esteem offered to girls growing up on such stories is certainly clear enough.

Young and old, the women gather and walk slowly to the foot of Tai Ma Shan—Great Horse Mountain. There they stand side by side in the light of the waning moon, the third moon of the new year, and by the flowing waters of the the river that wash the foot of the mountain, the riverbank lit by the twenty-one day old moon, they send their voices across the waters. Soft and loud, high and deep, the voices float off together into the night air—carrying with them the most wondrous of tales, the story of Loy Yi Lung, the dragon's daughter, and of the girl who had once lived in their village in times long ago, the brave and loving Gum Lin—Golden Lotus.

At first there is a sadness in the voices of the women, as they sing of the time of the dryness of the land, when the water was so scarce that the rice would not grow, when the bamboo withered and died in the drying mud of the gullies that had once been the beds of flowing streams. They sing of Gum Lin, when she was not yet a woman, and how she had gone about her work, her small hands cutting the reeds, her small fingers tying them together, making bamboo brooms, making bamboo mats—and selling all that she had made to help to feed her family:

As the land grew dryer and more barren, further and further from home did Gum Lin have to wander, searching for a few stalks of bamboo, when all that had grown close to the village had been stricken by the thirst of their roots. Miles from home she walked, into the deep forest thick with trees, making her own path between the great rocks, until far beyond the tall trees, at the foothills of the mountains, she saw what seemed to be an image in a dream. Thickets of bamboo, tall and yellow green, bent gently in the soft wind, clustering along the edges of a clear blue lake, a secret bowl of water in the mountains, one that she had never seen before. Gathering all that she could carry, Gum Lin returned to her village with her precious bamboo treasure.

All through the long night She tossed upon her sleeping mat. So much water in the forest where few can drink. So little water in the village where thirst was part of every day. The slender reeds of dream wove in and out through her restless sleep, until they wove themselves into a channel, a canal that the water could pour

36

through—a canal in which the waters of the forest lake could find their way into the thirsty village, there filling up the muddy ditches where other waters had once run.

In the light of the early morning, a shovel and a pick-axe balanced upon her small shoulder, her long black hair braided tightly to last the rigours of the hard day's work ahead, Gum Lin started on the way that led to the clear blue mountain lake. There she planned to dig a pitcher spout on the rim of the reservoir of water, so that it would pour from the foothills of the mountain, into the thirsty gullies of the village from which the rice and bamboo had once been free to drink their fill. But arriving at the water's edge, she noticed a thick grove of trees on one side, and rocky ledges and boulders along another. By the rim of the great cup that held the deep, gathered, mountain waters, Gum Lin walked and looked, hoping to find the right place—until, just a few steps before her, in a place where she had thought she might dig, she saw a great stone gate.

She pulled upon the door of the gate, but it would not open. She picked and pried with the tip of her axe, but the door was very thick and tightly bolted. Stopping for a moment to catch her breath and to think of what to do, Gum Lin was surprised by a strange voice, and turning to see from where it came, all she could see was a wild grey swan that had made its way almost to where she stood at the edge of the lake. Again she heard the voice. Could it be the red ringed throat of the swan that was saying, 'These waters are yours, once you find the key to the stone gate.' There was no one else in sight, but by the time she thought to ask the wild swan if it had been speaking, and if so, where this special key might be found—the graceful wild bird had already made its way far across the wide lake.

Needing time to solve the puzzle, Gum Lin wandered back into the forest, winding her way between the cypress trees, thinking about the strange gate, wondering about the key to its latch. She had hardly noticed the three brightly feathered birds perched up high on the branch of a gnarled cypress, until voices, that seemed to come from where they sat, sang out in perfect chorus, 'The daughter of the dragon. The daughter of the dragon.' But just as Gum Lin was about to ask the birds if they had truly spoken, three pairs of wings of brilliant colour slid into the air, waving as if in farewell. Gum Lin would have been more puzzled yet, had she not taken notice of the tail of a peacock, as it spread out against a tall pine, fanned open as wide as it could be. Suddenly the peacock shook its tail into a blur of blues and greens, and in the sound of the rustle of the feathers, Gum Lin heard these words, 'Go to the edge of Ye Tiyoh, Wild Swan Lake. Stand upon its banks and sing the songs of your people. Make your voice loud and clear, so that the daughter of the dragon may hear you, and if your songs please her, she will come to you.' And then the peacock folded its fan of eyes into a long tail, that followed behind its soft round body, and walked further into the dark woods.

The small legs of Gum Lin, still carrying the weight of pick and shovel, moved as fast as they could, back to the water's edge. Standing her tools beside her in the dirt, she leaned upon the handles, breathed deeply in, and then chanted out in a voice that was as clear as the blue lake water. She sang songs of the snow on the mountains, of the peaks that one could see from the village, of grass as green as that which she had been told once grew, of the loveliness of flowers that she had never seen—but though she sang song after song—nothing happened. The daughter of the dragon had chosen not to listen.

Determined to follow the peacock's instructions, Gum Lin thought of every song she knew. When she had finished the songs of the loveliness of nature, she began to sing the songs of the people of her village, of those who worked in the flooded fields of rice, of those who could not work now that they were dry. She sang the songs the women sang, as they wove the reeds, or as they repaired family huts after strong winds had blown them apart, or as they tried to feed the small but hungry mouths of new existence. They were proud songs, of people who did the best they could, but they were not the pretty songs of grass and flowers and snow capped mountains. Surely if the other songs had not brought the dragon's daughter forth, these songs would please her even less. Still Gum Lin sang.

Singing of the hardships of her people, of the loving kindness that they gave to one another, when there was little else to give, tears came to the dark brown eyes of Gum Lin, blurring her vision of Loy Yi Lung, the daughter of the dragon—as she emerged from the waters of the lake. Wiping the tears from her cheeks, Gum Lin soon remembered why she had been singing and called out to the daughter of the dragon, 'The key. Please may I have the key? My people are dying of hunger. They work very hard but without water they have no food, without water the rice cannot grow.'

'The key is in my father's cave on the deepest floor of the lake.', Loy Yi Lung answered. 'There he guards it, as he jealously guards all his worldly treasures—and would destroy anyone who might dare to intrude—even his own daughter.' Then growing from a moment of further thought, a scheme was devised by the daughter of the dragon, who knew the dragon as well as he could be known. 'Often when I sing just outside the cave, my father crawls closer to the entrance to listen to my song. Perhaps if we sang together, our voices would bring him to the entrance, and while I continued to sing, you could slip past him and search for the key.'

All proceeded just as the two had planned, but when the brave young Gum Lin found herself in the darkness of the cave, she was overwhelmed by the sight of trunks and vessels piled high with golden coins and precious gems. For a moment she thought to stuff her pockets with the jewels and gold, for with them she could move her family to better land, but then remembering the others of the village, the hungry crying infants, the weakened grandparents, those who still searched daily for any rice plant that might have survived the drought, she knew that she could not leave the cavern until she had found the key to the waters. Just at that moment, the edge of her shoulder upset a small ivory box that sat upon a rocky ledge. As it fell, it tumbled its contents out upon the watery stone floor—and there before her lay the key, golden and glowing, a carefully formed swan at its top, swimming in a sea of pearls that had long nestled against it in the box.

The key safely tucked inside her pocket, Gum Lin swam quietly past the dragon's side, and reaching the place where Loy Yi Lung still sang, she grasped her hand in joyous triumph. Side by side they swam to the edge of the mountain lake, to the place where the stone gate stood. Loy Yi Lung watched from the water, as Gum Lin climbed back upon the bank, and slipped the key into the long unused lock, turning it this way and that, pulling upon the handle of the door with all the strength of her small arms—until suddenly the door flew open as if being pushed from the other side! It was in this way that the water that had pressed upon the door rushed forth upon the grassy lakeside, digging deep into the ground—carving its own canal.

The water swam until it reached the dry waiting stream beds of the village. It sped along, diving over rocks, thinking only to quench the thirst of the ground where the rice and bamboo had once grown.

It danced joyfully about the ankles of the few remaining plants, and tenderly bathed the seeds and ailing saplings, tucking them in their moist bed to rest, humming lullabies of how tall they would grow as it bubbled by. It tunnelled beneath the earth to leap inside the stone walls of wells, pouring itself into the cups of the thirsty. Ye Tiyoh Lake had stretched out its merciful river arm, spread its blue palms and fingers open in offering, to share itself with the people in the village of Tai Ma Shan.

Gum Lin walked along the river banks, following the path that the water had chosen into the village, as Loy Yi Lung swam alongside, relieved that the angry bellowing of her dragon father was quieting with the distance. The broad river provided directions to a stream, that now flowed by the small home of Gum Lin, and in the fresh new mountain waters, there the dragon's daughter made her home. By that stream Gum Lin would sit upon the grassy edge, and spend the hours of her days tying the bamboo and visiting with Loy Yi Lung, both singing as they had by the entrance of the cave, the perfect mating of their voices ringing as celestial chimes throughout the village.

It was this ancient tale that the women of the village sang, as they stood upon the banks of Ye Tiyoh, Wild Swan River, at the foot of Tai Ma Mountain, their voices finally waning in the dark night, as the moon waned in the sky and the great starry dome of night filled with silence. But it was then that they heard the most marvelous music of all, though the women of the village made not a sound—two women's voices, joined in perfect harmony, rang out from beneath the deep blue waters.

and there before her

lay the key

mighty in magic, enchantment
and divination

As part of our exploration of the nature of the Goddess among the Celtic peoples, those whom we know best from Ireland, Scotland, Wales, Cornwall and Brittany today, we must first be aware of the vast geographical areas that the Celts once inhabited, and of the great number of quite separate tribes that formed the group we refer to as the Celts. In the third century B.C., large numbers of Celts were spread across Europe, from the mouths of the Danube in Roumania to the western coastlines of France. The Classical Greeks referred to the Celts as Keltoi; the Romans knew them as Galli or Gauls. Galicia in Poland, and Galicia in Spain, were once Gallic/Celtic areas. Perhaps most surprising is the evidence of Celtic tribes living in Turkey, forming the nation/state of Galatia, so well known from St. Paul's epistle to them in the New Testament.

Excavations of the Hallstatt culture of Austria (800-500 B.C.), and the La Tene culture of Switzerland (500-50 B.C.), reveal that these sites had once been Celtic settlements. Celtic tribes such as the Brigantes, Belgae, Helvetii, Sequani, Parisi, Boii, Iceni, Cornovi, Bellovaci, Trinovantes, Osisimi, Treveri, Silures, Demetae, Domnonoii, Cantiaci, Novantae, Aquitani, Remi, and many others, lived upon the European mainland until migrating or fleeing from Romans and/or Teutons, and finally settling in their current homelands. Those who had settled in Britain were driven even further

43

west by later Teutons (Angles, Saxons, and Jutes). From these Celtic tribes, European place names such as Paris, Belgium, Helvetia, Carnac, and Reims, still survive today.

Many archaelogists identify the homelands of the earlier Proto-Celtic people with the sites in France and Germany of the Bell Beaker culture (2000-1200 B.C.), and the Urnfield culture (1200-650 B.C.). These cultures may account for a great many of the Proto-Celtic people during these periods, but quite possibly not for all. Celtic references to very early Celtic settlers of Ireland, as Danaans, have raised questions and theories concerning possible links between the Celtic Danaans and the Greek Danaans of Homer's account who participated in the Trojan War in Turkey. There are further speculations on links between the Celtic Danaans and the early Danes, as well as with the Danuna, a tribe thought to be from Adana, Turkey, listed among the Sea Peoples who raided in the Mediterranean areas in the twelfth century B.C. These possible links, between the Celts and groups of Greece and Turkey, are further supported by a Welsh account that Celtic Llundein (London) had first been settled by a man named Brutus, described both as a worshipper of the Goddess as Diana, and as a Trojan from Anatolia (Turkey).

Though the possibility, that some Proto-Celtic groups may have been living in Greece and Turkey during the second millenium B.C., may be difficult to reconcile with our knowledge of the Celtic people of today, we should keep in mind that tribes speaking Indo-European languages did live in the southern regions of Russia, and that some of these tribes entered Turkey, Iran, and India, during the second millenium B.C. One current hypothesis suggests that Celtic society was the result of the merging of the Bell Beaker culture of Europe and the Indo-European Battle Axe culture of southern Russia. Although this theory is too complex to discuss here, for those interested, further study on these possible connections may provide answers to some of these puzzling links. To even further complicate the matter, there are the statements by Arrian, that the Celts of Galatia paid homage to Artemis, and by Strabo, that Gallic representatives attended a religious council in the sacred centre of the Anatolian Goddess Kybele (the city of Pessinus) in the second century B.C. This in turn brings to mind, although probably coincidental, that the castrated clergy that served Kybele in Turkey were known as *Galli*.

Since there is no written material from the Celts until the period of their arrival in their current homelands, the nature of the Goddess, as revered among the Celts, is drawn primarily from Irish, Scottish, and Welsh tradition and literature. This does not mean that these beliefs were not held by the Celts in earlier periods, but suggests that up until the time they were recorded, they were probably preserved through tradition and oral recitation.

One of the major themes found in the accounts of the Celtic peoples is the association of the Goddess with a particular body of water—usually a river, but at times a spring, a lake, or the ocean. The Divine Ancestress of the Celtic Boii tribe was known as Boann, and linked with the River Boyne in Ireland. The Divine Ancestress of the Sequani tribe was Sequana; the River Seine of France, once known as the Sequana, named in Her honour. A healing shrine dedicated to Sequana stood at the headwaters of the Seine near the modern day city of Dijon. There has been some hypothesis that the Sequani were also linked to the River Sankarya of Anatolia, the river that was known as the Sangarius to the Greeks, and cited by Homer as an area in which Amazons had lived. Sequana's name was later linked with the River Shannon of Ireland. The most ancient Goddess name on Celtic record is that of Danu, Mother of the Danaans. Her name is usually associated with the Danube (Donau and Dunava in areas of eastern Europe). There is some speculation that in Proto-Celtic periods, the name Danu had been linked with the River Don in Russia, Don also used as a river name in Celtic Scotland.

This association of the Goddess with various bodies of water, in turn appears to be linked with the Celtic reverence for the Goddess as The Great Mare. The white breakers of the ocean were described in Irish legend as the white mane of The Morrigan's head. The equine Goddess Macha, whose colt 'returned to the sea', is at times referred to as the The Daughter of the Sea. Epona, a name of the Mare Goddess in Celtic Europe, was at times linked with Neptune (Poseidon) in Roman festival. The connection is interesting in that Poseidon was regarded not only as a deity of the sea but described by Greeks as the inventor of horse racing. An account of Poseidon mating with the Goddess, as Demeter, both in the form of horses, may have been influenced by this Celtic imagery.

Though at first glance it may seem that the symbolism of the mare has little to do with the symbolism of river or ocean, it may be worth noting that both are important in transportation and mobility. The double imagery of horse and water may well be compared to that of a figure known as the Submarine Mare, in the accounts from India. This image of the Mare from India was said to have a divine fire in Her mouth, and to have lived in the ocean—to avoid burning up the world. This connection of sea and horse might help to explain the double use of the word mare, meaning sea in Latin and Russian (and the root of the English word marine), while at the same time used to designate a female horse. Both meanings of mare may have been derived from the same initial Indo-European source word, possibly the Sanskrit *mah* meaning mighty. This word may also be the foundation of the Goddess names—The Morrigan and Morgan—the roots *gan, gin* and *gen* meaning birth, as in genesis and begin.

Another prominent aspect of the nature of the Goddess, as revered by the Celts, is the ability to assume various forms and identities. In the material in this section, The Morrigan becomes an eel, a wolf, a heifer, a raven, and several diverse images of mortal women. Cerridwen transforms Herself into a greyhound, an otter, a hawk, and a hen, while Macha, the Caillech Bheur, and Rhiannon, take the form of horses. This shapeshifting aspect of the Goddess is one that recurs repeatedly in Celtic accounts, and unless it is to be viewed as purely poetic metaphor, which the texts do not really suggest, it may well have encouraged those who revered the Goddess to treat all animals with respect and caution. It seems to be this aspect of the nature of the Goddess that most insistently remained as Christianity gained power in Celtic society, this ability then transferred to the more acceptable image of Faerie Queens.

A less documented image of the Goddess among the Celts is the figure of the Goddess of Victory, invoked by Celtic Queen Boadicea as Andarta or Andrasta, a name quite similar to one applied to Egyptian Isis, that of Adrastea. The Goddess name of Tailltiu is mentioned briefly in some texts, as the mother of the god Lug. Tailltiu was honoured at the Feast of Lugnasadh (Lammas), August 1st, though at the period of the early Irish literature, as a secondary figure to Lug. Yet Her name was especially linked with Tailltean Games played during Lugnasadh, and the town of Tailltenn. There has also been some speculation that the famed prehistoric mounds of New Grange were at one time associated with the Goddess name of Grainne. This New Grange site that lies along the coast between Dublin and Belfast, just a few miles west of Drogheda, has been attributed to peoples as diverse as very early Celts—to Phoenician colonists.

Celtic accounts of legendary women as governmental and/or martial leaders, and soldiers, are found in the descriptions of Scathach, Aife, Medb (Maeve) and the nine Gwyddynod of Gloucester. Actual historical records of the powers and actions of Boadicea (Boudicca), Queen of the Iceni tribe, who personally led a rebellion against the Romans in 61 A.D., and Cartimandua, Queen of the Brigantes, who made the decision to sign a peace treaty with Claudius of Rome, suggest that the more legendary figures were based upon historic realities.

Along with these records of the martial prowess of Celtic women, Plutarch wrote that Celtic women often acted as ambassadors in battles and rivalries between the Celtic tribes, and sat upon peace councils when disputes were discussed. *Banfathi* (prophetesses) often accompanied troops into battle, and were relied upon for advice and strategy. Plutarch's account of women travelling with German troops, in much this same capacity, explains that the German women based their advice upon listening to the sounds of streams, and studying the eddies and currents of the waters. It seems quite possible that these methods were also used by the Celtic banfathi, who regarded rivers and streams as possessing the essence or spirit of the Goddess.

Mention of groups of Druidesses, in early Irish literature, appears to be connected to the references to women's islands, especially to those off the western coast of Brittany, such as the Druidesses of Sena on the Isle de Sein (just west of Pointe du Raz). Although no specific Goddess name is mentioned, early Christian tradition at Chartres Cathedral included the idea that Chartres had been built in the very place that was the major religious site of Druidic beliefs, its underground passages not unlike those of Mont Saint Michel's lower levels still dedicated to Notre Dame Sous Terre, Our Lady Beneath the Earth, while those at Chartres were remembered as the holy places of The Black Virgin.

DANU

Evidence of this most ancient Celtic Goddess, as Divine Ancestress of the Tuatha de Danaan (literally, tribe of Danu), is found primarily in the Irish *Lebor Gabala* (Book of Invasions), dated at about 1000 A.D. In the Welsh *Mabinogin,* Her name is given as Don. This image of the Goddess among the Celts is one that probably originated during the periods that Celtic tribes inhabited the mainland of Europe, the reverence for Danu being closely linked with the River Danube (Donau). As mentioned in the general introduction, the Celtic Danaans may have been related to the Danes, the Greek Danaans, the Danuna, or even, as some have speculated, to the tribe of Dan in Canaan. Considering the widespread movements of the Celts, any or all of these associations may be correct, but until further research is done, none can be stated with certainty. There is also the question of possible links between the name Danu, the name Dione as a Goddess name in Greece, and the Goddess name Diana, as known by the Romans. The name Danu may mean wisdom or teacher, as in the English word don, or giving, as in the root of the word donate.

Goddess whose spirit lives in the mighty waters that flow from snow capped Alpen mountains into the darkness of the Black Sea, ever flowing, ever giving, She is Donau, Dunav, Danube, Mother of all Celtic peoples. She brought the dawn of being for those who dwelled upon Her banks so that they understood that it was Danu who gave them sustenance and life.

The tribe of Mother Danu, the Tuatha de Danaan, most ancient of the Celts, those who were once spoken of as Gauls when they lived upon the lands that stretched from the coasts of the Atlantic to the triple mouths of the Danube, kept the memory of Mother Danu deep within their hearts and when fleeing from their Gallic lands, they carried Her with them to the British Isles.

Finally pressed by Teutons and by Romans to the lowlands of Cornwall, to the highlands of Scotland, to coastal western Wales where The Mother was called upon as Don, Her memory was also taken for safekeeping to the Isle of Erin where She was spoken of as Danu, Mother of the Tuatha de Danaan and long remembered as the most ancient Mother of the Celtic peoples.

In the twilight of the day whose light lingered longer than any other, there were prayers for abundance on Midsummer's Eve, the holiest of Danu's holy days. Worshippers carrying windblown torches of blazing bundled straw tied upon long branches made their way up the mountainsides, blessing the new cattle and the newly planted seed, explaining that they were commemorating the very day that the children of Mother Danu had first set foot upon the Irish soil.

THE MORRIGAN

The Morrigan is a major figure in the Irish epic *Tain Bo Cualgne*. The narrative of the epic makes it clear that The Morrigan's loyalties are with the Tuatha de Danaan and the Celtic tribes that had settled in the area of the large nation/state of Connacht. Though at times there is a tendency on the part of some to attribute a triple nature to Goddess images from all cultures, even when there is a complete absence of evidence of triplicity, there is no doubt about the triple nature of The Morrigan. This concept of the threefold nature of the Goddess among the Celts may also be seen in the Goddess as Bridget, as well as in the Three Matrons or Mothers who were often depicted in Celtic art, sitting side by side. But unlike the more sedentary images of The Mothers, The Morrigan was extremely active, even aggressive, and certainly always acting with a comfortable self assurance.

Triple imaged Morrigan, triple named Morrigan, Mighty Queen, Badb and Macha—it was She who protected the Tuatha de Danaan by cover of fog and rain and cloud so that the people of Danu could land safely upon the coast of Ireland. Those who say that She was three parts in one, say many things about Her: some say She was the three phases of the silver moon, waxing, full and waning, while others speak of the Three Mothers, The Divine Matronae who sat side by side with cornucopias of abundance upon their laps; some explain that The Morrigan was Maiden, Matron and Crone, saying that The Holy Trinity was once the Daughter, the Mother and the Grandmother.

Some saw Her as a vengeful crone, chortling in delight at spilled blood upon a battlefield, drowning enemy princes beneath Her white waves, battling against the Fomorians and the Fir Bolgs to protect those of the tribe of Danu. To others, She appeared as a young woman dressed in brightly coloured cloths embroidered with threads of glistening gold. Changing shape and form was but play to the mighty Goddess—and poetry and prophesy Her natural tongue.

Loud was Her war cry when She took the form of Badb; sharp were Her spears; powerful were Her enchantments; true were Her grim prophesies—as She flew across Celtic battlefields black as the sleek raven, making Herself visible only to those whose life would soon be over, Her raven caw filling hearts with dread, as death's call slid from Her widespread wings. And as The Mighty Queen, She took Dagda's body into Her own while Her feet were firmly planted upon opposite banks of a wide flowing river, from this joining giving birth to Mecha who had three serpents in his three hearts.

How filled with anger was The Morrigan when the lad named Odras used Her sacred bull to mate with his cow. Gathering up both bull and cow, She took them through the oak woods of Falga and brought them to the cave at Cruachan, not far from the River Shannon, where one might enter into the Otherworld. Desiring to retrieve his cow, Odras followed as fast as his legs would move but the fleet footed Morrigan, even with the burden of bull and pregnant cow, soon outdistanced the exhausted fellow—arriving at the cave of Cruachan while Odras was still far behind. When She later came upon him in the woods, his eyes closed deep in the sleep of his fatigue, She laid a magic spell upon him so that he changed into a pond, his spirit captive in the water of the oak woods of Falga until this very day.

But it was the warrior of Ulster, the arrogant Cu Chulainn, who most aroused the anger of The Mighty Morrigan. Some say that Her feud with him first began on the day that She had watched him bathing by a river bank and upon seeing his bared body, desired to lay him down beside Her. It was then that She approached him in Her finest robes, embroidered with all the colours of the rainbow. Though all the other soldiers could hardly look upon Her, so filled were they with awe and admiration, Cu Chulainn refused Her suggestion that he lie with Her in love, claiming that he was too weary from the day's battle.

Still, it was not this refusal that angered The Mighty Morrigan, who showed much patience and concern for the man that She desired, for She then suggested that She would help him in the battle and with the energy that he would save by Her conquests in the fighting, he would be able to accept Her offer of a loving bed. But this second offer was responded to with great disdain at the very idea of a woman helping in the battle and it was this reply that aroused the wrath of The Morrigan—thus making Cu Chulainn an enemy of the powerful Daughter of Eternity.

So it came about that on a morning when Cu Chulainn still lay fast asleep, he was wakened by a noise so loud and startling that it caused him to tumble from his bed on to the floor and to then rush half asleep through the door without a stitch of clothing. Jumping into his battle wagon, naked and unarmed, the mist of sleep began to clear and Cu Chulainn soon realized that although his intent was to ride to a battle, he did not know in which direction he had meant to go.

Sitting there in naked puzzlement, he saw another wagon approach, that one drawn by a single bright red horse that walked upon three legs and pulled the vehicle behind it by a pole that ran directly through its body—the tip of the wagon pole emerging from between the horse's eyes. Alongside the horse walked a footman, a forked wand of hazel in his hand. And upon the high seat of the wagon sat a woman whose hair and thick brows were the colour and brilliance of flame, Her long cloak of blood colour spread out about Her—as if She sat upon a throne.

Ever more puzzled and confused, Cu Chulainn asked their names and purpose. But he found that the riddles that he received as answers were far beyond his ken. As he added questions to his questions, the riddles grew in sarcasm so that his confusion soon became frustration. Just as he realized what a fool he must seem, sitting naked and unarmed in his own wagon, puzzled by words of his own language, holding the reins but ignorant of his intended destination—all disappeared except the woman, who suddenly became a great black bird, cawing in laughter at his plight as Her wings slid off into the morning air.

But Morrigan was not satisfied to have shown the man a fool. When next the warrior Cu Chulainn fought upon a battlefield, She gathered fifty white heifers and linking them together with a perfect silver chain, She took the form of a heifer without horns, thus leading the herd across the fields and waters—until the confusion they had caused among the troops of Cu Chulainn gave the advantage to his enemy. The Morrigan then made Herself into a long black eel and twisted about the arms and legs of Cu Chulainn so that he was unable to move in the waters but just as he was almost able to pull the eel from his body, She became a sharp toothed wolf, cutting deep and painful gashes on his arms. In this way they battled, until the dark of evening began to cover all. Then She left him on the battlefield—knowing that he would make his way towards home to heal his cut and broken body.

The Morrigan too had been badly hurt, especially about the face and eyes. Realizing that She could best be healed by the one who had caused the wounds, if She could win three blessings from him, She soon devised a plan. So it was that at the next noon, She became an old woman with a milking pail, sitting with a cow by the side of the road, the path that Cu Chulainn would have to take upon his journey to his home. When he came along the road, as She knew that he must do, his body as dry and tired as She suspected, She called out the offer of a cup of milk, suggesting that it might be pleasant to feel the wetness upon his throat. Not knowing who the woman was, he came gratefully to Her side and drank the creamy liquid from the cup, blessing Her for Her kindness as he took the empty cup from his mouth. When She poured a second time, again he drank and blessed the woman and yet a third time did he do the same until—thrice blessed—The Morrigan was healed.

Cu Chulainn was startled as The Morrigan then spread Her raven wings and more so when the old woman disappeared and the large raven that took Her place perched itself upon a nearby bramble. It was then that he heard the shrill cawing prophesies of a future grim and short in time, and watched as the wide black wings of The Morrigan disappeared into the distance—as he stood earthbound and fearful of Her wrath and magical powers.

MACHA

The name of Macha (literally meaning mighty) is given as one of the three aspects of The Morrigan, but in several accounts Macha appears almost as a separate deity. Thus we may regard the following material, primarily from the Irish *Noinden Ulad,* as the acts of Macha, while at the same time consider them to be the actions of one of the aspects of The Morrigan. Macha appears to be the embodiment of the equine imagery of the Goddess, suggesting a relationship to the Celtic Mare Goddess known in Europe as Epona. Two sites in Ireland's county of Ulster still bear the name of Macha, one an ancient capital of Ulster known as Emain Macha, literally Twins of Macha, the other, Ard Macha, the present day city of Armagh. The story of the curse that Macha laid upon the county of Ulster is one that might well linger in our minds upon considering the tragic plight of that county today.

In the days when dense forest still covered the earth, the mighty Macha came with Her great axe and cleared the land—so that the cattle could graze, so that the wheat could grow.

Again She came in the days of the two brothers, of Cimbaeth who was evil, of Dithorba who was cruel. Saviour of the people, She drove the brothers from the land and then ruled upon their throne for seven years. But the sons of Dithorba challenged Her rights; five lads lay claim to one throne, yet no better were they than their father had been and mighty Macha caused them to flee beyond the borders of the province.

When rumours gained entrance to the court that the sons of Dithorba made camp in the forest nearby, living for the day that they could defeat the mighty Macha and dominate the land as their father and uncle had done, Macha left the court, disguised as a leper. Deep in the damp green of the woods She spied the campfire, the wild boar roasting for dinner—and the five brothers who sat about it, plotting Her destruction.

Though the sight of the leper woman hardly pleased them, they allowed Her to stay at the edge of the warmth, uncomfortably withdrawing to the other side of the blazing logs to return to battle talk and brew. Four dry logs had been brought to the fire when the youngest thought, despite Her apparent disease, to use Her in the woods. Thinking Her a simpleton, he suggested a stroll but upon reaching a great oak, he fell upon Her with violent force—only to find himself tightly bound against that tree and left alone in the forest.

Returning to the campfire, Macha explained his absence by telling of the shame he must have felt for lying with a leper, until a hearty laugh was had by all, but soon the second youngest thought to do the same. Just as with the first, he was left in the woods secured to a great oak, not far from the one that held his captured brother. This time Macha told of the second lad's shame, yet it was not but the burning of another log before a third was tempted, and thus the fourth, and thus the fifth—until it came to pass that the five sons of Dithorba found themselves bound captives in the forest.

With Her magic She had tied them. With Her magic She then taught them, so that each became a faithful servant of the mighty Goddess. It was in this way that the five sons of Dithorba came to build the temple of Emain Macha, serving Her there for the rest of their lives.

Many years later, Macha took the form of a poor young peasant woman and after wandering through the forest, She entered the small wooden house of Crunnchu, a widower yet not much past a lad. Making Her way about the cabin, She soon fit it to Her liking. When She was satisfied with what She had done, She beckoned to the fellow—who was more than pleased to find such a woman in his home.

For moments that seemed as eons, for eons that passed as moments, so pleased was Macha with Her life that She made the life of Crunnchu one of joy and abundance—until his only wish was that children might enter into such bliss. In this way it happened that Macha, the mighty Macha, grew great with life.

It was not without a bit of surprise that Crunnchu glimpsed this mother-to-be darting about between the trees, so swiftly that Her feet seemed never to touch the ground so that when a time soon came that Crunnchu happened to be in Ulster and chanced upon the men of the Ulster Court, he told them of this wonder, of a pregnant woman who could run faster than the king's horses. Of course they laughed, with insinuations that the man was daffy, but Crunnchu continued to insist until the men of Ulster grew so angry that they cried, 'blasphemy that anyone should dare to so insult the name of the king by saying that his wife, full with child, could run faster than the steeds of the royal stable'.

'Blasphemy!', they cried and swore to take his head—and then relented just enough to let him try to prove the truth of such an absurd claim. So it was that upon his return to the mother of the yet-forming child he had desired, Crunnchu told Her of his days in

54

She sprang off so lightning quick

Ulster and insisted that She must save his head by proving that his claim was veritable truth. He looked upon the swelling roundness in which the child lay, never suspecting that the woman was other than mortal, yet so worried was he for his own head that even when She begged for time—at least until after the birth—saying that to run now might endanger the babe, perchance kill the mother, he ruled that they must go. Perhaps the men of Ulster, seeing Her so filled with new life, might see fit to postpone the challenged race—but go they must, for his head was in peril.

Almost in disbelief of Crunnchu's willingness to chance Her life for his, Macha arrived at the court of Ulster to be greeted with jeering cries of blasphemy, doubt and challenge. Nowhere, in the hearts of the crowd that had formed, was there anything that might keep them from watching such a race. Already the king's steeds pranced about, nipping at their reins, anxiously waiting for the moment that they would be set loose. The noise of the gathered crowd was thunderous. How dare a man claim that his wife could best the finest horses of Conchobar, the King of Ulster?

Right up to the starting line She tested their hearts as they thought to test Her legs. Not a 'stop' was to be heard among the thousands, though they swarmed by the place where the great horses waited, watching, as She stood for a moment to pull the pins from Her braided bun, watching, as hair coloured with the glow of burning embers blew behind Her as a mane in the wind. Then She sprang off so lightning quick that it seemed that She flew over the horses and pulled ahead with such a speed that the royal steeds were hardly to the halfway mark—when She calmly made Her way across the finish line.

But this is not the ending of this story, for the mighty Macha, as quickly and easily as She had run, then brought forth the set of twins that had grown in Her womb and took one up under each powerful arm. No one made a move. The air was dense with quiet as thrice victorious Macha, Her new born babes held close to Her sides, stood before the now frightened men of Ulster. With the resounding echo of prophetic words that will never be forgotten, Her voice rang out into the silence. Thus She cursed them for their pride and for the cold blood in their hearts and warned them that misery and suffering as painful as the labour of childbirth was to be Her punishment of Ulster for nine times nine generations. And with these words, Macha took Her twins and left the land of Ulster.

CERRIDWEN

The name of Cerridwen has been translated both as Cauldron of Wisdom and Fortress of Wisdom, *caer* meaning fortress, *cerru* meaning cauldron. Although references to Cerridwen occur as fragments in several texts, most of the information about Her is to be found in the work of the Welsh Elis Grufydd done in the sixteenth century A.D. Grufydd relied upon oral traditions and earlier texts in compiling his treatises on ancient Celtic literature. The powers attributed to Cerridwen, who was described by Grufydd as a witch, reveal Her nature as one imbued with great wisdom, prophetic foresight and magical shapeshifting abilities. This account, of the theft of these powers by the male Gwion, may offer some insight into the otherwise puzzling accounts of Merlin's capture by The Lady of the Lake (see Morgan le Fay and The Lady of the Lake).

Mighty in magic, enchantment and divination, the ancient Cerridwen lived upon an island in a lake, some say on the waters of Llyn Tegid in Penllyn in County Caernarvon in Wales, while others say that it was on the island of the Sidhe, the place known as The Land Beneath the Waves.

It was on the island that a son was born to Cerridwen, a boy that She named Morfran, because he was as black as a raven. But some called him Afagddu saying that his darkness was ugly, so that the dark Cerridwen worried that the life ahead of him would not be one of ease or pleasure. Thus Cerridwen decided to give Her son a birth gift of the magical powers that She knew so well, hoping that this might make Morfran's years on earth easier for him to live. For this reason She began to prepare the Cauldron of the Deep, the cauldron known as Aven, from which three drops of liquid providing foresight and magical powers could be given to Her son.

Some say that She followed the Books of Pherylt. Some say that She followed those of Vergil. Yet none say that the magic cauldron Aven was not Hers. Into it, She poured the water of prophesy and inspiration and then carefully observing the movements of the moon, the sun and each and every star, She was able to add each herb, each root, even the foam of the ocean, at the proper planetary moments. As the ingredients began to boil, cress and wort and vervain simmering in the waters, She arranged for a blind old man to keep the fire burning, and for a young lad named Gwion to stir the contents of the cauldron.

Nine women stood close by, just as the nine women of Bridget tended the ancient fire at Kildare. Some say that those at the cauldron of Cerridwen were the Druidesses of the Isle of Sein, sacred island off the coast of Brittany, lived upon by women who could take the form of any animal, ban filid who could blow the seas into a rage with their perfect poetry, ban fathi who could heal all wounds and illness and foretell the events of the future. All agree that the nine women breathed upon the magic cauldron as it boiled night and day for one entire year.

But a year and a day was the time the formula required. When the day finally came in which the three drops would be ready, Cerridwen placed young Morfran by the cauldron to receive the legacy that She had prepared for him. Then in fatigue, after all that She had done, Cerridwen fell asleep in the woods nearby. But young Gwion, seeing that the year and the day were drawing to a close and that Cerridwen was still asleep in the forest, shoved the child Morfran to one side and scooped the three precious drops on to his own fingers, which he quickly thrust into his mouth—as the poisonous remainder of the waters split the very sides of the cauldron apart and poured out upon the ground.

The thundering noise of the cracking cauldron woke Cerridwen from Her sleep. Soon realizing what had happened, She moved to punish Gwion who used his new gained powers to change into a hare and hop off as quickly as his legs would take him. Cerridwen took the form of a greyhound and followed in swift pursuit until She was just about to catch the lad—when he changed into a fish and slipped into a nearby river. Cerridwen then took the body of an otter and diving into the water She was soon close to the tail of Gwion, who in terror that he might be caught, changed into a bird and flew off into the sky, only to find that Cerridwen was still close behind him—in the form of a great hawk.

Fearing more than ever that the time of his punishment and death were growing near, Gwion noticed a pile of wheat upon the land below and changing himself into the tiniest of grains, he dropped upon the pile. Cerridwen's sharp eyes saw what he had done and taking the form of a black crested hen, She pecked at the grains until She found and ate the seed that had been Gwion— thinking that would be the end of him.

But the tiny grain of Gwion took root inside Her womb and soon began to grow. Cerridwen swore the nine months long that on the day that Gwion would be reborn, She would destroy the infant, yet upon the day of birth She relented, hesitating to strangle the new born child. So it was that with the intention of leaving him to his fate, She placed him in a leather sack and threw him into the raging waters—two days before the first of May.

*   *   *

The ancient poet Taliesin, spoken of by many as the wisest and most profound of Gaelic prophets, claimed that he had once been Gwion, born from Cerridwen's womb. Saying that his leather sack had been fished from a lake on All Hallow's Eve, holy Samhain when dead souls rise, Taliesin also claimed that he had once been the wizard Merlin, thus making it most clear that Celtic wisdom, poetry, magic and foresight, the riddles beneath which divine knowledge lies, had long ago been stolen from the cauldron of the ancient Cerridwen.

MORGAN LE FAY AND THE LADY OF THE LAKE

The image of Morgan le Fay is generally thought to have been derived from earlier Celtic beliefs in The Morrigan. Although Morgan le Fay and The Lady of the Lake are most often described and presented as two quite separate figures, the many curious links between them, that I have described here, suggest that they may both have been derived from a single, earlier, concept of the Goddess. Again we will want to remember the widespread habitation of the Celts in Europe, as we read of Morgan le Fay in England and Wales, Morgain la Fée in France, and Fata Morgana in Italy. Along with similarities of mystic isles, secret lakes and castles on crystal mountains, the events surrounding the Celtic accounts of Arthur, and the sword Ex Calibur, should lead us to a more careful exploration of the connection between these two figures, whether as Goddess or Faerie Queens. In exploring these connections, it may also be helpful to consider the other Goddess images associated with specific bodies of water; Sequana of the River Seine, Boann of the River Boyne, Danu of the Danube, Cerridwen of Lake Llyn Tegid and the magical Caer who lived on Loch Bel Dragon. (The lake of Caer may offer some insight into the traditions surrounding Loch Ness in Celtic Scotland, the Loch Ness 'monster' said to have been 'subdued' by the Christian missionary St. Columba at about 550 A.D.) The stories of the male wizard Merlin, being captured by The Lady of the Lake, may be the result of the confusion caused by transitions of the powers of the earlier images of the Goddess to a male, as more clearly described in the accounts of Cerridwen and Taliesien/Gwion.

Queen of the mystic isle of Avalon, Morgan le Fay, was woven with delicate haunting threads into the tales of Celtic Britain, yet was She not still remembered by those who lived upon the continent where tribes of Celts first made their home and there spoken of as the magical Morgain la Fée, the Queen of Faerie? And does Her memory linger in the one they described as Faerie Queen Melusina, She whose spirit was said to come forth from the bubbling springs in the Forêt Columbiers while memories of the Faerie Queen in Celtic Germany told of a wondrous palace upon a crystal mountain on an island in a lake where flowers bloomed throughout the year, a perfect paradise—inhabited by ten thousand women, yet visible to very few.

Celtic memories of the great Queen Morgan also lingered in Italian lands, where tales were told of Fata Morgana who lived beneath the waters of a lake. But Bojardo wrote that the powerful Fata Morgana was but another name for the holy Goddess Fortuna, She whose shrines once graced Etruscan towns where omens of the future bubbled forth from underground springs. And there are those who say that Fata and Fortuna were but other names for The Three who were known as The Fates, for are not Fata, Fay and Faerie simply other ways of saying Fate?

Some claim that Morgan le Fay was sister to King Arthur, and that it was She who took his body upon Her holy barge to the island of Avalon when he lay close to dying, yet some speak of the Faerie Viviane, She who was known as The Lady of the Lake in the Forest Broceliande in Brittany, and say that She too made that fateful ride. Many claim that it was The Lady of the Lake who gave the sword Ex Calibur to Arthur, that martial sceptre that allowed Arthur to sit upon the throne, yet they also claim that the sword of rule had first been forged in Morgan's Avalon. Still we hear that at the moment before Arthur's death, he returned the sword to The Lady of the

Lake, who thrice brandished it in the air, before Her hand, reclaiming the sword of sovereignty, slipped into the deep waters of Her home.

Tales there are aplenty of how The Lady of the Lake tricked the wizard Merlin into teaching Her his store of magic knowledge, just as he was said to have taught Fata Morgana. Yet he who is said to have been the cornerstone of Arthur's victories through his wealth of magic powers was later imprisoned by The Lady of the Lake, who supposedly made use of what She had learned, to capture the wizard Merlin. But Taliesin claimed that he had once been Merlin, as he had once been Gwion, thus confessing that the powers and the knowledge had been stolen from the cauldron of the wise Cerridwen. Was this why it was said that the shape changing Merlin at times took the form of a woman, as people still remembered the one who first held the knowledge of enchantment: remembering the powers of the mystical Morgana, Queen of the Isle of Avalon; remembering the powers of the ancient Cerridwen, Lady of the island of the Sidhe folk, Lady of the Land Beneath the Waves; remembering the powers of The Morrigan whose mane was seen in the foamy breakers of the ocean? For had Merlin's powers truly been the greater, why then was it said that he was captured by The Lady of the Lake—while She was ever free to roam?

There are many who still search for Avalon, the island ruled by Morgan le Fay, and upon hearing that it was an isle of glass, believe it to be Glastonbury, though memories of snow capped Alps of the ancient Celtic homeland may live in images of castles upon glassy crystal mountains reflected in deep blue mountain lakes—as ancient Britain's name of Albion reflected the whiteness of Alpen peaks. And there are those who follow brooks and streams or listen for the bubbling whispers of a spring in Brittany as Gallic priestesses may once have read the omens of the future in the eddies and the windings and the flowing speech of running waters. But those who search for Avalon remember that it was known as the land of Avalloch and looking for the home of mighty Morgan, they also search for the dwelling place of The Lady of the Lake.

Where to hunt for Celtic Avalon, or the island of a castle upon a crystal mountain that may be deep beneath the waters, for is not that island always to the west, ever rich with blossoming apple trees, reminiscent of the Greek Garden of Hespera sometimes described as the homeland of the Amazons? But perhaps the island is not to be found in England, France or Germany, nor in Switzerland or Italy, nor in Libya or Greece and not even in Ireland, Scotland or Wales, or off any coast upon the earth where islands may hover grey in the distance—but in those mystic waters where lie the Isles of the Blessed or the island of the Sidhe folk—where Celtic souls were said to go when they departed from mortal bodies, as Arthur went to Morgan's Avalon when life left his body.

Perhaps it is the Heaven Loch, eternal isle haven upon eternal waters and no matter how far to the west one goes, the island is yet further to the west, forever lit by the glow of the setting sun. For is it not there that the Mighty Regina, Morgan, Mistress of Avalon, waits for each of us to one day sail to Her—there to learn that beyond the setting sun is the Morgan that is morning.

BRIDGET

The transitions in the status and nature of the Brigante Goddess Bridget, whose powers were celebrated at the Celtic ritual of Imbolc on February 1st, help us to more clearly understand the continual process of the Christianizing of early Celtic deities. In the case of the information on Bridget, we are fortunate enough to have both the accounts of Bridget as the supreme Goddess of the Brigantes, as well as accounts of the later canonization of Bridget as a Christian saint—said to have been the midwife to the Virgin Mary. The fire at Bridget's shrine in Kildare, originally tended by priestesses, was later cared for by Catholic sisters—until the decree of a Bishop declared it to be pagan, and ordered that the fire be extinguished in 1220 A.D.

Across the lands that lie between the town of Nottingham and that of Leeds, nearly all the lands that now comprise the province of Yorkshire, the Gaelic Brigantes, driven from the shores of Gaul, called upon the name of the Great One, the Mother who was known as Mighty—as Brigantia, Briginda, Brigidu and Bridget, Divine Ancestress of the Brigantes who had given them so much for which to be grateful.

Some say that Bridget was born exactly at sunrise, and that a great tower of flame reached from the top of Her small head all the way into the heavens—thus signalling the birth of a holy babe. It was this very same fire that was tended by the Daughters of the Flame, the nine who are Ingheau Anndagha, those who lived inside the fence of Bridget's shrine and could be looked upon by no man, to insure that the purity and sanctity of the fire would be protected.

It was through these sacred women that the wisdom of Bridget was spread among the people, spoken by the priestesses to the women of the village, those who brought them food, and in this way heard of the healing herbs and which would cure what ailment. It was in this way that women also learned of the sites of the healing springs which became known about the countryside as Bridget's wells of healing, for the water of these wells could cure the leper or make the impotent husband able to join his wife in bringing children into their lives.

Bridget's wisdom reached the smithy, so that he learned how to forge the iron that would soften in the heat of the fire, and even how that fire might best be built and kept. And from Bridget came the tales that none had known before, and the Gaelic trick of painting pictures with words. With Her wisdom She revealed that sounds might be turned into written marks, so that another, though many miles away, could hear them with their eyes. Some poets call upon Her yet, inviting Her to speak inside their heads with her tongue so sharp and sweet.

One story is told—perhaps She came Herself and told it to the speaker of the tale, for she knew much about the sacred well, the one so filled with grey stones that it was no longer used to heal the ill. 'It was Ostrialoch, son of Indoch', she said, 'who so despised the well that he destroyed it, for in it his enemy, a son of Bridget, had been cured when he lay dying.'

Yet another tale about a well has crossed past many lips, the story of a time that a man, dying of leprosy, asked of Bridget that he might die owning a cow, a richness that he had never known since birth. But Bridget proposed a greater gift, and once agreed upon, his long ill body was made well with the touch of the well's waters from Bridget's own fingertips—so that the man kneeled in promises of everlasting gratitude. Two more, stricken with the leprous skin, heard rumours of what had taken place and travelled far to ask for Bridget's help. By the well of healing waters, She instructed one to bathe the other until that other watched his skin grow well before his very eyes, while he who had helped this to happen still lived with the disease. Turning to the one now cured, Bridget bade him to do the same as had been done for him, but now, repulsed by the disease he had once suffered, the healthy one refused to help the one who had bathed him—and upon his refusal was once more stricken—at the very moment that his friend was healed. Thus Bridget taught compassion.

Bridget's fire, carried from the land of Brigantia upon the British Isle to Hibernian Kildare not far from Dublin, burned brightly with the caring of the Daughters of the Flame—and even later when it was tended by sisters of the newer Christian faith who called upon the Goddess as St. Bridget. But there finally came a time when its flames were extinguished by those of the church who knew of its beginnings and spoke of it as pagan. How dark it was after the dousing of the ancient fire.

CAILLEACH BHEUR

Folk traditions of the Cailleach Bheur are found primarily in Ireland, though closely associated with a very similar figure, sometimes known as Mala Liath (Grey Mare), in Scotland. The name Cailleach is alternately translated as hag, crone, or wise old woman. Yet it is clear from the accounts of Cailleach's ability to move mountains, and to have carried the massive stones of the sacred circles and cairns in her apron, that She was viewed as far more than a mortal woman. The accounts explaining that it was the Cailleach who created the many stone monuments in Celtic areas may once again cause us to suspect the origins of the attributes credited to the wizard Merlin, one of which was that he alone had brought the stones to Stonehenge, and built the great monument himself. The images of both the Cailleach, and Mala Liath, as a grey mare, provide possible connections to the images of the Irish Macha and the Welsh Rhiannon, and we may once again look to the ancient Mare Goddess Epona for their origins.

The Old Woman of Bheur, Daughter of the Moon, ran with the wild animals of the woods, yet threw thunderbolts from the heavens, raised and calmed the winds and sometimes set the forests of Scotland and Ireland on fire, if the people aroused Her anger. Still, She cared for Her herd of deer with tenderness, as they roamed along the rockiest of western beaches, and even brought fish and seaweed to feed them when they could not find enough food for themselves.

She might take the form of an eagle or a sleek black cormorant to fly across the waters but whatever shape the Cailleach would take, She would carry her magic wand that brought frost and snow to the land, when its tip grazed the earth. It was a branch of such immense power that many tried to steal it or to gain possession of it by trickery but none succeeded, for the Cailleach easily outwitted all who dared.

Some speak of the Cailleach as Mala Liath, saying that She dwells in Scotland and that Her giant being can be seen along the most deserted beaches, while others claim that She makes Her home in Ireland—and pointing to her sacred site in County Covan. they tell of the time that Patrick destroyed Her cairn. Some claim that these circles or mounds of rocks had been poured out from Her apron on to the hills of Meath, pointing to the sacred stones at Knowth. Still others claim that She moved the mountains and the islands off the coast of western Kerry and that it is from the peninsula of Berre that She takes Her name, explaining that the rocks that She dropped upon the earth had been carried in Her creeling basket and that it was upon Berre that they first fell—yet those in Limerick say they know the Cailleach best, for She is none but the Queen of the Faeries of Limerick.

Nearly always appearing in some disguise, She takes all shapes and forms and might become a great grey stone or a pale grey mare, so enormous that She leaps from mountaintop to mountaintop. One can never be certain that any person, any animal, any rock, is not filled with Her being. One tale they tell of the Cailleach is about the three brothers who sat by their fire in the woods of Scotland at the end of a day's hunting, eating the catch that they had roasted on the spit. It was at that moment that an old and unkempt beggar woman came out of the woods, pleading for a bite to eat and to sit by the warmth of the fire. When the eldest ignored the old woman's requests, the woman turned to the next in age but was this time met with flat refusal. Before the woman even had a chance to ask the youngest, the lad stepped forth and offered the poor woman what meat he had left and made a place for her by the fire. When the time for sleeping came, the youngest brother worried that the old woman might freeze in the damp night air and thus offered half his blanket—and the place beside him on his bed of soft pine needles. They say that it was in this way that the youngest brother of the three came to spend the night with the Cailleach, the Queen of the Faeries—never regretting for a moment that he had been so kind.

But another story is of a man who did not fare as well, for when he chased a wild boar, determined to kill it for his dinner, he of course was unaware that it was the Cailleach, enjoying romping in the forest for the day. As the day went on, Her anger grew with each arrow that She diverted, but when the sun began to set and the man continued to give chase to the boar who had outwitted him all day, the Cailleach filled with rage and caused a thorn of poison to prick his foot—so that by early evening, it was that hunter who lay dead in the forest.

MAEVE (MEDB)

The image of Maeve is a somewhat unusual combination of a Faerie Queen and a martial leader of troops (see Scandinavian Section—Freya). Maeve's appearance in the *Tain Bo Cualgne* is as a mighty queen, and general of the army of the Irish county/state of Connacht. Both Her husband Aillil and Her lover Fergus rode alongside Her in battle, Maeve clearly leading the way for all three. In the *Fled Bricrenn* of the *Lebor na L'Uidre,* Maeve was portrayed as a judge of protocol and status among the Celtic peoples. As Queen of the Faeries, Maeve's tomb was said to be a cairn overlooking Sligo Bay, in an area that was once part of Connacht. Later images of Maeve as the Shakespearian Mab, Queen of the Faeries, were based upon these ancient traditions of the Celtic Medb or Maeve, as they remained in Anglo-Saxon England.

Tales of the mighty Queen Maeve still linger in memories of Celtic lands, some saying that She is the Queen of Faerie and that those who truly know Her, speak of Her as the magical Mab, the Queen of Elfhame: Others say that She was a mortal queen of County Connacht and wore the purple robes of royalty, Her sceptre a massive iron sword—yet upon the shoulders of this queen of mortal body, they say there perched two sacred golden birds whose magic voices whispered wisdom into the ears of Maeve.

Owner of the Sovereignty of Ireland, the throne was Hers alone, for only when Maeve chose a new lad for Her bed, might he then claim the title of a king. There are many who remember that until Maeve had slept with the fellow, even Cormac was not a king of Ireland, and that when She led the troops of Connacht to retrieve Her brown bull from Conchobar of Ulster, it was yet another husband, Aillil, who rode at Her right side, while Her lover Fergus rode at Her left.

Whether Faerie Queen or General, the spirit of Maeve still rides through the woods along the upper Shannon and floats heaviest in the mist near the cave at Cruachan, the cave to the Netherworld, the cave not far from the town called Elphin, the place where the words that She spoke when Ireland was but young may still be heard echoing through the trees:

> If I married a selfish man
> our union would be wrong
> because I am so full of grace and giving.
> It would be wrong if I were the more generous,
> yet I would not want to take more than I offered.
> I would not want a timid man
> for I must admit that I thrive upon action
> and believe that any couple must be equal in spirit.
> It would be wrong if I married a jealous man
> for never have I been with one man
> without another waiting patiently in his shadow.

The spirited courage of warrior Queen Maeve rides through the recollections of the many battles that ancient Connacht had with Ulster—just as many Celtic women warriors linger in other memories: the mighty Scathatch who lived beyond Alba, said to be a genius in both weaponry and prophesy; the courageous Aife who some say lived as far to the east as Greece; the Gwyddonod of Gloucester, the nine of them remembered as crones, warriors, prophets and witches; the Iceni's Queen Boudicca who burned the town of London down to defy the Roman army and then offered gratitude to the holy Andrasta, Iceni Goddess of Victory, revered upon the land where Norfolk now stands; Brigante Queen Cartimandua who decided upon a peaceful treaty with Claudius of Rome and so put aside her husband who opposed her decision—choosing to rule the people of Bridget as sole sovereign of the tribe.

Was it the ban filid, the poet/prophetess Fedelm, she who carried a golden weaving rod, saying that she was a student of vision and verse in Alba when her wagon chanced to pass Maeve's chariot upon the road, who wrote so many tales of the mighty Maeve? And was it the poetess Fedelm, she of the yellow hair and ebony brow, she who looked out upon the world with triple irised eyes, who told of Maeve leading the Connacht troops in battle and of how many fine children Maeve had brought forth from Her womb—and how Maeve assured them of Her mother strength by saying, "I can best thirty men a day—on the battlefield or on the bed."

RHIANNON

The name Rhiannon was derived from an earlier name for this image of the Goddess among the Welsh, Rigantona, literally translated as Great Queen Goddess. The importance of the pale-white horse of Rhiannon, and the magical bag of abundance that She possessed, both suggest that the image of Rigantona was in turn derived from the Mare Goddess Epona. Epona was often depicted at Celtic sites in Europe, carrying a similar bag or pouch, inscriptions beneath Her image carrying the epithet—Regina (Queen). The assertive wit, tinged with a bit of sarcasm, that is noticeable in the words attributed to Maeve, is also found in several of the passages of the *Cyfranc a'r Mab* of the *Mabinogin* that are concerned with Rhiannon. One passage records that as Rhiannon rode upon Her magical horse, a prince of Dyfed made many attempts to catch up with Her, each in vain. After several days of trying, always finding his horses slower than Hers, the prince finally called out, asking Her to wait. Rhiannon turned to the prince, still far behind Her, agreeing to his request, but not hesitating to add, ". . . and it would have been far better for the horse had you asked long before this."

ANCIENT MIRRORS of WOMANHOOD

The Great Queen Goddess, Rigantona, Regina, Rhiannon, rode upon Her pale white horse, canwelw coloured mare, ambling at a steady gait, seemingly as slow and aimless as the clouds that drifted by, yet no steed or stallion in the country could reach or overtake Her.

Within the holiness of Rhiannon live even older memories of Divine Epona, Her most ancient images carved in stone across the wide Gallic continent—woman sitting proudly astride the magic mare, in Her hand the bag of abundance, Her spirit and the animal as One, Her gentle foal close by Her side. This trinity of Woman, Mare and Colt, seen across the lands from France to Austria, was taken south into Rome and as far west as Uffington upon the British Isle. And wherever this triple image went, there the divinity of The Mighty Mare echoed as Regina, Queen, among the Celtic people, Her yearly feast a joyous celebration in expectation of the Winter Solstice.

Though some say that Rhiannon's home was near the magical mound of Arberth, not far from St. Bridget's Bay in Wales, and that Rhiannon was often seen there riding by in golden silk brocade; others say that Her home was on the island of the Sidhe folk where the souls of the dead resided and that it was there that She truly dwelled with Her three sacred birds that perched upon Her shoulders—as the perfect sound of their song lulled the living to death, woke the dead to life and healed all sadness and pain.

So clear and sweet were the voices of Her birds, so great their power over life and death, that many tried to capture them to keep them for their own. Thus the giant Buddaden ventured upon the island, to steal the birds from Rhiannon, but chancing upon their nest, he greedily ate the eggs the magic birds had lain so that when the Goddess came upon him, She saw feathers sprouting from his pale leathery skin. The sight was so ridiculous that Rhiannon bellowed with hearty laughter until Buddaden grew scarlet with embarrassment, and in his shame he felt the need to hide the absurdity of his feathered body. So it was that the giant Buddaden fled from the island of the Sidhe, forgetting all but his own foolishness.

Often taking Her pleasure in the woods, ever exploring and playing among the trees and in the meadows, in the form of any animal that She cared to take for the hour or the day, Rhiannon knew well the tiniest of roots to the greatest of oaks. Hopping as a hare across the bushy lowness of a field, a hunter one day spied Her

70

playful pace and thought to kill Her for his dinner, thus setting his dogs upon Her scented trail. So it happened that when the lad Cian saw a hare jump frightened at his feet, and saw many dogs in close chase behind it, he lifted the hare to his chest and carried it over a nearby creek. Upon reaching the far side of the waters, he was astonished to see the Goddess Rhiannon standing there before him, while the hare was nowhere to be seen.

Pleased with the lad's compassion for a small animal fleeing for its life, Rhiannon thought to honour his kind heart by welcoming him to join Her on the island of the Sidhe, for never was there a place more beautiful, air more clear or colours more brilliant. Thus Cian went to live upon the magic isle, passing his days in perfect hours, passing his months in perfect days.

Many moons had waxed and waned, and many hours had Rhiannon strolled with Cian, hearing always of his joy and pleasure in living upon such an idyllic island—until the day that the Goddess decided to enjoy the solitude of a long familiar grove bathed by thin streams of gold that pierced through the tree tops. So filled with peace did She feel that when a man crept silently up behind Her, and then tried to force his body upon Her own, She could hardly believe that such a thing was happening. Turning to see who had dared to attack Her in this way, She was more than shocked to see the face of Cian!

Anger rose from Her usually gentle being, wrath at the arrogance of such an act, a cowardly attack—without even the honour of a warning that any enemy warrior would give before engaging in a battle. Her rage doubled at the feeling of betrayal of the kindness and concern that She had shown him all those months. As if from the power of the anger, Rhiannon took the form of a great mare, whinnying with Her rage, stomping Her hooves upon the ground, until She raised a massive leg against Cian's body and splintered his thigh bone with her powerful hoof. So it was that Cian limped in pain for the remainder of his life—never able to forget either the kindness or the wrath of Rhiannon.

the oneness that lies beneath all dualities

As Mother of the corn and earth, shining as the moon yet found in the sacred caves of mountains, Her essence known in both eagle and serpent—Goddess images in Middle and South America are as rich and diverse as the many varied cultures in which they have been known and revered. But we can scarcely attempt an exploration of the nature of Goddess reverence in these areas, without first realizing that the people who settled in the more southerly areas of the two continents of the A- merican hemisphere, originally came from the same area of north- ern Asia as the Native Americans of North America.

Examinations of prehistoric sites throughout the two American continents, and in Siberia, suggest that the many waves of migrations of the Mongolian peoples who crossed the Bering Strait into Alaska, and gradually moved southwards, may have begun as early as 40,000 B.C. If recent studies at Fell's Cave are correct, some of the groups that crossed over from Siberia, from there making challenging and courageous treks over many thou- sands of miles, appear to have reached the southernmost tip of South America by 11,000 B.C. More conservative scholars state that this most southerly point was inhabited by at least 6000 B.C.

Although we have long been encouraged to regard the Native Americans of North America as quite separate from the Native Americans of Middle and South America, the archaeological and anthropological evidence suggests that early Native Americans traversed the two continents with quite different perceptions of the land than those accompanying contemporary views of national borders. It is somewhat ironic for U.S. citizens, especially those descended from Caucasians, whose ancestors lived in Europe until just a few centuries ago, to regard a Native Mexican or Native South American of today, one who is descended from people who had lived in and made their way through North America over a period of so many thousands of years—as an alien in North America. It is equally ironic that the Rio Grande River (at one time, a major route for those who had lived in what is now known as Colorado and New Mexico to the land that is now known as Mexico) today comprises such a major portion of the U.S./Mexican border.

It was long believed that most of the groups that had settled in the southerly areas of the western hemisphere had continued to subsist on food gathering, fishing, and small game hunting, until shortly before the arrival of Columbus and the Spanish conquerors. Now, several studies, such as that of the Tehuacan Valley of Mexico, reveal that there was an understanding of agricultural methods in this area, perhaps as long ago as 6000 B.C. Early cultivation of beans, maize, squash, and chili peppers, have been noted at several sites, suggesting that agriculture in the 'New World' developed relatively shortly after it did in the Near and Middle East—and prior to its development in northern and western Europe.

Although the dates of origin are as yet uncertain, the cultures of Mexico and Guatamala had developed a form of glyph writing that appears on stone carvings, and on accordian folded bark paper made from the fibers of the *copo* plant. Surviving fragments of this writing reveal that the peoples of this area possessed an extremely complex knowledge of mathematics and astronomy. Accounts, of Europeans from the sixteenth century, state that upon their arrival to this area, they were surprised to find that most major villages and cities kept archives of many books. Though some of the original writings have survived, much still undeciphered, the majority of them were destroyed. Unfortunately, most of the earliest sources of evidence about these cultures are accounts written by Catholic friars who accompanied the soldiers at the time of the Spanish conquests. Biased attitudes, towards the beliefs and customs of the people of Mexico and Guatamala, were made clear in the writing of Spanish Franciscan Bishop Diego de Landa who referred to the holy books of the Mayans as " . . filled with superstitions and lies." He ordered a mass burning of all Mayan books in 1562. Though he also recorded, ". . . we burned them all", several books survived, later surfacing in Europe, probably as a result of having been kept as souvenirs by Spanish soldiers.

Alongside evidence from the writings mentioned above, numerous Goddess images have been discovered at sites at least as old as 2000 B.C. Even older images may still lie buried in the vast areas of South America that have never been explored for archaeological remains. Though we have no written records of names, or information on the nature, of Goddess reverence in the earliest periods, one of the more ancient concepts of the Goddess may be that later embodied in the Goddess as Chantico. This Goddess of Fire, both of hearth and volcanic eruption, was included as a minor deity in Aztec beliefs. She may have been worshipped at the pre-Aztec open air altar, set upon a high adobe mound, built to face the volcanic Ajusco range of Mexico. Though little is known about Chantico, other than Her primary attribute of volcanic fire, She may have been the source of some of the symbolism associated with the Mother of All Deities as known among the Aztecs. Images of the Goddess as Mother Coatlicue, Her altars of cooled lava, Her birth of a child that was described as volcanic obsidian, and Her home upon the peak of a high mountain always covered with a dense cloud—each suggest volcanic symbolism in the worship of Coatlicue. Though it is certainly plausible that such imagery would naturally develop among people who lived in such a heavily volcanic area, comparisons with the Goddess as Mahuea in New Zealand and the Goddess as Pele in Hawaii, are difficult to avoid (see Oceanic Section).

The multiplicity of names, that we today identify with Goddess reverence in Mexico and Guatamala, may be partially the result of various languages and dialects, as well as of the many titles and epithets of the deities. Coatlicue literally means Lady of the Serpent Skirt. Tonantzin simply means Our Mother. Toci means Our Grandmother. Tonacacihuatl is the word for Goddess. Teteu Innan (Teteoinan) is translated as She Who Gives Birth, a title not unlike that of Coatlicue as Mother of All Deities. This last title is also applied to the Goddess as Tlazteotl—known to have received confession, absorbed the sins of the guilty, and to have thus purified all worshippers.

The Goddess known as Chicomecoatl was most closely associated with the growing of maize (corn), known to the Aztecs as *zea mays*. Ilamatecuhtli was known as Old Princess, symbolic of the maize at the time of its full ripening. The early stages of the maize crop were symbolized by the young Xilonen. Both Goddess images, Ilamatecuhtli and Xilonen, are aspects of Chicomecoatl, revered as The Great Corn Mother. The use of the word *coatl,* meaning serpent, in the names of Chicomecoatl and Coatlicue, suggests a possible linking between these two images as well.

Ideas, similar to beliefs about The Corn Mother of Mexico, may have been shared by those who settled in and around the Andes Mountains. Although in most studies of ancient Peru, the male Viracocha is named as the supreme deity of this area, along with the claim of his singular importance, it is often more casually added that Viracocha was the supreme deity of the ruling Incas, but that the worship of a Goddess of the crops, Pachamama, was the most common form of religious belief among the general farming population. Along with this reverence for the Goddess of the farming people, those who lived along the coastal areas also revered a Goddess of the Sea, whom they spoke of as Mamacocha, and envisioned as a great whale. The similarities of the names Mamacocha and Viracocha (*cocha* meaning sea), along with a prayer to Viracocha that begins, "Viracocha, Lord of the Universe, whether female or male, at any rate guardian of the sun and the making of new life . . . ", suggest that the deity of the sea may once have been regarded as a gynandrous being. Gynandrous, and closely coupled deities, were not uncommon in Middle and South America. The supremacy of the male aspect among the ruling Incas, while only the female aspect was called upon by the coastal population, may even reveal a complete change of gender by a clergy closely associated with the male dominant Inca regime. The moon was also revered as a Goddess image among the ancient Peruvians, Her name, Mamaquilla, translated as Golden Mother.

Although it is generally accepted by most scholars that the primary route by which Native Americans of both continents entered the western hemisphere was by way of the Bering Strait, there is some evidence of possible contact between the people of Central and South America and Polynesian groups. Extreme similarities in the construction and scaling of music pipes, the widespread use of the word *kumara* for sweet potato, feather mosaics, and specific weaving and dyeing processes, all point to possible connections. A minor strain of Australoid skeletal structure, common among Polynesians, has been noted in the Americas.

The general attitudes towards these links have been to believe that they are purely coincidental, or to assume that the people of Polynesia, even Asia, must have influenced the 'New World'. This last conjecture was supported by the drifting of a boat from Osaka to southern California in 1815. But it is just as possible, if these developments were indeed connected, that at least some of the knowledge may have travelled in the direction of Heyerdahl's raft, drifting from Peru to the Tuamoto Islands (northeast of Tahiti) in 1947. The nature of the Goddess as Chantico, and the imagery of the Goddess as Coatlicue, may certainly be compared to beliefs about the Goddess as Pele in Hawaii, the Goddess as Mahuea in New Zealand, and the Goddess as Fuji among the Ainu of Japan, while the cave of the Goddess of the Cuna of Panama may bring the rituals of the Australian Kunapipi to mind. But statements made about direct influence, and especially the source of that influence, would at this time be hypothetical at best.

Perhaps the truth to be gained from an exploration of the Goddess in Mexico, Central, and South America, is that travelling from one side of the planet to the other has been in vogue for some 40,000 years. Developments that were not the result of contact, or direct influence, may help us to better understand the astonishing similarities and ingenuities of the human mind, in relating and responding to specific environmental situations. The reverence for the Goddess as symbolized by maize, rain, moon, and volcano, are perhaps not too surprising. But the theological concepts embodied in the Goddess of the Cuna in Panama, who welcomes each girl into sacred womanhood, and the joyful Chibcha Huitaca, who beckons us from the chastity and sobriety demanded by Bochica—to sing, dance and rejoice in Her moonlight—may be images of Goddess that most deeply touch that elusive essence that we refer to as our souls.

MU OLOKUKURTILISOP

Knowledge of the puberty rituals for young women, and the reverence for the Goddess, of the Cuna peoples of Panama, is drawn from anthropological field studies done during this century, especially the work of Dr. Clyde Keeler. The painting of the red juice of the saptur fruit upon the face of the initiate, as a symbol of the menarche, is echoed in menarche rituals among the Navajo. The cave, as the burial place of the dead, offers an interesting parallel to the womb/cave of the Goddess as Kunapipi in Australia (see Oceanic Section).

Deep in the sacred caves of the mountain Tarcarcuna, overlooking the deep waters of the Gulf of Darien, the spirit of the Goddess Mu, Giant Blue Butterfly Lady, still lingers lovingly, protecting the women of the Cuna tribe.

In the days before the world began, Mu gave birth to the sun and taking Her sun as Her lover, She gave birth to the moon. Mating with her grandson Moon, She brought forth the stars, so many that they filled the heavens. Then mating with the stars, the sacred womb of Mu once again stirred with life so that in this way She brought forth all the animals and plants. It is for this reason that Cuna people remember that Mu Olokukurtilisop gave birth to the universe—created all that exists.

The first Cuna people made their homes in the caves of Tarcarcuna but even when they wandered as far as the Chucunaque River, still they brought their dead back to the caves of the mountain, there to rest in the womb of Mother Mu, the protective womb from whence all people came.

Close to the caves of Tarcarcuna, stands the sacred grove of saptur, trees whose fruit contains the juice of the menstrual blood of Mu. And close to the grove is the sacred hut of the Inna, the shrine of female puberty that each young woman enters at the time of her new womanhood, the time she celebrates the ceremonies of the Inna. On the ground near the Inna shrine, the young one lies being as one with the earth, as the older women toss the sacred soil upon her. Gathering in a circle about her, they sit on the benches to form the Ring of Protection, smoke rising from their pipes as incense invoking the spirit of Mu. Then removing the covering of earth, the women take the young one and paint the red juice of the saptur, the menstrual blood of Mu, upon her face—chanting their blessings on her life, honouring her with the dance of new womanhood.

Into the sacred Inna shrine, the young woman is escorted and there the black ribbons of her hair fall upon the earth, as her childhood falls from her in the woman shrine that no man has ever entered, the holy place of Mother Mu. Emerging from the Inna shrine as a full grown woman, her golden brown face glowing with red saptur is now framed within her small black satin cap of woman hair—as she awaits the time of the omens.

One sacred saptur tree is felled by the women as a gift of Mu to the initiate. Carefully studying the cross grain of the tree, the women read each and every line, foretelling the events of the new woman's life. Only now that the woman blood has begun to flow, only now that she is one with the earth, only now that the menstrual blood of Mu has brightened her face, only now that her head is free from the weight of the hair of her childhood—is the young woman dedicated to the Goddess Mu Olokukurtilisop, brought into the sacred fold of womanhood and provided with her secret Cuna name that she will tell no others to the end of her days on earth.

AKEWA

This unique account of women's arrival upon earth, from the Toba people of Argentina, is one that may linger in the minds of many women, as we struggle to comprehend the senseless violence of both rape and war. Though images of the Goddess in many cultures of Central and South America is as the moon, the Toba reverse the situation, regarding the sun as the Goddess, the moon as male. The ability of Akewa to grow young, as well as old, may be compared to the Navajo concepts of Changing Woman (see Native American Section). For those fascinated by theories about spacemen arriving on this planet, this account, and the account of the origins of Ishtar (see Semitic Section), suggest that if such an event ever occurred, it may well have been spacewomen, rather than spacemen, who stopped by to visit or settle earth.

Who has not heard of that most ancient time when women descended from the heavens, climbing down the great rope that hung from the sky to walk upon the earth, searching for new plants and roots that they might carry back to their home in the heavens?

And who has not heard that when the women arrived the men were still animals, their bodies covered with fur, walking upon their hands as well as their feet? So it was that chancing upon the rope whose end touched the brown soil, the animals jumped at it and snapped it with their sharp teeth—so that the women from heaven were forced to remain upon the earth. It was in this way that the women of heaven and the male animals of earth began to live side by side and upon their mating with each other, they brought forth the people who now live upon the Toba lands.

Yet one woman still lives in the heavens for each day we see the fiery Akewa as She climbs from the lowest part of heaven to walk across the wide skies, bringing us Her golden light and warmth, giving us the gift of Her brilliant being—until She travels so far to the other side that She slides into the abyss at the end of the world, leaving us for the night. Just like any other woman, Akewa grows old and tired so that She walks across the heavens slowly. At that time the days are very long for Her brilliant light moves as She walks along but unlike any other woman, Akewa also grows young and in Her youth moves quickly, so that when She is young, the hours of daylight are few.

When Akewa leaves the sky each evening and the world grows dark with night, out comes an old man, one with a potbelly too full of food. Although his belly glows with a silver light, when he lays down for the night he turns from side to side—but he has never found just the right position in which to keep the huge belly, so that he may sleep in comfort.

In the vast spaces of heaven, the Jaguar also dwells, always wanting to eat Akewa and the moon man. Thus Jaguar attacks the moon each month for the moon is fat and cannot run, but Akewa fights with metal weapons so that Jaguar seldom catches Her— except for the few times that Akewa was hidden in the middle of the day and all were filled with fear that beloved Akewa was being killed and that the world would end. For who could live without the nurturing warmth and light of Akewa?

HUITACA

This wonderfully rebellious, light hearted image, of the Moon Goddess Huitaca, from the Chibcha people of Colombia, is surely a unique and delightful concept of deity. Since Bochica is regarded as a teacher of spinning and weaving, both activities done by Chibcha women, ideas about Huitaca's role may have developed in reaction to an emphasis upon industry, chastity, and sobriety, that threatened the more relaxed pleasures of a woman's life. It is tempting to assume that these pleasures had once been quite acceptable before the arrival of the ever wandering Bochica.

Wonderful Huitaca,
wild and lovely Goddess,
appearing in the night,
some say as an owl,
some say as the silver moon,
leading us into merriment,
encouraging us us to drink
the juices of intoxication,
encouraging us to feel the wonder
of the touch of our bodies against another,
until the time Bochica spoke against you,
saying that life must be completely serious—
and that the joys that you offered
must be seen as wrongs.

This joyless Bochica,
who some call Nebterequeteba,
walked throughout the countryside,
preaching that the good drinks were bad
and pleasure from our bodies even worse,
crying out that to follow your ways
was a great mistake
but just as the people of the villages
began to consider his ideas,
you appeared, laughing and happy,
teasing the unsmiling one
so that his anger rose
but all who watched and listened

soon laughed along with you,
calling you Chie and Jubchas Guaya,
Mother of Joy—
and though Bochica frowned and glowered—
we danced about the moon
and called your name.

COATLICUE

The Goddess as Coatlicue, Mother of all Aztec deities, was associated with
Aztlan, legendary homeland of the Aztecs. Current day conjecture, on a
possible location for Aztlan, ranges all the way from just north of Mexico
City to areas in New Mexico and Colorado, the latter suggestions supported by the linguistic affinities between the Aztec language and that of
the Hopi tribes of the southwestern U.S. Aztec accounts describe the
mountain upon which Coatlicue lived as being surrounded by water. Such
a description may summon up images of Pacific islands, rather than any
area on the mainland of the two American continents, but the area
surrounding the two volcanoes located on Ometepi Island, in Lake
Nicaragua, may deserve some careful exploration. This is further suggested
by the names of a pair of deities, female and male (at times depicted as one
gyandrous being), who were regarded as original creators of life and the
universe by the Aztecs (a role also attributed to Coatlicue). Their names
were Omecihuatl and Ometecuhtli, suggesting their possible connection to
Ometepi Island. It is interesting that although the Aztec word *ome* simply
meant two, in the Hopi language *oma* means cloud, and *omic* means high
or up. The repeated relationship of serpent to fire, and serpent to cloud,
among many groups in Mexico, may be derived from the image of Coatlicue as Lady of the Serpent Skirt living upon a high mountain peak,
revered at altars made of volcanic lava. Such an image of the Goddess may
or may not have a connection with the volcanic Goddess imagery of the
Oceanic peoples, but the similarities certainly provide interesting comparisons.

In the most ancient days of the peoples of Mexico, Mother
Coatlicue hid Herself in a misty cloud upon a mountaintop in the
homeland of Aztlan, while Her serpent servants lived within the

mountain's caves. From this sacred home She brought forth both the moon and the sun, and all the stars in the heavens.

It was Coatlicue who gave all life and took again in death, the necklace of skulls that She wore about Her neck or those She sometimes wore as headdress, reminder of the certain time that each would return to Coatlicue, for each was the child that She held above Her altar of molten lava. Was She not the source of all being, the One who made the earth quake, giver of the goodness of life, She who enfolded the dead in Her bosom when their life on earth was done? Was it not into Her lava altar that each would one day melt again with Her, while in Her mirrors of cooled obsidian She would reveal what the future held?

It was upon Her sacred mountain in the land of Aztlan that Coatlicue had nurtured yet another new life deep within Her holy womb, some say from the swallowing of an emerald, while others claim that a ball of soft furry feathers fell upon Her and in this way She knew that another child was to arrive. Thus the warlike Huitzilpochtli was said to have been born, though some gave his name as Tezcatlipoca and said that a son of obsidian, a smoking black mirror, was born to Coatlicue, Mother of the Deities.

Upon learning of the expected birth, the older children of Coatlicue are said to have grown angry, fearing that the new one might replace them in the heavens. So it came to pass that soon after the birth the warlike son went forth, murdering each and every star, the many holy children of Coatlicue. But when Huitzilpochtli pressed his knife blade of obsidian to the throat of Coyolxauqui, the fairest daughter of Coatlicue, the one the Mother called Golden Bells, Coatlicue broke down in grief. Recovering the severed head of the daughter who had brought the Mother's greatest joys, the daughter who had tried to protect Coatlicue from the anger of the others, Coatlicue set the golden head in a most honoured place in heaven so that daughter Coyolxauqui would never be forgotten— as Her round and radiant face lit the night time skies—from that time until now.

Still the daughter Xochiquetzal lived. They say that it was She who brought the knowledge of the spinning and the weaving; the gifts for the eyes of the painting and the carvings; the gifts for the ears of the pipes and the drums. Especially was She remembered and honoured by the women who lived as they pleased, for they say it was Xochiquetzal who taught the goodness of woman's sensuality and that when a woman felt the pleasures of her body, it brought special joy to Xochiquetzal.

From Xochiquetzal they learned the message of the marigold, the petalled book of the cycles of life, of seed to leafy stem, of leafy stem to bud, of bud to flower fully open to the sun, of flower to drying petals that housed the womb pocket of new seeds, seeds that would take root in the earth and grow again. From Xochiquetzal's teachings the people came to understand the flow of life eternal, unchanging in its ever changing, as images of Xochiquetzal on the ocelot, quetzal bird feathers rising from Her head, two flowers set in Her long black hair, thin chains of glowing jewels stretched across Her golden cheeks, provided visions of this daughter of Coatlicue.

From Xochiquetzal's mouth came words like sweet flowers. From Xochiquetzal's mouth came words as sharp as the blade of a knife. Both emerging from Her bejewelled lips, She was called upon as the Obsidian Butterfly, soft and mobile as the bright winged being that was once the hidden unmoving chrysalis, while at the same time hard as the glassy black obsidian that had once been glowing, flowing, molten lava. And was it the knowledge that Xochiquetzal was the spirit of changing, the oneness that lies beneath all dualities, that caused the people to speak of Her as The Ruler of the Land of the Dead—for it was the statues and the temple sites of Goddess Xochiquetzal that were honoured on the Holy Day of the Dead Ones, pilgrims heaping sacred marigolds upon Her perfect feet.

Yet a third daughter came from the womb of Coatlicue, She who was known as Malinalxoch. This daughter was so filled with the powers of Her Mother that the wildest animals of the jungle grew docile in Her presence—as did the humans who revered Coatlicue. Yet was it not this daughter that Huitzilpochtli spoke against, envious of Her great powers, jealous of Her ease in leadership? So it was that he told the Aztec troops he led to leave all thoughts of Malinalxoch behind—as they marched and conquered the villages of Mexico.

So long had Coatlicue been known as Mother to the people, that great statues and temples had been built in Her honour. Upon Her sacred hill of Tepeyac on the western banks of Lake Texcoco, some came to call upon Her as Tonantzin. Thus when the arriving priests of Spain noticed the great importance of the ancient holy site that was each year visited by pilgrims who brought rounded cakes of corn to honour the ancient Mother on the twelfth of December, just before the rains were due, they claimed that the site belonged to Mary. It was in this way that the ancient shrine of Coatlicue became known as the shrine of the Black Madonna, La Virgen Morena, and some began to tell of sightings and miracles of Mary at the temple of The Lady of Guadalupe Hidalgo—while the spirit of She who gave birth to the sun and the moon still lingers about the sacred site of long ago.

CHICOMECOATL

The Aztec image of Chicomecoatl was primarily that of The Great Corn Mother, revered by many peoples of the southwestern U.S., as well as in Mexico. Although Her name is literally translated as Seven Serpents, *coatl* meaning serpent, the word coatl is also known among the Pueblo people of North America—as a digging stick used to plant seeds. The connection with childbirth, as well as the sun on the shield, both suggest an association of Chicomecoatl with the Goddess as Teteu Innan.

Along the path of the valley village, the young girls danced in gay procession, following the three who had been chosen as Corn Maidens for the year: the youngest with her hair cropped short as image of the newly rising sprouts; the second whose hair fell upon her shoulders as image of the corn half grown; the oldest and tallest of the three, her waist long hair tied into a braided bun, as image of the full grown crops. Each wore the opalescent glow of fish scales painted as discs upon her golden cheeks; each had brilliant scarlet feathers thonged to golden arms and legs—as they walked proudly along the path to the temple of Mother Chicomecoatl.

The first walking of the temple way was to bring the baby sprouts of corn, to lay them at the feet of Chicomecoatl. The second walking of the temple way was when the maize had grown half way to harvesting. Yet a third time did they go, on the day when the corn waved highest in the fields, the bundles of seven ears wrapped in tissue red coverings, carried upon the backs of the holy three, as mothers might carry their children. Thus were the seven ears presented to the Goddess, the Mother of Corn, She whose spirit had made it grow.

Feasting and celebration were accompanied by deepest gratitude from those who knew the true sanctity of the corn and regarded it as a gift from Chicomecoatl. They knew this was a time for thanksgiving, the time to take the seven ears that had been blessed and store them in the granaries until the days of the sowing would come again and the dried kernels of the blessed ears would be pressed into the earth—to fulfill the sacred patterns of the Goddess.

The corn was sometimes spoken of as Cinteotl, or known as Xipe Totec, the son of Chicomecoatl. Some said that it was his spirit that lived within the ears of corn after they had ripened, his body dismembered, his skin flayed—just as the kernels were taken from the cob, yet each year reappearing in the plants that grew.

As Chicomecoatl watched over each harvest, so too did She linger protectively over all women who died in childbirth. Such women, spoken of as heroes and warriors by the people of the valleys of Mexico, having given their life for a life, their very own life's breath extinguished in the battle of labour—were especially honoured and cared for by Chicomecoatl who kept watch over their souls that resided in the highest heaven.

Some say that this ancient Mother, Her skirt covered with white flowers, Her face covered with red ochre, Her shield emblazoned with the sun, the knife of obsidian in Her hand—was the First Mother of the people of the valley of Mexico. They tell of the time that She was known long before the Tenocha Aztec tribes arrived and that it was Her spirit that was called upon at the most ancient council meetings, for it was remembered that it was Chicomecoatl who had first taught the knowledge of the ancient temple ways and that the highest priestess, Snake Woman, had once attended the mighty Corn Goddess whose essence was in the Seven Serpents of Her name.

Still She lived in heaven, even after the Aztec tribes had come, caring for the wondrous crops of corn, caring for the woman warriors as they hung as spiders upon silken spider threads, menacingly swinging from their webs in heaven, daily escorting the sun to its western destination. But there are those who say that the spiders are angry and that one day they will cause the sun and the moon to collide, crashing wildly against the stars—so that the world as we know it will end, the spiders then dropping from their celestial webs to feed upon the people of the earth, perhaps even to take life as it had once been taken from them.

TETEU INNAN

The somewhat sparse information on the Goddess as Teteu Innan (Teteoinan), from accounts of the Aztec period, portrays Her as a Goddess of childbirth, healing, and prophesy. The word *innan,* meaning birth, may be related to the title of the menarche rituals of the Cuna, the *Inna.* Teteu Innan's skirt of shells perhaps reveals a connection with the Pueblo concept of White Shell woman, the youthful manifestation of Changing Woman.

Holy Mother of Birth and Healing,
Matron Spirit of all Midwives,
Goddess of the sacred totoixitl herb,
Teteu Innan wears the skirt of many shells,
as the sky wears many stars,
a golden disc in proud display upon Her shield,
appearing in glowing visions
to those who call upon Her powers.

It is Teteu Innan who fills the wombs
of those who wish to bear new children.
It is Teteu Innan who empties wombs
of the women who do not,
remembering always to ease the pain of childbirth
for Her daughters upon the earth.
Yet Her sacred spirit also dwells
in the magic springs of healing,
rising in the steamy mist
in answer to the pleas of the ill,
providing the curing waters,
while in Her vast wisdom
She arranges the patterns
of the tossed kernels of corn,
thus making known Her will and Her decree
to all who care to read the prophesies
written in the chance falling of the corn,
offering glimpses of the future
that She will bring.

CHALCHIHUITLICUE

The account of the great flood, caused by the Rain Goddess of Aztec beliefs, may be compared to the inundation attributed to the Mayan Moon Goddess Ix Chel. The concept of past eras of civilization, that had ended in total destruction, suggests comparison with the beliefs of many of the tribes now living in the southwest U.S. Though religious ideas common to peoples in Mexico and the southwestern U.S. are possibly the result of a common heritage, it is interesting to note that texts of India refer to four ages, *yugas,* existing in each eon of time, and that the Greek Hesiod also wrote that there had been four eras of civilization, each subsequently destroyed, before the one in which he lived. The Aztecs believed that the age in which they lived was reigned over by the sun god Tonatiuh, the one to whom they offered their sacrifices, perhaps suggesting that many of the other deities, to whom they offered reverence, were adopted deities of other groups, or ones they had revered before arriving in the area of Mexico City (probably as late as 1300 A.D.). A ten foot high statue, now simply known as Goddess of the Waters, had long been revered not far from where the Aztecs settled—perhaps explaining the origins of the belief that Chalchihuitlicue had reigned during the age that preceded the reign of the Aztec Tonatiuh.

In the garden of heaven where mist fills the air, and as far as eyes can see flowers dot the ground with brilliant colour, where an arching rainbow never fades—there lives the Goddess Chalchihuitlicue, Mistress of the Rains and Waters. There She sits upon Her celestial throne in Her crown of Quetzal feathers, in Her skirt of the bluegreen of the lakes, waterlilies floating upon it, jade adorning Her perfect neck, discs of turquoise framed by Her ears, while raging whirlpools circle round Her feet and all manner of precious gems swirl about in those wild waters.

In the most ancient of days when only jaguars had inhabited the land, Ocelot had ruled—for this was the time of the First Sun. Upon the emergence of the Second Sun, Quetzalcoatl sat upon the throne until the time that all living beings turned to monkeys as awesome hurricanes swept away their lives. Then Tlaloc came to rule by the light of the Third Sun which finally dimmed and died in the holocaust of storms of fiery rain. Thus came the time of the Fourth Sun—and the Goddess Chalchihuitlicue took the seat of rulership.

So it came to pass that Chalchihuitlicue sat upon Her heavenly throne in the light of the Fourth Sun until the time the Goddess

while raging whirlpools circle round Her feet

could no longer ignore the wrong that was being done to some by others. Choosing those who had been careful not to impose their wishes upon others, She built for them a bridge so that the people that She had chosen to save might cross over from the land of the Fourth Sun to live on earth in the light of the Fifth Sun. When the bridge was ready and all whom She had chosen had safely crossed, Chalchihuitlicue sent constant rains, flooding the land of the Fourth Sun with Her raging whirlpools, sweeping away those She had rejected—so that they floated as fish in the ocean. She raised the waves so high that any still afloat in their canoes were tossed into the icy waters and crashed upon the rocks. Then when all was done, She calmed the wild waters until they were as smooth as the feathers of a bird at rest—so that all that had been destroyed lay invisible beneath the still surface.

Thus was the Great Chalchihuitlicue remembered by those She had saved, so that each year during the month of Etzaqualitzli they came as pilgrims to Her temples to place jewels upon Her image, lighting incense and sweet smelling herbs in Her honour, joining in joyous celebration, praying to the Goddess of Rains and Water to send the water for the crops—but asking Her to please remember not to send too much.

BACHUE

The lake, described as the place of emergence, and the later habitation, of the Chibcha Divine Ancestress Bachue, is located a few miles northeast of the city of Tunja in Colombia. The image of Bachue as the protector of agriculture, as well as the teacher of peace and order, appears to be a somewhat universal concept—a similar combination of attributes described in the accounts of the Goddess as Demeter in Greece, Isis in Egypt, and Ala in Nigeria. The portrayal of Bachue as a woman—and as a serpent in the waters—presents an image that may well be compared to accounts of the Goddess among the Semites, e.g. Atargatis, Asherah and Tiamat, as well as the Sumerian images of the Goddess as Nina and Nammu (see Semitic and Sumerian Sections).

From the clear blue waters
of a small lake
near the village of Iguaque,
emerged Mother Bachue,
who some call Fura Chogue—Kind Mother,
and with Her came Her son of three years,
holding tightly to Her hand.

Living in the forests,
She raised the lad to manhood
until the time She took him as a husband
to bring forth all who live
along the banks of the great river
and on the mountainsides—
teaching them
as She had taught Her son
that they must live in peace
and with loving concern for each other.

When She saw that all was well
and that Her great family
knew how to care for themselves,
She returned to the lake,
taking Her son/husband with Her
and assuming the form of water serpents,
they slid into the rippling home
from which they had first come.

It was by the waters of this lake
the people came to offer
the sacred smoke of forest resins
to honour the First Mother,
asking for Her help in making the food grow,
asking for Her ever present protection,
thanking the Mother Spirit of the Waters
for the very joy of life.

MAYUEL

Though the name of the Goddess, as Mayuel, might suggest that She was worshipped by Mayans, rather than Aztecs, the name is known only from Aztec accounts. The similarity of Mayuel to Maya may simply be coincidental, or our lack of evidence from the Mayans perhaps a result of the obliteration of nearly all of the Mayan writings. Though revered by the Aztecs as the Goddess of the intoxicating liquid of the *maguey (metl)* plant, this account of Mayuel's discovery of the drink portrays Her as a mortal peasant woman. Mayuel, like Coatlicue, is described as having four hundred breasts, and as having given birth to the four hundred stars of heaven. Evidence that the pulque and mescal, made from the maguey, were used to ease the pains of childbirth, along with an Aztec account that the first two people on earth were raised from infancy on the juice of the maguey, may account for the imagery of the four hundred breasts to nurse the four hundred stars—the breasts of Mayuel perhaps regarded as having been filled with the magical and sacred drink. Mescal, better known as tequila, is distilled from the fermented juice (pulque) of the maguey, the century plant of the Agave species.

Astride the Great Tortoise, Mayuel rides, Goddess of Four Hundred Breasts, Mother of Four Hundred Stars, seen by all who drink Her sacred brew and intoxicated by Her spirit, they tell of a time when Mayuel was a woman living upon the earth:

Across the fields of growing crops, Mayuel walked in the dimming sunlight, tired from a long day's work, going to fetch the water as the last chore of the day. Passing the great maguey plant that towered high above her head, she noticed a tiny mouse nibbling at the lowest growth, strangely unconcerned by her approach. Much to her surprise the mouse began to dance about, as if in festive celebration, while Mayuel saw the wetness of the place from which the mouse had eaten, sap still dripping from the stalk. Wondering if the juice of the maguey was the reason for the mouse's joyful dance, she placed her water pot to catch the draining syrup and when the pot was filled with liquid, she continued on her long walk home.

Along the way to her thatched adobe na, her curious fingers dipped into the pot, her curious tongue then licking the liquid from her fingers. Much to her pleasure, despite the fatigue that she had felt, Mayuel found that she was in the mood to skip and sing, feeling a lightness in her step that she had not felt since childhood. So delighted was she with the wonderful discovery that she shared it with her family until their tiny home filled with the song and dance and laughter that each had long forgotten.

So it was that even after the time that Mayuel had finished her life upon the earth, those who knew of the magic of the maguey saw visions of the woman Mayuel as they drank the precious liquid to ease the pains of childbirth or sipped its magic at sacred celebrations to better understand the workings of the universe—remembering always to offer gratitude to Mayuel, She whose spirit lives forever in the Goddess given juice.

IX CHEL

Especially revered among women, the Mayan Ix Chel was closely associated with the moon. There is some question about whether the account of the moon's experiences with the sun was originally attributed to Ix Chel, or to another name of the Moon Goddess in Mexico and Guatamala, Ix Actani. The shrine on Cozumel Island, just a few miles off the northeastern coast of the Yucatan peninsula, is definitely associated with the name of Ix Chel. It was customary for all women who were pregnant or wanting to be, to visit the shrine of Ix Chel on this island. The astral bodies mentioned in the account are Venus (Chac Noh Ek), The Pleiades (Tzab), and the constellation of Scorpio (Zinaan Ek)—which, incidentally, was known as Scorpions to Mayan astronomers.

Ix Chel, sacred silver disc of the darkened heavens, first woman of the world, graciously gifted the people of the Yucatan, Campeche and Guatamala, with the easing of childbirth and the knowledge of healing. Mother of all deities, it is She who causes the blood to gather so that it may flow with the passage of the month.

So powerful was Ix Chel that when it was the time of the Hai-yococab, the flooding and remaking of the earth, it was She who sent forth the inundating waters. Some say that She sent great waves from the ocean that pounced upon the land and swallowed it, while others tell of a giant earthen vessel whose contents She poured down from the skies—so that the earth could be cleansed, so that life could start anew.

Crowned with the feathers of an eagle, eagle feathers carefully woven in intricate design into Her heavenly throne, Ix Chel was known as Eagle Woman and eagles were seen as messengers of Her moon essence. From Her home in the heavens, Ix Chel watched a spider carefully as it spun its gossamer web and in this way gave birth to Ix Chebel Yax, She who later taught the knowledge of the weaving to the women of the earth. Thus they say it was the wisdom of the spider that gave us the ways of the loom and the spinning of the cotton, this knowledge brought to Guatamala by daughter Ix Chebel Yax who also taught how to blacken the cotton with carbon, how to redden the cotton with the rust of iron, how to purple the cotton with the fluid of the prized purpura shell.

Coming to the mats of those who were ill, Ix Chel would appear at their feet, invoked by the sacred smoke of copal and tobacco, bringing with Her the finely ground powder of crab, the slowly brewed broth of turkey, guava tips and the haaz papaya, the sap of the rubber tree and the honeymead balche to quench the thirst of fever. And all the while, as Ix Chel stood by the mat of the one who was ill, She held the reed cradle in Her arms, signifying Her power over life.

Among the Mayan people, the tale was told that in the very beginning of time the heavens were filled by two great lights—for at that time the moon was as bright as the sun. Ix Chel, glowing in all Her radiance, fascinated the sun so that he became determined to win Her love. To trick Her grandfather, who guarded Her jealously, the sun borrowed the body of a hummingbird and in this form, the sun flew to the home of the gracious shining Ix Chel. Upon the sun's arrival, he was welcomed by the Goddess with a drink of the honey of tobacco flowers but sitting there, sipping upon the cool drink, the hummingbird sun suddenly felt the sting of a clay pellet that had been sent with the force of a blow gun, piercing deep into his feathered side.

Who could have done such a thing but my grandfather, thought Ix Chel, as She carried the wounded bird to the privacy and safety of Her own room. There She nursed it gently until it could once more spread its wings and fly about the room. But caring for the wounded bird had aroused a tenderness within the Goddess, a feeling that She had never known before and when the sun suggested that they fly off together, into the empty spaces of the great heavens, to escape the jealous grandfather—though somewhat reluctant, Ix Chel agreed.

Clear across the heaven flew the two luminous bodies . Finding a cedar log canoe, they slipped it into a marshy stream of heaven and began to paddle as fast as they could. But the jealous grandfather, bursting with rage, called upon Chac, he who controlled storm, to hurl a lightning bolt at the two who had defied him. In hope of some protection, Ix Chel jumped into the water and became a crab. The sun soon followed close behind Her, taking the form of a mottled turtle. But the strategy was to no avail as the lightning bolt aimed at Ix Chel found its target—and the Goddess lay dead in the slow moving waters of the reed filled stream of heaven.

The buzzing of heavenly dragonflies mourned hymns around Her body. Wings fluttered in ripples of grief. But lamentation transformed into action when the dragonflies prepared thirteen hollow logs and for thirteen days they hovered about the dead Ix Chel—so many dragonflies that no one could see what was happening, not even the sun. On the thirteenth night the logs broke open. Out of twelve crawled the great and awesome snakes of heaven but from the thirteenth, Ix Chel emerged—once again alive and brilliant in Her regained wholeness. The sun was overjoyed and this time proposed marriage to which Ix Chel agreed. Thus the pair set up their home in heaven, side by side.

But it was not long before there was trouble, for soon they had a constant visitor in their new home. The brother of the sun, the delicately beautiful Chac Noh Ek, stopped by all too often for the comfort of the sun, often lingering closer to the moon and quickly disappearing when the sun arrived. The sun grew hot with jealousy, accusing the radiant Ix Chel of encouraging his brother, accusing the glowing Ix Chel of succumbing to his brother's charms, finally accusing the Moon Goddess of making love with Chac Noh Ek. And refusing to listen to Her words of reply, in insanely jealous rage—the sun threw the moon down from the heavens!

Landing not far from the Lake of Atitlan, scarcely missing the peak of the nearby volcano, Ix Chel fell upon the grassy banks, Her frustration and hurt at unjust accusations changing to anger and defiance. Just at that moment a vulture came gliding down and landing close by, the vulture's compassion for the moon caused it to offer Her a ride to the high mountain peaks where the vultures made their home. It was in this way that Ix Chel met the King of the Vultures and in Her sorrow and confusion accepted his offer to stay there with him as his lover.

But the sun soon learned that far from suffering, his wife was now well treated by the handsome black bird and in his jealousy, he grew even hotter—until he finally devised a scheme to find the vulture's nest. Hiding in the hide of a deer, the sun waited for a vulture to spot the carcass. Even sooner than he expected, vulture wings swooped down upon the deer, whereupon the jealous sun hopped upon the vulture's back—and so was taken to the summit where Ix Chel now lived.

Once there, the sun begged, he pleaded with Ix Chel, poured out apologies like drops of water in a flooding river, spoke perfect pictures of all they had experienced together to first become husband and wife. In even deeper confusion than before, Ix Chel bade the handsome vulture farewell and flew back into the heavens with the sun—to resume Her celestial throne beside him.

Hardly had She settled back into Her heavenly home, when again the sun grew hot with jealousy. Angrily, he shouted at Ix Chel, 'Why do you move so close to Chac Noh Ek? Why do you allow Zinaan Ek to brush against you and why do you stay in the house of the Tzab? Everyone sees you embrace them before you part. How can I call myself your husband and still keep my pride before all the others of heaven? It is true that you are beautiful, lustrous and radiant, wise and gentle, but if I cannot have you for my own, no one else will have you as you are!' Thus shouting and raging, the sun began to beat his wife, trying to destroy the beauty of Her being, to scar Her so badly, no other would want Her. Ix Chel stood firm with defiance as the blows fell upon Her. But as Her brilliance dimmed with the severe assault, Her will inside grew stronger—until, finally, with an anger of Her own, She flew off into the night!

Never again did She marry another, though many offered marriage as She passed by. 'The sun is my husband', She would say, though She quickly disappeared whenever he arrived. Wandering alone in the dark night sky, She thought about the women of the earth, those who paddled miles in small canoes to pray at Her shrine on Cozumel Island, those who asked for Her help, those who truly needed Her, those who had loved Her always. Thus among the many gifts of knowledge that Ix Chel gave to the women who knew Her best at Cozumel, was Her example that a woman must be free to come and go as she pleases—just as Ix Chel comes and goes, even disappearing for days at a time. But women trust that Ix Chel will return, for no matter how often She leaves, She soon reappears in the night time sky, Her image most brilliantly reflected in the waters that caress the shores of Cozumel.

IAMANJA

Although this account of the Summer Solstice ritual for the Goddess of the Sea, Iamanja, comes to us from Brazil, it is one that is believed to have been brought to South America by enslaved African peoples. It is generally assumed that it was originally a custom of the Yoruba groups in Nigeria, though it may have developed in South America from the tragedy of having been kidnapped and enslaved in a foreign land, and long remembering the ancient homeland across the sea. These ceremonies, now incorporated into the customs of many people of varied ethnic and racial backgrounds, are still enacted annually along the coastlines of Brazil on the eve of the Summer Solstice.

Your holy spirit floats
along the cresting waves of the water,
as we walk out upon the sands,
night time closing on the longest day of the year,
and join together in small circles
around the sacred boats
that we shall send you,
each whispering our prayers to a flower
that we lay upon the boat,
for Iamanja, Holy Queen Sea.

Flames set to floating campfire logs
flicker on the mounting flowers,
as our boats of prayers are set afloat
upon the edges of your being,
your gently caressing waves
washing about our bared legs,
cleansing away our sadness and our troubles,
bathing away any wrongs that we have done,
and as we watch the sparks of dancing light
dimming in the growing distance,
we know that you are waiting
for the messages we send,
Iamanja, Holy Queen Sea.

Fire reflections in your gently rocking darkness,
light above, so light below,
chanting chorus keeping time
to the rhythm of your being,
I stand to one side
to watch the others
toss their last flower prayers upon the moving boats,
thinking that you have enough to do
without my adding to your work.
But just before the last boat
floats out too far for change of mind,
I too toss my flower upon the others,
with prayers for your health and long years
and that you may always be
just as we have known you,
Iamanja, Holy Queen Sea.

and from chaos She has led us
by the hand

Along the great rivers of the Tigris and Euphrates, and across the northern sands of Syria to the lands that lie along the Mediterranean's eastern waters, Semitic people called upon the Creator of Life as She who descended from Venus, yet emerged from the waters upon the shore at Ascalon. Whether the result of creative invention, or embroidered memories of the ancient beginnings of human life, the nature of the Goddess of the Semitic peoples has been made known to us by the many treasures Her worshippers left buried in the earth, upon which they had lived.

The evidence of Goddess reverence, presented in this section, is drawn from a vast number of translations of tablets and texts written in the Semitic languages of Akkadian, Ugaritan, Phoenician (Canaanite), Amorite, Aramaean, Hebrew, and Arabic. Becoming more familiar with the geography of the areas inhabited by early Semites, helps to clarify the religious beliefs, and helps us to better understand both the similarities and the differences in these beliefs, as they appear in different areas of the Near East. Much of the evidence, of the worship of the Goddess among the Semites, comes from the area that stretches along the eastern shores of the Mediterranean, lands now known as Lebanon, Israel, and Syria. This area is referred to as The Levant. The other major area, in which written evidence of the worship of the Goddess by ancient Semitic peoples has been discovered, is that of the north

99

and central sections of present day Iraq, ancient Mesopotamia. Between The Levant and Mesopotamia lies the vast Syrian desert, as far as we know, largely uninhabited in ancient periods, except for a few settlements along the Euphrates River. The Euphrates, which is the major link between The Levant and Mesopotamia, starts in Anatolia, crosses the northern section of Syria, flows southeast across Syria, into and through Mesopotamia, until its waters pour into the Persian Gulf. Both The Levant and Mesopotamia reveal evidence of settled sites, and Goddess imagery, that date back to the earliest neolithic periods. (The Tabun Cave, on Mt. Carmel on the Levantine coast, is one of the most ancient sites at which full homo sapien remains have been discovered.)

The worship of the Goddess as Ashtart (Ashtoreth, Astarte), Atargatis, Asherah, Anat, and Shapash, was primarily known in Levantine areas. The worship of the Goddess as Mami, Aruru, and Ishtar, was best known in northern and central Mesopotamia. The images and nature of Ishtar may have been derived from, or influenced by, religious beliefs of Anatolia (Turkey). A larger body of evidence reveals that the worship of Ishtar was integrated with the worship of the Goddess known as Inanna among the Sumerians of southern Mesopotamia. The name of Ishtar eventually replaced that of Inanna at the Temple of the Queen of Heaven in Erech, a city not far from the Persian Gulf. While Semites of northern Mesopotamia had many links with Anatolia, and Semites of central Mesopotamia had many links with the Sumerians—Semites of the Levantine coast had access to Egypt, Cyprus, Crete, southern Anatolia, and the many islands of the Mediterranean. Ports all along the coast of The Levant—such as Ascalon, Sidon, Tyre, Byblos, and Ugarit—are especially noticeable in accounts of Goddess worship, and provide a great deal of information about Goddess reverence among the Semitic peoples, both in the Levant and throughout the Mediterranean area.

Under each Goddess name, I have included the material specifically associated with that name. The epithets and titles are from translations of carved or clay cuneiform inscriptions. Place names of shrines and temples, and specific information about them, are based upon the records of archaeological excavations. The prayers are from translations of cuneiform tablets, some combined adaptations, when I had access to two or more slightly differing translations of the same tablet. The narrative accounts are from translations of sacred epic poems found upon the clay tablets of ancient libraries and temple archives. Cuneiform, wedge shaped marks pressed into damp clay, was a method of writing almost certainly first developed by the Sumerians of southern Mesopotamia. Soon after its development, it was used by Semitic Akkadians, who adapted it to record their own language. After a long period of use and change, Semitic Phoenicians (Canaanites) of The Levant passed this knowledge of writing on to the Indo-European Greeks, who then further adapted it to record their own language.

I have tried to present as much information as possible about Goddess reverence among Semitic peoples, in a volume such as this, but this is by no means all that is known about each specific Goddess name. Connections and influences between the Semitic people and the Sumerians are discussed in greater detail in the Sumerian section. Connections between the Semites and the Anatolians (Turkey) are further examined in the Anatolian section. Although each Goddess name, and accompanying information, is presented separately, even within this section we cannot help but notice the overlapping concepts of certain religious customs and rituals such as: the presence of eunuchs who castrated themselves to serve in the clergy of the Goddess; the sexual rituals (more fully described and explained in *When God Was A Woman);* the sacred marriage rites; and perhaps most abundant are the translations of the legends and rituals surrounding the annual enactment, or commemoration, of the death of the son or brother consort of the Goddess. These connections may be observed not only within the Semitic accounts of Ishtar, Ashtart, and Anat, but also in those of the Anatolian Kybele, the Egyptian Isis (Au Sept), the Sumerian Inanna, and the Greek and Cyprian Aphrodite (see Anatolian, Egyptian and Greek Sections).

For far too long, psychologists, mythologists, philosophers, and theologians, have written and developed numerous treatises on the 'inherent' nature of woman, often basing their theories upon references to ancient Goddess imagery. Many of these theories have revolved about structured dichotomies of either good or bad. Reading over the actual prayers, narrative accounts, titles, and epithets, of the Goddess as She was worshipped by Semitic peoples, it is clear that theories of dualistic archetypes are not only simplistic, but actually in conflict with the multi-faceted nature of the Goddess, as She was known by those who revered Her.

Some scholars have referred to the Goddess of the ancient Near East as a fertility figure, the central figure of a fertility cult. Others have opened their eyes just a bit further (though categorizing all evidence of fertility attributes under the label Goddess of Love, rather than sexuality and creation of life) and have also mentioned the heroic or martial aspects of the Goddess of the Semitic people, by the additional label of Goddess of Battle. Most of those who bother to mention both of these attributes, often add a comment about this as a strange, or improbable, pair of traits, describing them as 'paradoxical'. This paradox remains a paradox only as long as the reader is unaware of all the *other* aspects attributed to the Goddess—such as prophesy, judgement, divine decree, law, divine guardianship of the right to rule or lead the people, creation of life, and concern for the oppressed and mistreated. It is as if one were to claim that Jehovah's creation of life as told in Genesis, and the leading of Joshua in the invasion of Canaan, as told in the Book of Joshua, presented a paradox, excluding mention of all other stated attributes and actions of Jehovah.

Only with a thorough familiarity with the actual texts available from ancient periods, can any meaningful or intelligent discussion of Goddess reverence in the ancient Near East even be initiated. There is a vast, diverse, and complex body of beliefs, about the ancient Goddess of the Semites, one that we simply cannot ignore, if we are to approach any analysis of the nature of womanhood through ancient Goddess imagery.

While reading of the various types of records and evidence, certain topics may present themselves as areas for further research and examination, beyond what I have been able to present here. One subject, that has been largely ignored, is that of the existence of the oracular shrines of the Goddess, wherein priestesses provided predictions and counsel, as interpretations of the word of the Goddess—thus influencing political and governmental issues, well into periods in which Goddess reverence was losing ground. Another is the nature of the *Ibratu* shrines, which are mentioned in various texts and proverbs, described as gathering places for women both in Sumer and in Semitic Akkad (Babylonia). The reader may be interested in a further exploration of the repeated mention of the sacred stones in the worship of Ba'Alat at Byblos and Al Uzza at Mecca, comparing these to the worship of the sacred stone of the Amazons at Colchis, and the one associated with the

Goddess as Kybele in the city of Pessinus—a stone considered to be so important that it was later brought to Rome at the decree of the prophetic Sibyls (see Anatolian Section for these last two references). The claims that Ishtar and Her women had descended from Venus, and that Ashtart arrived as a fiery star that fell into the lake at the sacred shrine of Aphaca—alongside African beliefs about the star Sirius (see African Section introduction), and the association of the Egyptian Goddess as Isis with Sirius—may provide topics for speculation for those with broader imaginations.

Along with the material from Sumer, Anatolia, and Egypt, evidence of Goddess worship among Semitic speaking peoples is some of the earliest written material that we possess. Since Goddess worship in these areas both predates, *and* coincides, with biblical periods, this information allows us to examine statements about the religious beliefs and customs that surrounded the early Hebrews, later the early Christians, and even later the early Muslims. This more knowledgeable point of view allows us to examine the political and religious biases about so called pagan religions, and certainly to question the gender biases inherent in the biblical diatribes against the most ancient religion of all, that of the Mother as Creator.

Current excavations in the area of northwestern Syria (in The Levant), have recently revealed the ancient culture of Ebla, and the name of the Goddess there as Eshtar. The Semitic language found on Ebla tablets, tentatively labelled Eblaite, appears to have been used at about 2400 B.C. The name Eshtar, in northern Syria, further links the worship of Ishtar of Mesopotamia with Ashtart of The Levant area.

MAMI ARURU

These two names of the Goddess, as Creator of Life, were most often used separately, but in the *Babylonian Theodicy,* an Akkadian discussion of theological concepts, the names Mami and Aruru are used interchangeably. The information on the Goddess, as known by these names, is rather minimal, but references found in several different texts of Akkadian Babylonia provide the information included here.

Aruru, Oldest of the Old
Creator of Life,
Mami, Divine Mother of All,
Womb that created all humankind
and still creates all destiny.
They kissed Her holy feet
and called upon Her
as Creator of Humanity,
Mistress of all Deities.

Sweeter than honey and date wine
was the ancient Mother,
for it was She who made all life
by pinching off the fourteen pieces of clay—
and laying a brick between them,
She made seven women
whom She placed to the left,
She made seven men
whom She placed to the right.
Forming them into people
She then placed them on the earth.

ISHTAR

There are several conjectural origins of the worship of the Goddess as Ishtar. The site of Arpachiyah, from the Halafian culture of about 5000 B.C., was situated on the Tigris, within a mile of where one of the most sacred centres of Ishtar, Nineveh, later stood. It may be of interest that other Halafian sites were in Anatolia, perhaps settled by descendants of the even earlier Catal Huyuk culture. Excavations of Arpachiyah have provided us, not only with very early Goddess statues, but a Goddess accompanied by images of doves, serpents, and the double axe—symbols that reappear repeatedly in later Goddess imagery. Since the son/lover of Ishtar, Tammuz, is almost identical with the Damuzi of the Sumerian Goddess as Inanna, it is also suggested that the symbolism, stories, customs, and rituals, associated with Ishtar, were derived from Sumerian beliefs. Whether these various aspects of the religion, known to have been connected with reverence for Ishtar, were derived from Anatolia, Sumer, or the Semites of The Levant (as the accounts of Ashtart might suggest), Ishtar became the most popular name and image of the Goddess, as She was known among the Semites of northern and central Mesopotamia.

Ishtar, Queen of Heaven, said to have descended from the planet Venus, thus arriving upon earth accompanied by the Ishtaritu, Ishtar's holy women, was revered as Mother by Semitic peoples who lived along the banks of the Tigris and Euphrates.

Many claim that Ishtar was one with Inanna, for when Semites went to Sumerian Erech, they called upon the Goddess of the ancient Erech temple as Ishtar, though Erech had long been known as the holy place of the Sumerian Mother. And it is true that at Telloh, Kish and Ur, the name of Ishtar replaced that of the Sumerian Inanna, but Ishtar's name had long been called upon in Nineveh, Aleppo and Arbela, in Assur, Mari and Ischali, and in the great city of Babylon at the temple known as E Kidurinum. Both Ishtar and Inanna were known as Queen of Heaven, but in ancient Sumer it was said that Inanna had eight Ibratu, eight smaller wayside shrines where women gathered daily for prayer and meditaton, or even to exchange the news of the day—while Ishtar had one hundred and eighty.

Images of Ishtar were known throughout Semitic lands: horned as the holy heifer of Egypt; armed with bow and arrow; wearing the tiara crown upon Her head; holding the double serpent sceptre; holding Her hands beneath Her breasts; standing upon the lion beneath Her feet; mushrusshu dragons by Her sides; riding in Her chariot drawn by seven lions; holding a bull by the horns; seated upon Her lion throne; riding upon the back of a large bird; holding the sacred branches in Her hands; brandishing sword or scimitar; priestesses sitting on the ground before Her—knowing Her as the most sacred eight pointed star, the guiding light of the planet Masat Venus, Star of Prophesy, Her holiness shining in the heavens.

Many were the sacred titles that She bore: O Shining One, Lioness of the Igigi; Mother of Deities; She Who Begets All; Producer of Life; Creator of People; Queen of Heaven and Earth; She Who Guides Humankind; She Who Holds the Reins of Royalty; She Who Possesses the Law of Heavenly Sovereignty; Guardian of Law and Order; Mistress of Ordinances; Ruler of the Heavens; Director of the People; Light of Heaven; Shepherdess of the Lands; Possessor of the Tablets of Life's Records; Source of the Oracles of Prophesy; Lady of Battle and Victory; Lady of Combat Who Carries the Quiver and the Bow; Exalted; Glorious; Heroic; Supreme; Malkatu; Gingira; Belit Mati—Queen, Lady of the Lands.

Across the ancient lands many carved inscriptions revealed the nature of the holy Ishtar:

Mother of the fruitful breast,
when at the front of combat She is seen,
She is a flood of light whose strength is mighty.

When at a quarrel She is present,
it is She who understands the matter.

It is Ishtar who renders all decision,
Goddess of all that occurs,
Lady of Heaven and Earth
who receives our supplication,
who hears our requests,
who listens to our prayers.

It is Ishtar who is compassionate
because She loves righteousness.

She is Ishtar the Queen,
oppressing all that is confused,
holding full powers of judgement and decision.

AND FROM CHAOS SHE HAS LED US BY THE HAND

Prayers that passed across the lips of many people, prayers inscribed on stone and clay, still echo Her sovereignty as sacred songs in memory's ears:

Queen of Heaven, Goddess of the Universe,
the One who walked in terrible chaos
and brought life by the law of love
and out of chaos brought us harmony
and from chaos She has led us by the hand.

Woman of women, Goddess who knows no equal,
She who decrees the destiny of people,
Highest Ruler of the World,
Sovereign of the Heavens,
Goddess, even of those who live in heaven.

It is you who changes destiny
to make what is bad become good.
At your right side is justice,
at your left side is goodness.
From your sides emanate life and well being.
Ishtar, how good it is to pray to you;
there is concern in your glance,
your word is the light.
Please look upon me with affirmation.
Please accept my prayer.

With Ishtar there is counsel and wisdom.
The fate of everything She holds in Her hand.
Joy comes from Her very glance.
She is the power, the magnificence.
She is the deity who protects.
She is the spirit that guides.
Be it maiden or mother,
women remember Her and call Her name.

O Lady, glorious is Thy omnipotence,
Thy exaltation above all other deities.
Thou art the mighty One, the Lady of Combat,
strong enough to suppress the mountains.
Full judgement and decision are in Thy power
as are the ordinances of heaven and earth.
In Thy chapels, in Thy holy places,
at Thy sacred shrines,
we come to listen to Thee.

O Shining One, Lioness of the Igigi,
You stop the anger of all other deities.
You care for the oppressed and the mistreated,
each day offering them your help.
You are the One who gleams brightest
in the midst of all other deities.
You are the holy One of women and of men.

Praise Goddess, the mightiest of deities.
Let us revere the Mistress of People,
more exalted than all other deities;
Praise Ishtar, the mightiest of deities.
Let us revere the Queen of Heaven,
more exalted than all other deities.

O Ishtar, Sovereign Mistress of all people,
You are the light of heaven and earth;
heaven and earth move because of you.
All people pay homage to you
for you are great, you are exalted.
All humankind recognizes your power,
for you are the bright torch of heaven and earth,
the light of all living,
One who cannot be opposed,
whirlwind that roars against all that is wrong.

Her lips are sweet,
Life is in Her mouth.
When She appears, we are filled with rejoicing.
She is glorious beneath Her robes.
Her body is complete beauty.
Her eyes are total brilliance.
Who could be equal to Her greatness,
for Her decrees are strong, exalted, perfect.
Ishtar—Who could be equal to Her greatness
for Her decrees are strong, exalted, perfect.

All other deities seek Her counsel,
unique is Her position
for Her word is so respected,
it is supreme over them.
She is their Queen.
It is they who carry out Her decrees.
All of them bow down before Her,
receiving their light from Her.
Thus women and men hold Her in highest reverence.

AND FROM CHAOS SHE HAS LED US BY THE HAND

At Assur, at Arbela, at Mari, at Kalah, at Nineveh, at Kissuru, priestesses of Ishtar called upon Her wisdom at these shrines of divine prophesy, speaking of Her as The Lady of Vision, speaking of Her as The Prophetess of Kua, answering questions of life, deciding mortal problems whether great or small. Thus the names of priestesses were marked upon the ancient records of the oracles, names of the holiest of women who had spoken the words and decrees of Ishtar, names that resound with the echoes of the years— Belit Abi Sha, Ishtar Bel Daini, Sinkisha Amur, Urkittu Sharrat, Ishtar Latashiat, Baja and the woman known as Rimute Allate, priestess of the shrine of Goddess prophesy in the village of Darahuja in the mountains.

On the night of the full moon, the holy night known as Shapatu, special offerings of food and drink were made, as they were on the night of the new moon, when joyous celebration filled the temples. The sacred Qadishtu, the women who came to live as priestesses in the temple's Gagu quarters, took lovers in the Bit Ashtammi of the temple, expressing the sacredness of sexuality as the gift of Ishtar. Of these holy women it was said, "Respect and submission to a husband are not to be found among them." Men who joined in reverence of the Holy Mother offered their organs of maleness joyfully, in the midst of highest festive celebration, using razor, sword, or knife of stone, later wearing these upon their sash as symbol of their consecration to The Mother, thus joining the ranks of Kurgarru and Ishinu who served as eunuch attendants at the temples of Ishtar.

In the month of Tammuz, on the twenty-eighth day, the Day of the Sheepfolds, highest holy rites were celebrated by those who revered the mighty Ishtar—a vulva of lapis lazuli and an eight pointed star of gold placed upon Her altar—for was She not the star from whose vulva all life had come forth?

Those who called upon Ishtar knew well the story of Her son, he who had also been Her lover and Her consort, Tammuz, he who had died when but a youth. For it was Tammuz who was spoken of as keeper of the cattle stalls, leading goat of the land, tamarisk tree that could find no water, he who had been given the shepherd's staff by Ishtar, the one whom Ishtar had chosen for the sacred marriage rites celebrated during the holy days of the great Akitu festival, the one chosen as the shepherd for the year, after he had proven himself upon Her couch.

But the shepherd Tammuz was then removed from Her by death, causing sorrowful lament throughout the land, as flutes and drums accompanied dirging voices, as women mourned in sympathy for Ishtar, who grieved that Tammuz had been taken from Her—as Inanna grieved when Damuzi died, as Ashtart grieved when Tammuz died, as Isis grieved when Osiris died, as Kybele grieved when Attis died, as Anat grieved when Baal died, as Aphrodite grieved when Adonis died. But as the Goddess continued to rule upon Her throne in heaven, so did Her priestesses continue to convey Her word to those on earth, each year choosing a new Tammuz, each year celebrating the sacred marriage rites, each year mourning at the chosen shepherd's death.

In days when invaders conquered Ishtar's cities, Gilgamish prepared to take part in the rites of the sacred marriage, thus to gain the divine right to shepherdship, that which was bestowed by Ishtar—for knives and swords and spears are not the tools of the shepherd. But Gilgamish sought immortality, permanence upon the earthly throne. Thus the legend formed, the story of the changing of the rites, telling all that when the mighty Ishtar proposed to Gilgamish that he lie upon Her bed of pleasure; tempting him even further with promises of a chariot of lapis and gold drawn by the swiftest of storm demons; saying that all others would bow down before him; saying that tribute from field and orchard would be his—Gilgamish feared that his death might be included in the bargain, and that his life would end, as that of Tammuz had ended.

Thus Gilgamish challenged Ishtar with these words, "What mate would thou love forever? What shepherd boy would please thee always?", adding that each former mate of Ishtar had met a tragic end. Refusing to join Her in the sacred marriage rites, Gilgamish then killed Her bull of heaven, crying aloud that he wished that he could do the same to Her. Gilgamish, with warrior army behind him, defied the ways of those who worshipped Ishtar, the consort whose life ended with the year, so that the consort shepherd no longer met his death after a year of temple life. But those who then declared themselves as king, in deference to the ancient rites and customs, yearly had their hair shorn from their head, yearly had their royal insignias and jewels removed, yearly had their robes of royalty stripped from their bodies, as they were struck upon the face with a cord of seven knots and thrown into the river, afterwards walking about in the sackcloth of mourning for three days of lamentation—in memory of the time they would have died.

So it came to be that those who first gained kingship by sword, instead of shepherd's staff, gained seats of permanence upon a throne of rule. Still they continued to speak of themselves as The Beloved of Ishtar, the one who received the reins of royalty from Ishtar, the one who received the staff of shepherdship from Ishtar, the one who received the year of reign from Ishtar. In this way, the High Priestess of Ishtar was left with hollow symbols of power, as the new kings placed Ishtar upon a crumbling pedestal of worship—while they sat firmly upon the seat of rule.

Yet memory of the time, when the shepherd would have met his death, still lingered in the minds of many, who knew that the shepherd king was but a servant of the Goddess, the one who must convey Her wishes and decrees to keep Her love. Thus were the oracular priestesses still consulted for advice and counsel, as the word of Ishtar. And when the time of year arrived, the time that the shepherd would have met his death, the king was yearly struck by the cord of seven knots. In this way, all were reminded that the king must show humility, for it was said that if tears streamed down his face, all would be well—but if the signs of humble atonement did not come, Ishtar would lay evil fortune upon the land.

ATARGATIS

The name of the Goddess as Atargatis was especially associated with the temple at Ascalon on the Mediterranean coast, about 50 miles west of Jerusalem. This temple was famous for its dove cots, and as a shrine of oracular prophesy, yet the primary image of Atargatis was as a Goddess of the Sea, sometimes depicted with the tail of a fish. Her name and image were also connected to the Hierapolis temple on the Syrian Euphrates, a shrine that was said to have been founded after a great flood (see Ashtart). The association of Atargatis, not only with Ascalon, but with the Euphrates, and with the city of Nineveh on the Tigris, suggests a great antiquity for the fish tailed image of the Goddess, possibly connected to very early Sumerian images of the Goddess as Nina or as Nammu (see

Sumerian Section). It may be that this ancient portrayal of the Goddess led to later accounts of mermaids, and sirens, and mystical islands in unknown waters that were populated only by women (see Celtic Section). The Goddess name of Attar also appears in Arabia, described as a male deity in later periods.

Ancient Goddess of the Sea,
swimming in Mediterranean waters,
climbed upon the shore at Ascalon,
bringing Her infant daughter Shammuramat
and leaving her to the care of tender doves,
She slipped back into the sea,
there to live as Holy Mother.
Thus they honoured Her with sacred lakes
on whose shores were built Her shrines,
purity to be gained from Her holy waters—
while pilgrims swimming as the fish of the lakes
were touched by Her eternal presence.

Some say that it was Her earthly daughter
who founded the shrine for Her at Ascalon,
sacred site of doves of prophesy,
and that Shammuramat then made her way east
to build the city of Nineveh
along the waters of the Tigris,
while others claim that Atargatis had first been born
in the waters of the wide Euphrates,
Her priestesses upon the earth
offering fish upon Her altar
as Sumerians had done for Nina
by the waters of Euphrates at Eridu—
for the sign that meant Nineveh
was the same as the sign that meant Nina.

Thus was Atargatis honoured at Ascalon,
thus was Atargatis honoured at Hierapolis,
as Sumerians spoke of Nammu
as The Primeval Goddess of the Sea,
as Canaanites spoke of Asherah
as The Primeval Goddess of the Sea,
as Egyptians spoke of Nuneit
as The Primeval Goddess of the Sea.

ASHTART

The connections between Ashtart and Ishtar are obvious in the similarities of the names, as well as in the identification with Venus, and the title Queen of Heaven. The name of the son/consort of the Goddess, as Tammuz, occurs in worship of both Ishtar and Ashtart. The claim, by the people of Byblos, that the Goddess first descended to earth as a fiery star that landed in the lake at Aphaca (near Byblos), and that Aphaca was also the actual site of the death of the original Tammuz, made the area of Aphaca and Byblos one of exceptional importance, even to Egyptians. Byblos is in an area rich with human history: situated not far from the site of extremely early homo sapien habitation at Mt. Carmel; close to the Eynan site of the Natufians of about 9000 B.C.; and not far from the Ghassulian mural of the eight pointed star, dated to about 4500 B.C. Worship of the Goddess at Aphaca continued until about 300 A.D., when the shrine was closed by Christian Emperor Constantine, along with other Goddess temples of Syria, Lebanon, and Israel.

The worship of Ashtart on Cyprus, and many other islands and coastal cities of the Mediterranean, helps to explain the origins of many of the shrines that were later known as sacred sites of the Greek Aphrodite. The legend of Europa, being abducted from the Levantine city of Tyre and taken to Crete, may well be an allegory of the spread of the worship of the Semitic Goddess. The reverence for Ashtart in The Levant lasted well into biblical times, as Hebrew Scripture passages reveal. (see Sam. 7:3,4; Judges 2:13, 3:7; I Kings 11:5 and Jer. 44:15-19) It was during the Greek occupation of Syria and Lebanon that Ashtart came to be called Urania (Greek for Queen of Heaven), the title also used for Aphrodite, whose worship was initially derived from that of Ashtart. The Pyre ritual, described by Lucian at Hierapolis, appears to have been a synthesis of Greek and Semitic rituals, *pyre* being the Greek word for fire.

As many named Sovereign of Heaven, as Guiding Star watching over all, some say that Ashtart first came from an ancient homeland in Arabia, where children were once known only by their mother's clan. They say that there Her name was Amma Attar, Malkatu Ashar Amaim, or Allatu. But others say that Semitic people had long lived on the lands of Syria, and along the Mediterranean shores, suggesting that their ancestors were the Goddess revering settlers of neolithic Jericho, and perhaps even the community of Natufians, who lived not far from Nazareth some eleven thousand years ago.

Those who later lived at the port of Byblos, along the Levantine coastal waters, did not explain their own arrival on that land, but treasured a sacred stone that they said fell from heaven—

as they also said that the Goddess Ba'Alat Ashtart had descended from the heavens, as a fiery falling star. Byblians long remembered that it was in this way that the Mother of Deities had first arrived, spinning round like balls of fire in the sky, skimming over the peak of Mt. Lebanon, Her fiery mass then cooling in the waters of Aphaca. Thus they built Her most sacred shrine at the site of Aphaca—close by this holiest of lakes. The people of other towns and villages long honoured this sacred inland shrine, building the great Byblos temple some five thousand years ago, at the place where the waters from Aphaca flowed out to the broad sea. And there in this temple at Byblos, they kept Ba'Alat Ashtart's sacred stone.

Pilgrims from far off places visited Aphaca, to pay honour at the ancient holy site, casting jewels of gold and silver into the Aphaca waters, saying that the Aphaca shrine was doubly sanctified, for it was also the place where the son lover of the Goddess had died. Once paying their respects at Aphaca, the pilgrims then made their way to Byblos, following the westward waters of the river, until they reached the Byblos temple that looked out upon the waters of the Great Sea. And there in Byblos, they stood in the presence of the ancient stone that was said to contain the souls of all people, to heal upon the touching, and to whisper with the knowledge of all future events—for those who could understand Her words.

Egyptians said that it was to this port of Byblos, on the shores of ancient Canaan, that the grieving Goddess Isis travelled, while searching for the murdered body of Osiris, and that She discovered it there in the trunk of a tree, that had been used as a pillar in the Byblos temple. Yet Byblians claimed that when Egyptians sailed to their port so rich in timber, they came to know of the holy rituals for the dead shepherd Tammuz, and they then took these ancient rites back with them to Egypt. For do not even Egyptians say that Isis found the pillar tree, whose boughs and winding trunk had grown about the coffer of the dead youth, in Byblos of Canaan—Byblians adding that the pillar of the Byblos temple was a tree that grew on the hills of Lebanon.

It is true that Egyptians of most ancient days had wandered far into The Levant, leaving silent proof of their travels at Megiddo and Bethel, at Ugarit and Byblos, but it is also true that Ba'Alat Ashtart was often seen wearing the horns of Egyptian Isis upon Her holy head. The truth of the matter may never be ours to know, for all the way from Egypt to Canaan the Goddess was known as Queen of Heaven, Mother of Deities, Guardian of the Land, while images of Her upon Her lioness were oftimes simply marked with Her title—Quadesh—That Which is Holiness. But Isis was said to be seen in the light of the bright star Sept/Sirius, while Ashtart was looked upon as the light that some call Venus, The Eye of Heaven known as Masat, Prophetess.

Many were the images that conveyed the presence of the Mother of Semitic peoples. At Beth Shan and Beth Shemesh, at Beit Mersim and at Gezer, at Tir Dibba and Ain Shems, and at holy Byblos, sometimes known as Kepni or Gebal, images of Ba'Alat Ashtart were formed with the sacred serpent entwined about Her body, or emerging from Her perfect forehead, between holy heifer horns, that held the disc of the sun. At lonely Serabit El Khadim, upon the sands of Sinai, Semitic words were inscribed upon the walls, to Ba'Alat as the ancient Serpent Lady. At the Canaanite city of Sidon, Ashtart was known as Queen of Heaven with the Crescent Horns, while the name of the town of Ashtoreth Karnaim simply meant Ashtoreth of the Horns. In other towns of The Levant, priestesses of Ashtart sat upon thrones flanked with lionesses, or even sphinx, some inscribed with the words, "To my Goddess Ashtart,", while a stone carving of a doe, suckling her fawn, was marked with the inscription, "Ashtart is my strength."

*   *   *

In later times, Greek Lucian wrote of the holy city of Syrian Hierapolis, that stood by the waters of the Euphrates, not far from Anatolia. To this shrine too, pilgrims came from distant towns, to hear the oracles of prophesy at the temple that was said to have been built after the great flood—tradition claiming that a chasm had opened at that very spot, and the waters of the flood had poured into it and disappeared. As reminder of that eventful time, waters from the wide Euphrates were brought into the temple twice a year. And although the temple was dedicated to the Queen of Heaven, tales were told on holy days of the ancient Atargatis, She who had the tail of a fish, yet gave birth to an infant daughter who walked upon two legs. Thus was the Mother Ashtart, She who had arrived from heaven as balls of fire, linked with the Holy One of the sea. At the sacred lake of Hierapolis, pilgrims bathed close by an altar stone that emerged from the centre of the waters, fish glowing with golden lines swimming all about them.

On the first day of the month of Nisan, to welcome the event of the vernal equinox, the festival known as Pyre began at Hierapolis, celebrated among the trees that had been erected as a grove in the courtyard of the shrine. Just as in earlier times, priestesses still took lovers from among the pilgrims, but only on these holiest of days of Pyre. And males who chose to remain among the clergy, still made themselves as eunuchs at this time, offering their organs of maleness, donning only women's robes, to gain entry into the clergy of the Queen of Heaven.

There were many who simply cut their hair, placing the shorn locks in great silver vessels, and though not initiates to the clergy, they attended the rituals of Pyre that were held twice a day. The first was in silent mourning meditation for the dead son lover, whom they now spoke of as Adonis, the one who had been Tammuz—though there were those who whispered that Osiris was his name. The second was spent in joyful song and dance, to the music of flute and sistrum rattle, as they called upon the name of the mighty Queen of Heaven. So it was, Lucian wrote, that they watched the smoke of sweet smelling incense rise from Her altar, and ascend to the golden ceiling, later floating through the doors of gold that crowned the cedar steps of the Hierapolis temple of the Queen of Heaven.

Semitic people, spoken of as Canaanites or Phoenicians, those whom Philo said took the names of their mothers for they cared not who their fathers were, lived along the shores of the Mediterranean waters. Knowing well the ways of sails and oars, they wandered far from their Levantine home, carrying the memory of Ashtart in their hearts. To the northern coast of Africa, to Carthage and Sousse Djerba, to Rousadu and Rachgoun, they brought the name of Ashtart—where She came to be called upon as Tanit, perhaps in memory of ancient Libyan Neit, though Her priestesses took the names of Bod Ashtart and Abda Ashtart in Carthaginian towns, close by the site where the Lake of Tritonis was said to have been, site where some say Amazons once lived.

Phoenicians honoured Ashtart on the isle of Thasos, and on rocky Delos, where Hellenic Greeks later said Lato had given birth to Artemis—Phoenicians leaving inscriptions there 'To Ashtart of Philistia'. To the isle of Callista they brought Her, Thera of the fiery volcano, island that some claim gave rise to the memories of Atlantis sinking. At Phoenician colonies on Sicily, Her name was inscribed as Ashtart of Eryx, perhaps in memory of the famed

Goddess temple at Erech, temple that had long honoured the Queen of Heaven as Ishtar or Inanna. At Nora, Sulcis, and Tharros, on the island of Sardinia, Phoenicians left shrines and images of Ashtart. And touching upon the isles of Gul and Malta, once known as Ma Lata, some say that it was these Canaanites of the waters who built the great temples of Hagar Qim and Hal Tarxien, where massive stone images of Goddess permeated all.

Trading along the coast of Spain, at Almeria and Los Millares, Ashtart revering Phoenicians made their way past the Gates of Gibraltar, settling a colony at Cadiz. There are even some who say that Phoenicians reached the coast of Brittany, and from there sailed to the British Isles searching for gold and tin, perhaps bringing with them the sanctity of great stone circles, like those of Ghassul and Wadi Dhobai in The Levant.

Horned as the holy heifer of Egypt, was it Ashtart who was carried from Phoenician Tyre to Crete, for though some give the name as Europa, and claim that Zeus, disguised as a bull, carried Europa to Crete—sacred horns adorned Cretan shrines long before the followers of Zeus arrived. At Paphos, Kition, and Amathus, ancient towns upon the Cyprian isle, Ashtart was known among Phoenician colonies; while upon the sacred isle of Cythera, so close to Grecian shores, the Queen of Heaven was worshipped at a great Phoenician temple, until Greeks spoke of Her as Urania, the Greek way of saying Queen of Heaven. It was Urania that Greeks came to know as Aphrodite, explaining that the light of Venus was sacred to Her, and that Her Cythera temple had been built in ancient times by Phoenicians from Ascalon. Though memories of Atargatis had faded with the many years, Greeks remembered that Aphrodite had been born in blue Mediterranean waters, but said that She had climbed upon the land on the southwestern shore of Cyprus—island where Ashtart had so long been revered.

TIAMAT

The name of Tiamat, as a Goddess name of Mesopotamia, does not appear to have been used other than in the Babylonian epic legend, the *Enuma Elish,* the account of the *murder* of Tiamat as The Great Mother of the Sea. The imagery appears to be associated with the Goddess as Asherah, Atargatis, and the Sumerian Goddess as Nammu and Nina (see Sumerian

Section). The *Enuma Elish,* quite a favourite among scholars of the twentieth century A.D. (if we judge by the number of interpretations and references to it), is believed to have been written during the period in which Indo-European led Kassites conquered and controlled Babylon (about 1600 B.C.). The explanation in the epic that Anu and Enki (two male deities who were associated with the arrival of specific groups at Erech and Eridu in Sumer) had made previous attempts to dispose of Tiamat—and failed—while as the direct result of the successful murder of Tiamat, the male Marduk gained supreme power—certainly provides fertile ground for an exploration of the demise of the supremacy of the Goddess in Mesopotamia.

> Mother of all Mothers,
> She who gave birth to all,
> though known as Tiamat
> by those who rejoiced at Her murder,
> rippled as distant echo
> of mighty Mother Goddess Sea,
> Nammu, Asherah, Atargatis, Nuneit.
> Well remembered as Creator of all,
> first owner of the Tablets of Destiny,
> Her omnipotence sat as challenge
> to those who worshipped others—
> and thus both Anu and Enki
> were sent to depose The Great Mother.
>
> Cringing before Her powers,
> unable to complete the gruesome mission,
> Anu and Enki returned in defeat,
> until in Babylon under Kassite yoke,
> Marduk demanded promises
> of power and supremacy,
> if he succeeded in murdering The Mother.
> As Indra had murdered Danu,
> so Marduk took the life of Tiamat,
> proud and joyous in the matricide
> that allowed him to sit on heaven's throne,
> bragging of how he had pierced Her belly,
> split Her in two with his evil winds,
> and from Her mutilated body
> had made the heaven and earth—
> thus distorting memory's echoes
> of Goddess Sea's creation of heaven and earth.

ASHERAH

Biblical references to the Goddess as Asherah, and to Her sacred tree or pole symbol, known as the *ashera,* reveal that Asherah was still worshipped in biblical periods. (See I Kings 15:13; II Kings 13:6, 17:9, 21:3, 23: 4-15; Deut. 12:2,3 and Judges 6:30.) The name Asherah probably means Holy Queen, while Her title as Lat, Elat, Elath, or Allat, literally means Goddess. Though most of the information about the Goddess as Asherah comes from the tablets of Ugaritan Canaan of about 1400 B.C., in them Asherah is often invoked as the Goddess of Sidon and Tyre, cities that were also associated with the names of the Goddess as Ashtart and Ishtar, thus linking the reverence for Asherah to Ishtar/Ashtart. Evidence of a Goddess name of Ishara was found in northern Mesopotamia, while at the northern Mesopotamian city of Assur, the most ancient shrine was known as the Asheritu. Located some fifty miles south of the towns of Nineveh and Arpachiyah, this Asheritu was later known as a temple of Ishtar. The epithet of Asherah, as the Goddess Who Walks the Sea, repeated several times in the tablets of Ugarit, suggests possible links with the imagery and traditions of the Goddess as Atargatis.

From ancient settlements along the waters, the Tigris, the Euphrates, and the Jordan, Semitic peoples spread across the Levant, often calling upon the Holy Mother as Asherah, Highest Queen—knowing Her as Lat, Elat or Elath, Exalted Mother, Goddess. She was the Holy Lady Who Walked the Sea, remembered even in Arabia, and at Mesopotamian Assur, where the most ancient shrine was the sacred Asheritu.

Mother of all Wisdom, Her ancient oracles of prophesy renowned, She gave the knowledge to diviners, helping them to see far into the future, while they remembered that She alone gave birth to the Seventy Deities of Heaven. In Her sacred groves, they knew Her as She Who Builds, providing the timber of Her trees, teaching Her people the art of carpentry. On the flatness of the land, they knew Her as She Who Builds, providing the clay of the earth, teaching Her people the knowledge of the bricks. So it was that Asherah taught those who revered Her how to build shelters from the heat and cold, and how to build the sacred shrines in which they called upon Her name.

There were those at Ugarit who said that She was married to Thor El, though never did they say that She moved from Her home of the sea, and when they dared to say that Thor El had created creatures, never did they dare to claim that he had been the father of Her seventy holy children, the deities of heaven.

In the many temples that housed Her holy presence, even in Her temple at Jerusalem, Her dedicated women wove the woollen bands of mourning that were wrapped about Her tree, the sacred ashera—as the women of Anatolian Kybele wrapped the woollen mourning bands about the tree upon which Her son lover had died. Thus the sacred ashera tree stood by Her altars, Her holy fruit hanging upon its branches, Goddess symbol so threatening to Gideon and Hezekiah that they rejoiced in destroying it—as they tried to destroy the very memory of Asherah.

Israelite Queen Maacah tried to speak of Asherah to tell the people of Jerusalem that Asherah was The Mother, but for her religious beliefs she found herself evicted from her Judah throne— by those who said that only a father made life.

ANAT

Accounts of Anat (Anath) appear to have developed as a result of the diversity of ethnic groups living in the coastal port of Ugarit, just south of Anatolia. Most of the information about Anat comes to us from the Ugaritan tablets of about 1400 B.C., a time when this city had large populations, not only of Semitic Canaanites, but of Mycenaeans and Hurrians as well. This may explain the increased importance of the consort Baal in the accounts of Anat, as compared to the Tammuz known in the worship of Ishtar, as well as the introduction of the more patriarchal Thor El as a husband to Asherah in the same Ugaritan tablets. There may also have been influence from Ugaritan allies in Hittite Anatolia, and possible links to the image of the Goddess as Anait (see Anatolian Section— Anahita). There is still much scholarly disagreement over the origins and nature of the Hyksos, the group that appears to have introduced the name of Anat into Egypt. Some claim that the Hyksos were Indo-European, while others believe they were Semitic. They may well have been a combination of the two.

Mighty Lady of northern Canaan, infinite and varied was Her holy nature, for even as the accounts of Her power in battle were told in the city of Ugarit, still She was called upon as Mistress of the Lofty Heavens; Ruler of Dominion; Controller of Royalty; Virgin, yet Progenitor of People; Mother of All Nations; Sovereign of All Deities; Ba'Alatu Mulki; Ba'Alatu Darkati; Ba'Alatu Samen Ramen; Strength of Life; She who kills and makes alive again; She who makes union upon the earth, spreading love throughout the land; She who provides well being and increase, even as She carried spear and shield, even as She carried the arrow and bow of battle, even as the earth quivered beneath Her footsteps. And even as Her divinity and name were best known in northern Canaan—still Hathor horns adorned Her holy head, and the sacred symbol of life, the holy ankh of Egypt, was often shown in Anat's hand.

Though Her memory echoes strongest where Semites called upon Her name on the Mediterranean shores of Ugarit, naming cities holy to Her—Anathel, Anathoth, and Beth Anat, there are those who say that She was one with Anahita of the Iranians, with Anait of the Anatolians, with Anatu of the Sumerians, and even with Athena of the Greeks. Pointing out these many connections, it is said that the legends of Her mighty feats, in the town of Canaan-ite Ugarit, had been embroidered upon by invading northern tribes—still Her most ancient sacred images revealed Her Hathor nature, and declared Her oneness with the Mother of Egypt.

It is true that Mycenaean Greeks from Crete lived in the town of Ugarit, as did their Hurrian cousins, settling as immigrants and merchants in this cosmopolitan trading post. And it is true that they may have brought Her Athena nature with them, for Anat sometimes wore the battle helmet—still She also wore the horns and disc, the wings and headdress of Egypt's Holy Mother, and there are many who say that She was also one with Ba'Alat Ashtart, ivory carvings of Her features reflecting Canaanite images of the Queen of Heaven, as She was known in The Levant.

To confuse the matter further, most claim that it was the Hyksos, the mysterious shepherd kings who invaded Egypt in horse drawn chariots, that brought Her Anat name to Egypt, where it was inscribed in the temple of Denderah, as yet another name for Hathor. So it was that Ramses II and Seti of Egypt called upon Anat's name in battle, while Thutmose the Third spoke of Her as The Strength of Life—even after the Hyksos were expelled. Centuries later, at the Egyptian city of Elephantine, Hebrews prayed to Anat-Jahu, some saying that Jahu was the consort of Anat.

There are those who claim that Anat was the daughter of Asherah, yet it was Anat who pleaded for a temple for Her brother

121

consort Baal, Anat jealous because Asherah and Her kin had many sacred courts of worship, while Baal had none at all. And was it not Anat who predicted that Asherah would rejoice when Her brother Baal was murdered? Though it was written, in the texts of Ugarit, that Asherah entered the Field of Goddesses with Her daughter, to perform the holy rites, there steeping a kid in milk seven times over, the tablets do not speak of the daughter as Anat—but call upon the daughter of Asherah by the name of Rahmai.

Though some prefer to say that Thor El was the leader of all the deities revered at Ugarit, surely we cannot forget the time when he heard Anat approach his home, and in fear and apprehension, he hid himself in the innermost chamber of his house. Nor can we forget that when Anat discovered him, in his place of hiding, She threatened to trample him like a lamb, swearing to turn the grey of his beard red with his own blood—if a temple was not built for Baal.

Great were the powers of Anat, for when She heard of the slaying of brother consort Baal, he who had quaked with fear at the approach of threatening Mot, then met his death at Mot's hands, it was Anat who was strong enough to punish Mot. So it was that Anat seized Mot in Her two great hands, cleaved him in two with a blade, burned him with fire, ground him with a millstone, and threw his remains into a field. Yet Anat's gentleness was seen in Her sorrow at Baal's death. Her grief was said to be as a cow grieves for her dead calf, as an ewe mourns for her dead lamb. And Her revenge against Mot was not without purpose, for soon after Her battle with Mot, Baal was reborn, returning to kneel before Her in a field, admiring Her horns of strength, saying how pleased he was to again be able to look upon them.

Mighty Anat, Mother of Nations, annihilated the god River, muzzled the great dragon, slew the crooked serpent, vanquished fire and flame, and conquered the waters of the flood. When the men of the sunrise, and the men of the seashore, invaded the sanctity of Her temple, Anat hurled chairs and footstools at them, killing those who dared to challenge Her, with the perfect aim of Her bow. And when the battle was over, Anat laughed aloud with the joy of victory, bathing Her hands in the blood of battle, and then in the sacred oil of peace—washing them yet again in the fresh dew of the morning sunrise.

Perhaps as warning, for those who might dare to challenge the powers of the mighty Anat, the story was told of the youth Aqhat, and how Anat had once coveted his bow. Upon the request of the

Goddess to purchase his bow with gold or silver, Aqhat challenged Anat, by asking what need a woman would have for a bow. Thus Her wrathful anger was aroused, Anat swearing to meet him in his path of arrogance, to challenge him in his path of presumption, to hurl him down at Her feet in humility—for suggesting that his marksmanship would surpass that of any woman. Turning to leave Aqhat in the woods, the ground quivered with Her footsteps, as Her words floated sweetly, yet with warning threat in Her farewell, to "my darling he-man."

It was then that She arranged with Her assistant Yatpan, for Yatpan to fly as an eagle over Aqhat's head, and to swoop down from the air to snatch the bow from Aqhat's hands. But the plan did not go well, for as Yatpan descended upon Aqhat, Yatpan's eagle wings struck him so hard that the youth soon died from the blows. Sorrowing at the accident, for Anat had only meant to teach the lad a lesson, Anat hesitated to use the bow of tragedy, and snapped it in two, as symbol of Her mourning—as Aqhat's life had been broken by his lack of humility and respect for the powers of the Goddess.

Reverence for the Goddess as Anat found its way to the island of Cyprus, where Anat was called upon as Lady of Idalion, yet also spoken of as Anait on inscriptions that were later built into the walls of a Cyprian Christian church. Still other stones of Cyprus spoke of the Goddess as Anat-Athene, and Anat-Artemis, while the worship of Anait flourished in the towns of Zela and Ascilicena in the land we know as Turkey, the land once known as Anatolia— perhaps in honour of the invincible Anat.

ALLAT, AL UZZA AND MANAT

Our evidence on the names of the Goddess in Arabia is sparse, most of it coming from accounts of the final destruction of their shrines in the seventh century A.D.—upon the introduction of Islam. Herodotus referred to Allat as the primary Goddess of the Arabians, giving Her name as Alilat. The name Allat is cognate with the title of Asherah as Elat in Canaan. Al Uzza, though most often associated with the planet Venus, was at times described as the star Sirius, sacred star of the Egyptian Goddess as Isis. The name Al Uzza may be connected to the name of the pre-dynastic Egyptian Cobra Goddess, Ua Zit, who was closely linked with the image of Isis, especially at the site of Buto (Per Uto), on the Egyptian Delta.

Along the western coastline of Arabia,
the holy three were known:

Allat, Goddess who glistened
with the brilliance of the sun,
long had Her altars stood in Ta'if
where Her name was called upon as Mother,
until the day Her holy places were destroyed—
and Her ancient Mother being
was all but forgotten.

Al Uzza's light was seen
as the Morning and the Evening Star,
The Mighty One of Mecca,
Her strength emanating
from the Black Stone of the holy Ka'bah shrine,
stone said to be from heaven,
set into the Ka'bah wall
in the heart of sacred Mecca.
As the treasured stone of Ashtart at Byblos,
as the treasured stone of Kybele at Pessinus,
were revered as holy relics of the Goddess,
so too was the Black Stone of Mecca,
visited by pilgrims from far places,
who, naked, walked around it seven times,
kissing or stroking its sacred surface,
then making their way to Hill of Arafat,
to offer holy sacrifice at Mina.

Holy Manat spoke the words of destiny,
deciding fortunes, whether good or bad,
giving life and health as She saw fit,
taking in death when She declared the time.
Thus Her images were kept
upon the altars of each home,
so that all within might call upon Her name,
asking for safety and protection.

124

HOKHMA

Hokhma (Chokhma, *ch* as in the Gaelic *loch*) is the Hebrew word meaning wisdom. The following piece is adapted from excerpts of *In Praise of Wisdom*, from *The Wisdom of Solomon* in the *Apocrypha* of *The New English Bible*. The Apocrypha contains many texts that were removed from the main body of *The Bible*, the word apocrypha literally meaning hidden. We may want to question why this particular piece of writing, dated to the period of Israel's Solomon (about 900 B.C.), was not included in *The Bible*, in light of the exalted and powerful image of Wisdom as female. Even within *The Wisdom of Solomon*, as it appears today, we may observe possible evidence of attempts to alter the role and status of Hokhma. Such attempts may be the cause of the puzzling sixth paragraph of *In Praise of Wisdom*, which starts out by Solomon explaining that, "wisdom is under God's direction", and "He himself gave me true understanding of things as they are", but ends the long list of all that he had learned with, " . . . for I was taught by her whose skill made all things, wisdom". Throughout the piece, wisdom is repeatedly referred to in anthropomorphic terms, even described as seated by the door. Thus I have taken the liberty of capitalizing the name of Wisdom, whose role may be compared to that of the Egyptian Goddess known as Maat (see Egyptian Section).

Wisdom, She who knows all, shining bright and never fading, is recognized by all who love Her, quick to make Herself known to any who seek to find Her, for She is often seated upon the doorstep, just waiting to be invited in. The prudent will set all their thoughts upon Her, for to lie awake at night, with thoughts of Her upon the sleepless mind, is to find peace of mind more quickly—as She wanders about seeking out those who search, appearing with kindly intention, always meeting each halfway in their purpose.

That which comes from loving Her is the keeping of Her laws, the first of which is to forego pale envy, for from envy there is spite. Wisdom will not make Herself known to the spiteful, but only to those who realize, that compared to Her, all the gold in the world has the value of the sand upon the desert, and compared to Her, all the silver in the world in as common as the clay of the river bank. Her brilliance is greater than the sun, for She never disappears from view, but following Her to each place that She leads one may find riches greater than gold or silver, yet riches beyond count—and that which may comfortably be shared, for always She is there, to lead to more.

It is She who teaches the knowledge of the structure of the world, and of the constant changes of its elements: of the beginning and the end of eras, and the path of going from one end to the other; of the solstice and the equinox; of the changing of the seasons; of the patterns of the years, as the stars create their designs in the heavens; of the natures of animals and beasts, of the wild winds, and of the thoughts of people; of the many wondrous plants, and the purpose of each root—for whether visible or hidden, Wisdom teaches of all that She had made.

Wisdom is the Holy Spirit. She is one and yet She is many, so loose and free moving, so subtle and so light in touch that She is like the mist of the air, moving as easily as motion itself, loving what moves as easily as Herself, beneficence and kindness—as She permeates all with Her ethereal essence. Though they say that She is the brightness that comes forth from the eternal light, and that She is but the flawless mirror of the active power of God, they also say that it is She who continually renews all, as Her power spans the universe and Her kindly orders are always fulfilled; that She decides what God shall do, and that She is the cause of all that occurs.

Temperance and thoughtfulness, justice and strength—these are Her teachings. It is well worth listening to Her advice for She knows all that has happened in the past, as She also knows what is yet to come, and can thus explain the solving of all problems and the settling of all conflict, providing us with the knowledge of what to do through Her many signs and omens. If one follows to each place that She leads, each time doing as She suggests—afterwards there is rest with Her, rest without bitterness or pain, rest with only gladness and joy.

To begin to know Her is pure delight, to become with Her as family is the gaining of immortality. Understanding and eternal honour are won by those who hold converse with Her. Though they say that She sits by throne of God, and that She is his to give or to withhold, yet they also say that She was there in the beginning, at the time of the creation of the universe, and that She is the Holy Spirit that has since stood by us in our needs, forever teaching what would not otherwise be taught.

LILITH

The name of Lilith appears in several Sumerian tablets: in one text as 'the hand of Inanna'; in another as a female figure forced to flee from her home in a tree on the bank of a river. The Sumerian accounts may be linked to the Goddess as She was known in the Sumerian city of Nippur—as Ninlil (see Sumerian Section). Later Babylonian references describe a Lilitu, as a demon of the night air, again suggesting a link with Ninlil, whose name literally means Lady of the Air. The Lilitu texts occur at about the same period as the *Enuma Elish,* the account of the murder of the Goddess as Tiamat, and may be another manifestation of the suppression of Goddess worship. Accounts of Lilith, as the first wife of Adam, appear in the *Talmud* and the *Kabbalah,* but may well be based upon the Babylonian Lilitu—and in turn, a distorted version of the Goddess Ninlil.

How the many reflections of Lilith flicker upon the layered mirrors of time. Her name was once known as the hand of the Goddess Inanna, the one who brought the men of the fields into Inanna's holy temple at Erech. Yet they say there was a Lilith who lived within the huluppu tree, around which a serpent did entwine, until Gilgamish cut down its mighty trunk, from the bank of the river where Inanna had planted it.

Was the woman essence, that we've come to know as Lilith, taken from the ancient holy Ninlil, Goddess who gave the gift of grain, keeper of the divine Dukug grain chamber of the heavens, She who birthed the moon, in the darkness of the Netherworld, She who chose the lad at the holy Tummal shrine in sacred Nippur, Ninlil alone appointing him as shepherd?

Still they give the name of Lilith as the first wife of Adam, saying that she had been made of the dust of the earth, as Adam had been made, but that she left to live a life of her own, when Adam insisted that she lie beneath him—for she refused to be regarded as one inferior to any other. Angered by her independent ways, they then spoke of Lilith in her long absence, deriding her decisive woman strength, her insistence that she would have love only with mutual respect, or would not have love at all, by then saying that it was Lilith who came as a demon of the night, encouraging men to spill their sperm, defying their ideas of the legitimacy of each child who was born. So, into the Kabbalah it was written, that Lilith encouraged children to be born outside of marriage contract, to tug upon the father after he was dead, demanding an inheritance. And

127

though they said that it was the father of such a child who was to bear the pain, they said that it was Lilith who was to blame.

Looking deep into the layers of Lilith mirrors, I see an ancient Goddess, She who brought the gift of agriculture, transformed into a demon; the image of woman as strong and independent degraded for her strength—thus distorted into a temptress of men—even as they admitted that she had chosen well between oppression and freedom.

SHEKHINA

The Shekhina does not appear in *The Bible*, or in the *Apocrypha*, but is regarded as part of Hebrew lore, as described in the *Talmud* and the *Kabbalah*. The Shekhina, which may literally mean being, is used almost synonymously with the figure known as The Bride of the Sabbath, the divine woman image that is to be welcomed on the eve of the Hebrew Sabbath. The word sabbath is derived from the Semitic Akkadian word *shapatu*, meaning the night of the full moon, though some would relate it to a seldom mentioned Sun Goddess known as Shapas, who was entitled Torch of the Deities in Ugaritan texts. Although Shapas was described as a Sun Goddess, the Akkadian Shapatu rituals were held on the night of the full moon, later on both full moon and new moon. The concept of The Shekhina appears to be a combination of a desire for the return of a divine female image within Judaism, while simultaneously embodying the hopes for better days for the Jewish people.

Holy Shekhina,
perfect reflection of woman being
whose image appears upon seeking the highest holiness,
too long has She been in exile,
too long have Her people
sorrowed at Her absence,
for since the burning of Her sanctuary,
She has been seen at the wailing wall,
clad in black and weeping.
Yet She may be found
in the field of holy fruit trees,
Her orchards ever sacred in memory—
and thus She is begged to return.

Perhaps She is one
with the Queen of the Sabbath,
Shabbat Bride of the Kabbalah,
perhaps once known as Shapatu
and seen in the silver of the moon,
for was She not once welcomed by Semitic peoples
and honour paid to Her sacred being
when first She arrived
as a thin young crescent
in the dark heaven,
and again, when in Her full glory,
Her perfect glowing roundness
cast silver flecks upon the leaves
of Her sacred grove?

Still the candles are lit,
still the sacred braided loaf is baked,
in hopes that Her ancient Sabbath spirit
will enter each home—
filling it with the Mother love
that is the very presence of the Shekhina.

remind them of the Sekpoli

If any area of the world was to be regarded as the true home of the Goddess as The Mother of people, the extreme antiquity of human development on the continent of Africa must give highest priority to this area. Among the lakes and snow peaked mountains of Tanzania and Kenya lived the ancient ones who were the foremothers of the human species. Whether She was called upon as Mawu, Ala, Songi, Mbaba Mwana Waresa, Bomu Rambi, Jezanna, Mboze, Ngame, Nyame, Nuneit, Niachero, Amauneit, or Neit—it seems quite certain that it was on the soil of Africa that life came forth from the first human mother—the Divine Ancestress of all people.

In reading the accounts of reverence for the Goddess, and the legends of heroines from Africa that are included in this section, it is important to keep in mind that Africa is a vast continent. It stretches over five thousand miles from east to west and over five thousand miles from south to north. The material included here is but a small representation of the religious lore of the many diverse cultures that inhabit the African continent today. Perhaps even more significant is the fact that Africa has a history of human habitation (of homo sapiens and pre-homo sapiens) longer than any other area of the world. Since the accounts to which we have access are those which have been recorded over the relatively recent period of the last two centuries, it seems only reasonable to assume

131

that they have probably undergone considerable transitions since their initial development; yet within them may be the core of very ancient traditions and beliefs.

Evidence of pre-homo sapiens in Africa takes us back several million years—to the hominids of Olduvai Gorge in Tanzania and Kafuan in Kenya. The earliest human made tools, so far discovered anywhere on earth, were made in these areas. The members of the Lower Paleolithic culture known as Abbevillian, which originated in central Africa, are generally regarded as descendants of those most ancient hominids. It was the Abbevillian culture that spread across Africa, eventually introducing the concept of toolmaking into Europe and the Near and Middle East.

Some scholars suggest that later groups from Africa may have influenced the Upper Paleolithic Age of France and Spain, the era of cave paintings and Goddess Venus figures of about 30,000 to 15,000 B.C. These suggestions are based upon the evidence of paintings and incised drawings found in caves of southern Africa, Zimbabwe, parts of Morocco and Libya, and around the Sahara. The characteristics of the bone structure of skeletal remains found in Europe, such as the burial at the cave of the Grotte des Enfants in Grimaldi which show definite black African characteristics, support these hypotheses. The Grimaldi burial was of an elderly woman and a young male, both richly decorated with necklaces, while the woman had worn a skirt and headdress ornamented with shells. The combination of the very early Abbevillian entry into Europe; the evidence of later skeletal remains; and similarities between the cave art of Africa and that of France and Spain, suggests the need for a more careful examination of the role that groups from the African continent played in the cultural development of both the Lower and Upper Paleolithic periods of Europe.

In considering the following accounts, we are then aware that we are discussing many widely separated, extremely diverse cultures, some apparently of exceptional geographical stability. Thus it is not too surprising to find that the images of the Goddess, and the actions and symbolism attributed to Her, vary from the exalted position of the Goddess Mawu as Creator of the world and life among the people of Dahomey, to the Goddess as the Moon in the accounts of the Mashona and Buhera Ba Rowzi people of Zimbabwe, while the Zulu of Natal and the Woyo of Zaire both regard the Goddess as She who sends the rain. Still, we may do well to keep in mind that these were the attributes and symbols stressed in the accounts as they have been recorded—most often by people of Caucasian European heritage—and do not necessarily provide us with a full picture of the Goddess as She was actually known by each group of people.

A theme that seems to thread its way through these particular accounts is that of a testing of human values. Nsomeka was unique in her helpfulness at home and in her independent fortitude. Mella was endowed with similar qualities with the addition of exceptional courage and perseverance. Notambu, High Priestess of the Moon Goddess Jezanna among the Mashona, trusted her own inner sense of morality and challenged the very structure of her own religious beliefs—to find that she alone had truly understood and properly interpreted the wishes of the Goddess. Men were not exempt from this testing. The chosen mate of Mbaba Mwana Waresa, Goddess among the Zulu of Natal, was tested to assure the Goddess that his values would allow him to perceive the difference between what is important and what is superficial. Awe, and the brothers of Mella, found that bragging and stealing were not acceptable to those who revered the Goddess. The concept of being tested by divine powers may be observed in the religious beliefs of other cultures, such as in the account of the near sacrifice of Isaac by his father Abraham, as recorded in the Bible, but in the accounts of the Goddess in Africa the test is usually in connection with an explanation of a moral truth, rather than a test of the blind obedience of a worshipper. In this context, the story of Notambu is all the more interesting in that the inner sense of morality is held higher than the following of structured religious ritual.

As in the spiritual or religious imagery of many cultures, the dwelling place of the Goddess in Africa was often described as being much like the shelters or environments of those who revered Her. Thus the Goddess may live in a small house, such as Mbaba Mwana Waresa or Songi, or in a jungle in heaven, the description of the home of the mighty creator Mawu. But the audience or reader of such descriptions soon realizes that these dwellings were understood to be endowed with qualities beyond the worshipper's earthly home—Mbaba Mwana Waresa's with an ever glowing rainbow on the roof, Songi's filled with a strange light.

Another point of perspective, on the antiquity of the cultural heritage of the African continent, may be gained from the accounts of the worship of the Goddess in ancient Egypt (see Egyptian Section). Quite a few references in Egyptian texts associate the worship of the Goddess as Hathor, especially in the form of a lion, with the land of Nubia. The Goddess as Hekit, well known to the Egyptians, was described as having come from Nubia. Connections between Egypt and the lands surrounding it should not be overlooked. Few people realize that the name Libya, mentioned repeatedly in Classical Greek texts, did not always indicate just the land we know as Libya today. At about 450 B.C., Herodotus wrote, "As for Libya, we know that it is washed on all sides by the sea except where it joins Asia." (Book 4). Herodotus explained that a ship sent by the Egyptians, though the crew was Phoenician, left from the Arabian Gulf, sailed " . . . around the tip of Libya . . . ", and re-entered the Mediterranean by sailing eastwards into the Straits of Gibraltar. In Book 2, Herodotus wrote, "The Nile flows from Libya . . . ", adding that "nobody knows anything about the source of the Nile because that river runs through a part of Libya which is uninhabited and desert." Thus, according to Herodotus, Libya (with the exception of Egypt) was the name for *all* of Africa to the extent that it was known to the Greeks.

Once aware of this ancient use of the name Libya, the accounts of Diodorus Siculus, that the Amazons of Anatolia had originally come from Libya—as well as the many other Classical references to Libya—may be seen in a different light. Nineteenth century accounts of the woman warriors of Dahomey, and of women warriors among the Lunda and Gager tribes of Zaire, should be examined more carefully. Any exploration of Amazons in "Libya" might do well to include the account by Apollonius, that Amazons lived and worshipped the Goddess in the area of Colchis. Although Colchis is located on the eastern end of the Black Sea, Herodotus recorded that the people of Colchis had come from Egypt. This ancient definition of Libya may also be of interest in studies of accounts of the origins of the Goddess as Athena, who was said to have been *born* on the shores of Lake Tritonis in *Libya*. It may be significant that Greek accounts mention Libya as the name of a female figure linked to the tale of Europa, the woman who was taken from the city of Tyre in Canaan to the island of Crete, a legend that has most often been explained as an allegory of the migration of the worship of the Goddess from Canaan to Crete. The woman named Libya was described as Europa's *grandmother*.

In many areas of Africa, carved ceremonial figures of the Goddess reveal the widespread reverence for Her, though various names, attributes and legends may be described. Studies among the Ashanti of Ghana reveal their reverence for the Goddess as Nyame, a name closely related to the Akan of Ghana's worship of the Goddess as Ngame. The matrilineal descent patterns among the Ashanti, known as the *abusua,* results in the special importance attached to the birth of female infants among them.

One intriguing sidelight, of the exploration of Goddess reverence among the many peoples of Africa, is the association of religious ritual with the bright star Sirius by the Dogon peoples of Mali. Sirius (Sept) was regarded as the sacred star of the Egyptian Goddess Au Sept (known as Isis to the Greeks). The reverence for Sirius brings to mind the accounts of the Semites of Mesopotamia, that the Goddess as Ishtar had descended from the planet Venus, along with Her retinue of holy women. The connection of the Goddess with a star is also to be observed in the Semitic account from Canaan—that the Goddess had descended as a fiery falling star that landed in the lake of Aphaca, near Byblos in Lebanon. This lake was later regarded as sacred, and an important shrine was built nearby. The Alur people of Zaire also have an account of a divine woman descending from a star. Niachero, known as 'The Daughter of the Star', was said to have arrived upon earth near a great mountain, later returning to heaven by standing upon the mountain peak. These concepts may also be compared to the Goddess in India as Tara, Tara meaning star.

The sacred lake, the Davisa, that was so inherent a part of the worship of Jezanna among the Mashona, offers an interesting parallel to the sacred lakes of the Goddess among the Semites. The recurring image of the Goddess as a being of the waters, or emerging from the waters, lake, river, or ocean, exists in cultures as diverse as the Woyo of Angola, the Chibcha of Colombia, the Sumerians of southern Mesopotamia, the Peruvians of the Andes, the Semites of Canaan and Mesopotamia, the Tantric groups of India, the Greeks of Cyprus and Greece, and the Celts of western Europe. The relationship of the star to the sacred lake appears specifically in the accounts of Semitic Aphaca, but Egyptian texts from Hermopolis,describing the original creation as occurring on a flaming island in a lake, may be linked to the Aphaca accounts. One cannot help but be reminded of an epithet often applied to the later Virgin Mary of Christianity, Stella Maris, Star of the Waters.

Whatever the original meanings or intended symbolism of the imagery of star and waters, it is perhaps the human values of honesty, courage, and concern for others, that emerge most clearly in the accounts of the Goddess on the continent that saw the dawn of human life.

MAWU

The powers of Mawu are those of the omnipotent creator of all life. But the accounts of Mawu also reveal specific theological concepts that are an integral part of the belief in Mawu among the Dahomey peoples of western Africa. The concept of the *Sekpoli,* which may best be defined as soul, goes beyond western theological contemplation of the soul in the explanation that it is because of the existence of the Sekpoli, as a *part* of Mawu in every person, that aggression and fighting are wrong. The account also makes it clear that although magic may be useful or impressive, it is insignificant in comparison with the overwhelming powers of Mawu. So important is the emphasis on human humility, and acceptance of the fact that it is the Goddess Mawu who holds supreme power, that when the miracle of new life is not enough to convince the unbelieving, death is then added as further proof. The account of Awe challenging the powers of Mawu may bring to mind the recent efforts to gain control of the birthing of new life, a desire that has apparently been on the minds of some men for a long time. We may want to consider why the fertilizing of an egg (from a woman) in a test tube (then returned to the womb of a woman to gestate for nine months) has been hailed as such a marvelous and astounding feat, while the daily repeated miracles of pregnancy and birth have been so trivialized in our society. If Awe is once again throwing his balls of thread into Mawu's heaven, what results will his challenges bring this time?

Riding high in Aido Hwedo's mouth, as if on the back of an elephant, Mawu, Mother of All, Mawu, created the mountains, the valleys, the rivers. She created all, all, all! Do you sometimes wonder why the mountains curve? Why the valleys dip? Why the rivers twist and wind as they flow? These are the paths that Mawu took as the primeval serpent, the faithful Aido Hwedo, slithered over the earth, carrying Mawu in its giant reptilian jaws.

At first it was dark, so very dark that one could hardly see. Then with Her magic, Mawu made the fire, great wondrous light that brings each day, and set it in the heavens, high over the earth— so that She might better view all that She had made. In the light, Mawu saw the vastness of Her works, felt the joy of Her creation, tingled with the pleasure of contemplating the beauty She had made. But soon She worried about how much weight the earth could hold and thus She spoke to Aido Hwedo, 'Crawl beneath the earth. Curl yourself up as round as a reed mat and like a platter that holds the food upon it, hold up the weight of the earth so that it shall never fall. I have created massive mountains, heavy hills and tall trees, elephants and giraffes, lions and zebras. The earth is heavy with my creation and you must hold it up.' Thus Aido Hwedo crawled beneath the earth and lies there still.

Mawu called to a monkey as he sat upon a branch and these words She spoke to him: 'Out of the clay I have formed you, breathed life into your earthen body; carefully did I shape your fingers and now the time has come for you to use them. From the clay you must form other animals. They may be of your own design, with feathers or with fur, with two legs or with four. I shall return to breathe the breath of life into each. When you have completed your task, you shall be rewarded well for I shall help you to stand as erect as the humans I have formed, so that your hands shall be free to use, even as you walk.'

But when Mawu returned to see the work that the monkey had done, the monkey was not there. She stood before the pile of clay. Not a leg, not a feather—the clay remained as clay. The monkey had scampered off to brag to the other animals in the jungle of his great fortune-to-be. What use are hands, Mawu wondered, to one who only cares to twine his tail about the leafy branches and to boast to all his neighbors of what he has not yet accomplished? What use are hands, Mawu wondered, to one who has allowed his chance to aid in the Creation to slip by unfulfilled? Forever shall he remain a monkey and use his hands to walk. So Mawu then decreed—and so it has been for monkeys until this very day.

Gbadu, Holy Daughter Gbadu, She who Mawu made first, sat upon the tallest palm guarding Mawu's work. Up She looked and saw the heavens. Out She looked and saw the sea. Down she looked and saw the earth. Everywhere, Gbadu saw sadness and turmoil, fighting on the earth, fighting on the sea. The people of Dahomey had forgotten the teachings of Her Mother, the divine words of Mawu. Thus Gbadu spoke to her children, 'Your Grandmother Mawu has made the people. She has given them life and the earth on which to live it—but they have forgotten Her wisdom. You must go and teach them as I have taught you, as Mawu once taught me. Remind them of the Sekpoli, that essence of life that is the gift of Mawu—so that to fight with another is to fight with another part of Mawu.'

Then Gbadu spoke to Her own eldest daughter, 'Minona, you shall be known upon earth. You shall be holy among women for teaching the omens of the palm kernels so that the people may know what is to come and who is to die and who is to be born. She who learns to read the palm kernels shall gain the knowledge of the unfolding of each day and thus will Mawu's word be known, so that the people of Dahomey will be wise once again.'

The children of Gbadu wandered the lands of Dahomey, teaching of Mawu and the Sekpoli, Minona teaching of the omens, until the wisdom of Mawu was known by nearly all. But Awe, boastful braggard Awe, said that he was as great, as great as Mawu, as powerful as the Mother of All and that he too could make life, as everyone believed that only Mawu could do. Soon the others began to listen to Awe, for he made miracles and strange magic. 'Can Mawu's magic be superiour to mine?' he asked. 'I shall stand before Her in heaven and prove that I am as mighty as Mawu!' Awe challenged the powers of Mawu. Awe challenged the powers of Mawu. Was Awe as great?

Into the sky Awe threw two balls of thread. The others stood and gasped as the threads of cocoon silk rose further and further into the heavens until Mawu's great hands reached out and easily caught the balls of thread whose ends still touched the earth. Truly Awe was great, they said, for who else could throw so high and with the same astonishment, they watched as Awe climbed the silken threads up through the clouds until he reached the heaven of Mawu. And there, in the highest heaven of all—Awe challenged the powers of Mawu. Awe challenged the powers of Mawu. Was Awe as great?

In the jungle of heaven, Awe chopped down a fine round tree. Back and forth with a sharp rock, Awe made the branches leave the tree and in the trunk that was left, he made eyes, he made a mouth, a belly, arms and even fingers. Awe was making a person. When Awe had finished down to the toes he looked up at Mawu and said, 'I have created a person.' Only Mawu could make a person. Was Awe as great?

'Why does Awe's person not smile? Why does Awe's person not walk? Can it dance and chant for you?' asked Mawu. 'Breathe into it Awe. If you are truly as great as Mawu, give it the breath of life. Give it a Sekpoli.' Awe took a deep breath so that his chest grew large and then he breathed out so hard that the leaves of heaven quivered for miles—but his person still lay upon the ground, not moving. Again he made his chest great and again he blew. This time his breath made such a wind that the statue stirred. But when the wind calmed down the person of Awe lay as lifeless as ever.

Two more times he tried, then bent his head in shame and defeat. Awe had failed. He had to admit that only Mawu could make life. But Mawu was wise. She knew that boastful, braggard Awe would soon forget his shame and once returned to earth, his boasts would be bigger than ever. Those who listened might again be deceived. Thus Mawu cooked a meal for Awe. First planting a seed in the ground, the instantly sprouting wheat was made into a bowl of cereal for Awe and Awe ate until the bowl was empty—not knowing what he had eaten.

In his porridge had been the seed of death.
Awe had eaten the seed of death.

His belly filled with the cereal, Awe began to descend the ladder of threads to return to the earth below. It was then that Mawu told him of the seed and why She had fed it to him. 'Remind them', She said, 'Remind them that you may use your human charms and potions, that you may make your amulets and magic but only Mawu, only Mother Mawu, can breathe the breath of life into each—and will suck it out when She chooses.'

So it happened that Mawu, Mother of All, sent the first seed of death down to earth with Awe so that people would never again doubt Mawu's omnipotent power. Thus those who are wise, treasure the Sekpoli in each and know that it is from Mawu, *only Mawu,* that we receive the gift of the breath of life.

ALA

Though the information that I was able to find on the Goddess of the Ibo people of Nigeria is scanty, it does reveal several major attributes of the nature of Her importance. Ala is both the provider of life and the Mother who receives again in death, both attributes revealing Her high position among the people who revere Her. It is also Ala who proclaims the law that is the basis for all moral human behaviour. In this last attribute, we may see a concept of the Goddess such as that found in the images of Demeter and Isis as providers of the law, or perhaps the understanding that the Mother of all explains the law through Her works, a theological concept close to that found in China. Most interesting is the custom of having life-size images of Ala sitting on the porch of a small wooden house in the village, visible to all who pass by. This custom may well be one that grew from the worship of the Goddess as ancestress or grandmother, Her image and spirit still dwelling in the village.

> Holy Mother Earth,
> She who guides those who live upon Her,
> She whose laws the people of the Ibo follow,
> living in the honesty and rightness
> that are the ways of Goddess Ala;
> it is She who brings the child to the womb
> and She who gives it life,
> always present during life
> and receiving those whose lives are ended,
> taking them back into Her sacred womb,
> "the Pocket of Ala".

> Along the Benue River
> where the waters slide into the mighty Niger
> and through its many fingers,
> flow into the sea,
> the women and the men
> join in building the Mbari,
> sacred houses where Goddess Ala
> may sit upon the porch,
> child upon Her knee,
> sword sometimes in Her hand,
> looking out upon the Ibo world
> as the Ibo look upon Her—
> glad that She dwells close by.

JEZANNA

The practice of human sacrifice appears in accounts of many ancient peoples, in cultures as diverse as the Celts to the Carthaginians. Here we have the sacred narrative of how this ritual came to an end among the Mashona people of Zimbabwe. The ritual of mourning, for the one sacrificed, invites interesting comparisons with the ritual mourning ceremonies of Sumer, Egypt, Babylon, Anatolia and even the Christian Easter. What is of particular interest here is the reverence for the Goddess as The Moon, and that the primary representative of the Goddess on earth is Her High Priestess. In considering the concept and purposes of the sacred lake, the Davisa, we may find interesting parallels in the Near East, especially among the worshippers of Ashtart (see Semitic Section).

Among the elders of the proud Mashona people, lingers the oft told memory of times so long ago, of the holy woman Notambu, High Priestess of the glowing Jezanna, She who shows Herself as the golden moon. Standing by the waters of the sacred Davisa where golden Jezanna's image dwells at night, the women and the men gather by the shore and listen as they have listened so many times before, to the ancient story of Notambu and how she gave Jezanna's wisdom to the great Mashona people:

In the quiet rippling waters, filled with the darkness of the night, the wetness of Notambu's body glistened in the moonlight, her skin as wondrous dark as the sky, her voice as soft as the gentle cresting of the sacred lake, as she recited the prayers of the Mashona, asking Jezanna for abundant crops, plentiful cattle, healthy children. Notambu knew Jezanna's answers when She joined Notambu in the waters, Her perfect circle being glistening close to where Notambu stood.

When the time for the holiest of festivals arrived, that which would pay Jezanna greatest honours, when each would say their prayers of gratitude and ask Jezanna for one more year of blessings, Notambu readied herself for her role in the procession. It was she who would lead the rest, she who would conduct the sacred ceremonies, that which she had never done before, for only seven moons ago had Notambu been chosen as High Priestess to Jezanna.

As Notambu made her preparations, the Nganga too made ready for the ancient rites. Watching for the fullness of the moon, the one that preceded the roundness of the full moon of the festival, the Nganga entered the jungle when Jezanna's light glowed brilliantly in the heavens, to live there for the full month's time— eating only the meat of the crocodiles, sitting in silent meditation, hearing no human voice, not even his own, thus purifying his body and his mind.

The ceremonies began in the sunshine as the people gathered in the village clearing, each finding their place in the line that was forming. Young ones, old ones, women with children at their breasts, followed the lead of the Nganga, who, knees bent, danced from side to side, shaking and swinging the zebra tail switch, his high piercing wail spearing into the brightness of the day. He in turn, followed the holy Notambu whose body stood as the straightest tree, whose head was held high as if her graceful neck might reach the heavens, the golden disc upon her forehead glistening in the sun, as she led the long procession along the path that wound its way to the Davisa.

The mournful cry of pipes of reed mingled with the shrill sound of the Nganga, while sobbing drumbeats fell upon the earth, as the heaviest of fruits cry out when they fall from mother tree. Voices sympathized with instruments of sorrow, singing the familiar hymns of the child that would die for others, the holy child, the per- fect child, bright and healthy, with the promise of the future gleam- ing from its deep brown eyes. And there were songs of the sadness of the mother, whose tears of grievous lamentation would bring the tears of the very heavens to rain upon the planted seeds—so that the crops would grow and bountiful abundance would be ensured for the Mashona.

As Notambu grew closer to the waters of the Davisa, her vision of the mother and the child, standing in solemn silence at the shore, grew larger, ever larger, until the mother's size was as her own in closeness. Halting the procession where she stood, the eyes of Notambu touched those of the mother and the child. The pipes and drums and voices made a sudden silence that was louder than any sound that she had ever heard before. She watched the Nganga as he reached to take the child's hand, laying her down on the flat rock altar, drawing out his sacred knife, an act that once again raised the sound of the drums, beating even louder, even faster than before.

143

Notambu remembered other years and other tears but never had she been so close, as her eyes locked with the eyes of the little one who lay upon the flat grey stone, shining brown circles of terror betraying the calmness of her mouth. Questions rose in Notambu's heart for who knew Jezanna better than she and knew that the gentle light which had joined her in the sacred lake so many times, could never, would never, have asked that this child's life be taken to make the lives of others better. From Notambu's throat, where holy sacrificial chant was expected to rise, no sound came forth— but to Notambu's body came the message that she must speak with her arms.

Quickly sweeping the child from the altar, she held its shaking smallness to her chest. Notambu's strong brown arms wrapped about the little one in defiant gesture as the Nganga shrieked his anger, wildly waving his zebra tail in menacing threat to any who would dare to defy the ancient ritual. Notambu took not one step forward. Notambu took not one step back. But those who stood close by saw her look up into the afternoon sky and heard her whispered plea, 'Jezanna! Jezanna!'

Deep breaths of astonishment, backward steps of awe, rippled among the villagers, those who had now gathered about the empty altar, while in the sky where the sun still shone, the holy circle of the moon, glowing as the flames glow, marvelously luminous and large, suddenly appeared in the heavens, closer than Jezanna had ever been before. As Notambu raised her face to the scarlet moon, the disc upon her forehead reflecting Jezanna's fire, a gentle smile formed across her mouth and in the stillness of the moment, Notambu's voice came forth as clear and as gentle as the ripples of the sacred lake.

'Listen. She speaks to us. Jezanna tells us that the child must live—that never again should the life of any child be taken for our own comfort and abundance. These are the wishes of the great Jezanna.' As Notambu's voice floated over the waters and echoed back again to all who were gathered by the banks of the sacred lake, she set the child down to stand upon the earth. It was then that she saw that the terror and the anger that had covered the Nganga's face just moments earlier had been replaced by a surprising relief at Jezanna's word.

Ceremony turned to joyous laughter as those who had sung in lamentation now clapped their hands and moved about in a dance of exultation, gratefully rejoicing at Jezanna's decree. The little one stood close by Notambu's side until the darkness of the evening sky crept in from the east and when Jezanna saw that all was well, She floated back up into the heavens, Her fiery redness calming to a distant glow, Her satisfaction with the Mashona people sparkling like diamonds in Her radiant being.

Some say that when the little girl grew old, long after Notambu had been laid to rest, it was she who was the grandmother who saved the cattle of the tribe from the flames of the great fire. Others say that when the moon is full, those who walk to the Davisa might still catch a glimpse of Notambu and the little girl bathing in the holy waters, while Jezanna, filled with pleasure, dances by their side. But all agree that what they once believed were tears of sorrow that rained upon the crops of the Mashona, must now be known as tears of joy, for no life has been taken since that time, yet rains still fall from heaven—and the crops of the Mashona grow even taller than before.

SONGI

The large nation of Bantu peoples are represented throughout central and southern Africa. The name Bantu (Ba Ntu) is actually a language distinction such as Celtic or Semitic. It literally means the people. The languages known as Swahili and Zulu are part of the Bantu groups. This account, of why the women of the Bantu peoples developed the custom of notching their teeth, is one that speaks on many levels. Not only does it explain the origin of the custom, and the beliefs associated with it, but we may also observe the emphasis on the correctness of Nsomeka's actions— why she of all the young women of the village was singled out for such a special mission. We may also observe the knowledgeable acceptance of the fact that when the women own the lands, the home, and the property, men are more careful to treat them with respect.

ANCIENT MIRRORS of WOMANHOOD

Making the porridge, grinding the grains—poor Nsomeka, tired Nsomeka. All the children have run off to play but in the home of her mother, Nsomeka makes the porridge, Nsomeka grinds the grains—poor Nsomeka, sad Nsomeka. The work is done; she looks about but they are gone—swift Nsomeka, fleet Nsomeka—bounds as a zebra across the yellow grass, like a bird she flies over the ferns of the jungle—the almost invisible path reappearing, disappearing, reappearing. Tired from the morning's work, she runs and runs and runs, hoping all the way for a glimpse of the last straggler of the friends who could not wait.

Deep in the jungle, there is someone—but not the friends she seeks. A tall woman, an old woman, stands in the middle of the path. 'What is the rush, Nsomeka?' the woman asks, 'What makes you gallop as if you were on four legs instead of two?' Grateful for the chance to rest, Nsomeka stops to take a deep breath into her small chest and asks the old woman if she has seen the children pass by.

It is the wrong path, the wrong path, Nsomeka thinks, noticing the small house by the side of the road, wondering if it was there when she first stopped running. The offer of a cool drink takes Nsomeka through the doorway, her eyes greeted by a strange glow, her feet greeted by the softness of a reed mat. 'I have been here all day and no one else has passed by', the woman tells her gently, and then as if Nsomeka had spoken her thoughts aloud, the woman adds, 'But this is not the wrong path. You have come the right way. You have come to the house of Songi—The Mother.'

Sipping upon a cool drink, Nsomeka hears the woman say, 'The path was yours, made by your swift feet and your good heart. Someday you will lead your tribe but there is work that you must do first. No more shall the husbands beat their wives; no more shall they order them about. No more shall the women cry. Songi will protect Her daughters, if Nsomeka will help. Come sit down, my child.'

As Nsomeka sets her eyes upon a basket, Songi lifts the lid, allowing a small spotted snake to crawl about Her arm. Nsomeka sits in silence as Songi takes her hand—and shoulder to shoulder, Songi presses Her great arm against the child arm of Nsomeka, the snake winding about to bind the two arms together and thus entwined they sit. Then taking a rough white stone from a small wooden box, Songi begins to file notches in the teeth of Nsomeka— brave Nsomeka, fearless Nsomeka.

146

what is the rush,
Nsomeka?

Making her way back to the home of her mother, once the notching had been done, Nsomeka takes her mother's hand, gently pulling her as the child pulls the one who has given them life. Nsomeka leading, they walk along the path to her grandmother's home. And calling to her mother's mother, soon all three, daughter, mother, grandmother, stand together in the field, the sun cut in half by the great western mountain, welcoming the arrival of evening. So it is that the three stand together in the darkening field and when Nsomeka says that they must sing—three voices sing in chorus.

Hardly has the evening star arrived, when from between the notches of Nsomeka's teeth come cattle, come chickens, come pigs, come goats. The three continue to sing. Great fruit trees pass through the notches and root in the ground before them. The three continue to sing. Large reed houses, tied well and strong, fly out through Nsomeka's teeth, landing near the trees that will shade them from the hot daytime sun—sweet voiced Nsomeka, perfect voiced Nsomeka.

In the morning when the sleeping villagers awake, they can not believe what they see with their eyes. Hearing that this great wealth has come from Nsomeka, the men begin to beat their wives for not having brought them such riches, but Nsomeka calls to the crying women, beckoning them to join her. Thus the women gather with her in the field, the field where the three had sung, the field now filled with houses and trees and livestock—listening as Nsomeka tells the story of Songi and how and why Songi notched her teeth.

From the oldest to the youngest, one by one, the teeth of the women are notched by Nsomeka, her mother and her grandmother—so that each will be marked with the sign of Songi's protection. Filling with uncontainable curiosity, one by one, the watching men begin to enter the women's field. It is then that they see The Notches of Songi and know that it is Songi's village. Here they can not beat their wives nor order them about but so great is the desire of the men for the houses and fruit and livestock, so much do they want to stay, that they promise to treat the women with respect.

So it is that to this day the Bantu women are grateful for the life of Nsomeka who brought them under the protection of the Great Mother Songi—sacred Nsomeka, blessed Nsomeka.

MBOZE AND BUNZI

This image of the Rain Goddess, as the daughter of the original First Mother and Her son, from the Woyo people of Zaire, suggests that this account may have developed to explain the name of Bunzi replacing that of Mboze. Yet the image of the rainbow serpent, as the deity of rain, may be extremely ancient. It brings to mind the Rainbow Serpent of Australia who helps The Mother by providing nurturing rain. There are also hints of the relationship between the serpent and rain in the account of Fire Woman from Borneo (see Oceanic Section). Though the likelihood is rather slim, it is tempting to wonder if the concept of the Rainbow Serpent may be as old as the period in which the Australoids of Africa, Australia and Borneo, were a more cohesive group of people. Fire Woman also takes Her son as a mate, but with less dire consequences.

First there was The Mother,
fertile nurturing Mboze,
who watched over the people
who lived at the mouth of the great river
where it mingled with the waters of the ocean.
Taking Her son Makanga as Her lover,
Mboze swelled with new life
but as She brought forth
Her sacred serpent daughter Bunzi,
Her husband Kuitikuiti,
he who had changed his black skin for a white one,
grew furious upon learning
that Makanga was the father
and beat Mboze with such violence
that She finally sought peace in death.

As Bunzi grew older,
She learned to do the work
that had once been Her mother's,
pouring the rain from the heavens,

causing the fruit and nuts to grow.
Her brilliance was seen
in the many colours of the rainbow
as it arched across the sky,
Bunzi watching joyfully
after She had sent the welcome rain.
Yet those who sing and dance for Bunzi
and call upon Her gracious gifts,
do so in the wondrous darkness of the night
when Bunzi can be seen in the reflections
upon the opalescent serpents of the river,
the rainbow shining upon their skin,
as Bunzi promises the rains of abundance.

MBABA MWANA WARESA

This account, from the Zulu people of Natal, of how the Goddess came to
take a mate, includes a detailed description of the careful preparations
made for a marriage among the Zulu peoples. But the theme of the
narrative is the testing of the abilities of the one chosen, to be able to see
through the superficialities of such elaborate preparations, thus explaining
the greater importance of recognizing what is truly valuable. This account
may offer us some insight into a system of basic human values that western
thought has either forgotten or has yet to learn.

Sacred Goddess of the light that streaks across the skies, sacred
Goddess who beats upon the drums of heaven, sacred Goddess who
pours the waters from Her heavenly home roofed with rainbow
arches, sacred Goddess who makes the forest green, filling the fields
with grass for grazing, making the crops grow ever taller, sacred
Goddess who taught us how to sow and reap, sacred Goddess who

gave us the gift of beer so that we might celebrate our times of joy—
Holy Rain Goddess of the Heavens, Mbaba Mwana Waresa, how
dear to our hearts you are.

In the roundness of the thatched hut, listening to the rain that
falls upon the leaves, the story of the marriage of the Rain Goddess
pours forth from the mouths of the elders who remind us of the time
when the Goddess decided to take a husband and when none in
heaven took Her fancy, She chose a mortal youth, the most
beautiful, the most wise, that She could find upon the earth. Thus
the holy ones of heaven arranged the marriage that would take
place in his village, before they returned together to Her home in the
heavens:

When the sun of the wedding day peered above the eastern
mountains, the Goddess prepared for the ceremonies in a way that
astonished those who lived in heaven, choosing to shave the feather
soft black hair of Her head, choosing to smear Her perfect black
body with pale grey ashes, choosing to cast off Her rainbow coloured skirt and to dress in the torn skin of a zebra hide—while the
friend that She had chosen to be attendant at the wedding was
dressed as a Zulu bride is dressed.

The finest cloths were wrapped about the body of Her friend,
her hair was twined into delicate braids, each braid laced through
with precious beads; gold and silver bands circled about her wrists
and ankles; sacred dyes were painted carefully upon her cheeks and
forehead; a beaded belt was tied about her waist; glistening stones
hung on thin copper wires in the warmth beneath her arms to jingle
gently when she moved; great golden hoops were hung upon her
ears; and the sacred curving wombshell of life was hung upon her
forehead.

When all was ready, the Goddess and Her friend began their
heavenly journey that would lead them to the village where the lad
that was the chosen one of Mbaba Mwana Waresa lived, waiting
for the day that the Goddess would arrive. Suddenly the sky above
his home grew dark with storm; sharp branches of lightning shot
through the heavens; thunder crashed above his head—and in this
way the anxious lad knew that She who was to take him as Her
husband, would soon be by his side. Looking up into the darkened
sky, the fellow saw two women approaching and as he stood and
watched, filled with the wonder of his wedding day, the rains of
plenty and good fortune fell cool upon him as he waited.

The lad bowed low with reverence as the two women finally stood before his home, while the women of the village, those who had been chosen as the earthly attendants of the bride, watched to see if he would know which of the women was to be his wife. So it was that smiles broke upon their faces when he put his hand out to the Goddess, though Her head was shaved, though ashes made Her body grey, though She wore the torn hide of a zebra, and he softly said, 'Welcome Mbaba Mwana Waresa, Holy Goddess of the Rain, you need no beads nor gold nor silver, nor fine soft cloths wrapped about your body, for in your sparkling eyes I see the richness of the earth, the fruitfulness of the growing land, the beauty of the joyous harvest, the power of the thunder and the lightning—how deeply I am honoured that you have chosen me.'

Thus the ceremonies filled the day, dance and food and drink of celebration surrounded the Rain Goddess as She stood upon the earth and when the wedding day had ended, She took the lad, whose wisdom was in seeing truth, back to Her home in the heavens and lives there with him still.

MELLA

Although the moon, as the Goddess Bomu Rambi, is mentioned tangentially in this account of the heroine Mella, this is primarily a story of the courage that grows from deep concern about a loved one. It is both the courage and the integrity of young Mella that allow her to succeed, while those lacking these elements of human character fail. This account of Mella may be based upon an oral history of the Buhera Ba Rowzi people of Zimbabwe, since Mella's later role as tribal leader is stated so specifically.

In a bright sunny clearing on the edge of a deep green forest, were the homes of reed and fiber in which the people of the village dwelled. On a mat inside one home was the father of Mella, lying close to death, while all the offerings and sacrifice, while all the music of the pipes and drums, while all the magic of Nganga healers, could not rouse him from his weakness and his dying.

Into the forest Mella walked one night, stopping in the rich moonlit dampness of the ferns, her fingertips about the crescent amulet that hung about her neck, her young woman body holding thoughts of age and sickness in its heart. There she called upon the merciful Bomu Rambi, She who watched over the village, begging for any word of what she might do to help. The leaves above her trembled with the presence of the power of the moonlight as it shone upon them, until Mella heard these words echoing over and over within her head, 'You must go to the Python Healer. You must go to the Python Healer.'

Mella's heart beat quickened. Her body grew cold in the warm night air. Fear crept into her worried heart. Had not her older brothers sought the help of the Python Healer many moons before and had they not fled in terror from the entrance of the python's cave, returning to the village so shaken with terror that their voices had died within their throats when they tried to speak of their visit to the Python Healer?

Lying on her straw mat in the dark of that night, Mella's eyes would not close; Mella's mind would not rest as thoughts of the Python Healer crawled in and out of her thoughts. When the dimmest rays of the morning sun fell upon her wakeful eyes, Mella rose from her mat, quickly gathered roots and grains, putting them into a small sack of elephant hide, and set off for the place that she had never been, the cave of the Python Healer, the cave set into the foothill of a mountain in the covering of the deepest, thickest jungle.

Four times the sun disappeared from the sky. Four times the sun returned to cross the heavens. All this time Mella walked through ferns as high as her head, up and down the many rock strewn hills, making her way through wooded mountainsides, sleeping in unfamiliar groves, crossing streams whose currents challenged the expert balance of her body, crossing clearings high with yellow straw that felt both soft but piercing beneath her feet, all the while bravely singing songs while her thoughts roamed between the eyes of the animals whose paths she used and anxious worry about her father, lying still and weak upon his mat at home. Then all thoughts were pushed from her mind by the sight of the spiral carved upon the rock at the entrance to the cave of the Python Healer!

In the darkness of an early evening sky, lit only by a thin crescent of the moon, Mella tried to find the voice that seemed to have fallen deep into her chest and would not rise into her throat to reach her lips—until she reminded herself of the reasons for her long journey. Taking three deep breaths of evening air, she finally called out to the hollow in the rocky cave, 'I am Mella, sent to you by Bomu Rambi. I have come to ask your help, for my father has lain ill for many moons and his weakness is the weakness of my people.'

Waiting in the silence for an answer, Mella noticed that even the birds had stopped their talking. They too seemed to be waiting for an answer during the time that was passing, a time that felt longer than all the days and all the nights that she had walked. And then in the darkness at the entrance of the cave, she saw a pair of eyes in the dim moonlight, heard a voice as hollow as the cave, a voice as frightening as that of Bomu Rambi had been reassuring. 'The bravest of your people have fled in terror from my door. Does such a small young girl as you are have no fear that I might strangle you and leave your bones about my cave?'

'It is not a lack of fear that I possess,' replied Mella to the hissing voice that seemed to be without a body, 'but a love and a caring that is louder than my fear, a love and a caring for my dying father who has done no wrong, yet neither the Ngangas nor the spirits of the ancestors can rid him of the illness that lays upon him as he lies upon his mat. So deep in sorrow have I been that Bomu Rambi came in answer to my prayers. It was She who sent me to seek you out, to beg for your help if any can be given.'

'Your love and caring more powerful than fear of me?', Python Healer questioned in reply. 'Would you be willing to turn your back and let me crawl close to where you are standing?' Mella spoke no word but turned her back to the entrance of the cave, the pride of her people keeping her head high, though she saw only the jungle night. 'Your loving and caring more powerful than your fear of me?' the Python Healer repeated, the hollow hissing voice now close behind her heels. 'Would you let me twine myself about you as I might do if I chose to take you for my dinner?' Though the frantic cries of animals and birds pierced through the trees in worried, anxious warning, Mella allowed the python to wind itself about her body and when only the legs, the arms, the head, of what had once been Mella, could be seen apart from the many rings of the python that coiled about her body, Python Healer instructed Mella to begin the long walk home.

155

Still she held her head up high, despite the serpent's weight upon her, despite the fear she tried to quell, until from a depth of courage in her heart, a sound rose up into her throat and floated out as song into the air so that all the animals and birds that came to gape along the path on which the serpent laden Mella walked, watched in awe of her bravery, each uttering growls or chirps of deep respect along the way. In this way exhausted Mella arrived at the edges of her village—with the Python Healer still wrapped about her body.

When the members of the village saw the monstrous creature walk into the clearing between two houses, they ran for their arrows and their spears but Mella raised her arm and called aloud, 'It is Mella, inside the Python Healer! Do not harm us for I have travelled a long way to bring healing to my father.' Thus they walked into the door of Mella's home, where the python soon uncoiled itself, slithering down upon the earthen floor, making its way to the mat of Mella's father.

From the small scaled pouch that hung about its neck, Mella took the healing bark as the Python Healer instructed her to do. From the small deer horn that hung about its neck, Mella took the muchonga oil as the Python Healer instructed her to do. With it she made a fire that sent the vapours of the healing bark floating into the air of their home while the Python Healer recited holy chants of the Buhera Ba Rowzi people. And then to Mella's great astonishment—her father began to kneel upon his mat, then stood erect and tall and finally began to walk about the room, something he had not done for all these many moons of illness.

Though the father spoke with many words of gratitude, providing festive food and drink for Mella and the healing serpent, the voice of the Python Healer now was silent. Once again it began to wind about the body of Mella, so that she knew she must again repeat the walk to return the Python Healer to its cave. Once again reaching the spiral marking on the entrance, Mella sighed in great relief as the python crawled down from her exhausted body and moved in silence into the darkness of its home. But as she turned to leave, the Python Healer called out and invited her to enter the deep cavern in which it lived—as animals and birds again cried out in even louder warning.

So much fear had Mella faced that once again she chanced to trust the healer who had helped her father, and step by step she made her way into the granite darkness of the cave. Suddenly a light glimmered in the distance, glowing brighter as she walked. Though she dreaded seeing broken bones lying about the cavern floor, she opened her hesitant eyes and was amazed to see pots of gold and silver, baskets of ebony and ivory and precious jewels nestled upon soft silken cloths and woven tapestries. But more astonishing than all the unexpected treasures were the words that came from Python Healer. 'Take what you wish, for your courage and love should surely be rewarded.'

Mella's eyes lowered with embarrassment, thinking it was she who should reward the Python Healer, and in a voice not much louder than a whisper, she asked the Python Healer to do the choosing. From a great wicker box that sat upon the rocky ground, the python quickly took a golden chain into its mouth, upon whose links was hung a golden crescent of the moon, sacred image of the Buhera Ba Rowzi, holy Ndoro emblem that matched the one that Mella always wore, the one she had touched to call upon Bomu Rambi—thus she knew that Python Healer truly was a friend.

Returning to her village, Mella told her family of the treasure of the cave, proudly showing the golden Ndoro she had won but greed soon entered into the hearts of her brothers who began to plot the python's murder, so that they might steal the riches. Overhearing the quiet scheming voices, Mella ran quickly along the now familiar path to try to protect her friend who lived by the sign of the spiral, to warn the Python Healer of her brothers' plans—so that when the brothers arrived, they were greeted by bursts of hot, unpleasant smelling smoke, frightening thunderous roars—until they again fled in terror as they had so many moons before.

When the people of the village heard of what had happened, they sent the three boys from their home, to live alone forever in the jungle. And when in later years Mella's father died, the people of the village appointed Mella as their leader, thus honouring her courage, her honesty and her love. Mella led the proud Buhera Ba Rowzi for all the long years of her life, visiting the Python Healer as often as she could. So it came to pass that it was Queen Mella who arranged for the great wooden carving that stood in the center of the village, a perfect likeness of the trusted Python Healer, the one **who knew the magic of the Ndoro Crescent moon of Bomu Rambi—and cared for those who lived with courage, honesty and love.**

to watch over the people of the islands

eep in the caves of the mighty volcano we may find the Goddess in Oceania, half of our spirit soul entrusted to Her for safekeeping while we are alive, the other half to return to Her when we die—so that we may rest with our spirit united before we are reborn again. Such is the essence of Goddess reverence among the Australoid people of Australia, and the Polynesians of the Pacific islands, as revealed in their rituals and sacred lore.

The Australoids, most familiar to us as the 'Australian Aborigines', are part of a larger group of people that not only live in Australia and some of the nearby islands, but also survive in southern India and the southern coastal area of Saudi Arabia, while remains of Australoids reveal their one time habitation in Africa. These racial connections between Australia, India, Arabia, and Africa, reveal extremely ancient ties between the Australoid people of these widely separated areas, and suggest the possibility of actual physical connections between some of these land masses at a very early period. Skeletal remains of Proto-Australoids, prehuman forerunners of the present day Australoid people, have not only been discovered in Africa, but also in Talga (Queensland, Australia), attesting to the extreme antiquity of migrations from Africa to Australia. The existence of Australoid people along the southern Hadramaut coast of Arabia suggests that these people may have crossed the Red Sea long before Moses did—probably at the Strait of Bab El Mandeb.

In 1800, the Australoids of Australia were represented by some 500 different tribes. Over the last two centuries, Caucasians of European descent colonized the continent of Australia, most of them settling in the eastern sections where the land is most fertile and supportive of life. Much of the indigenous population was gradually pushed into the almost uninhabitable desert lands of the central sections. Many of the arriving Caucasians claimed that the original inhabitants of the land were at a lower level of evolutionary development than themselves, an arrogant and erroneous idea that often allowed them to treat the Australoid people as less than human. Primarily as a result of the Caucasian colonization, the estimated population of about 300,000 Australoids in 1800 dwindled to today's population of about 40,000.

Though regarded as 'primitive' and 'savage' by most of the arriving Caucasians, a few of them were curious enough to explore and record the social structure and religious beliefs of the Australoid people. They were astonished to discover that many of these so called 'savages' lived almost completely without war or group violence. Despite the physical evidence of Australoid people having inhabited Australia for many thousands of years, a surprising number of their sacred legends included accounts of their arrival from across the sea, suggesting many waves of migrations, perhaps over many thousands of years.

The rituals and sacred legends that were recorded, reveal the Australoid contemplation of their lineage, origins, spiritual concepts of birth, death, reincarnation, and ideas about the nature of the universe. Much of the theological contemplation was associated with images of The First Mother or Divine Ancestress, the survival of these beliefs most prominent in the area known as Arnhemland, the northcentral section of Australia. Religious rituals were often connected to sacred caves, the sanctity of the cave based upon the understanding that it was 'the doorway to the spirit'. Though most of the nineteenth and early twentieth century writers simply stated that the Australoid concept of the 'spirit' was of the 'spirit of the ancestor', and that it was 'ancestor worship' that was the foundation of Australoid beliefs, a few explained that entering the sacred cave was described as going into 'The Womb of The Mother'.

Churingas, sacred objects of stone and wood, incised or painted with religious symbols, were kept in the special caves, much as holy relics are kept in churches and temples of other cultures. Some of the caves in the western area of Australia had paintings on the walls of the caves, the Karadjeri people periodically repainting over the cave images as part of the ritual to honour and invoke the 'spirit' of the cave. This practice of repainting has been linked to caves in what is now France and Spain, the images on the walls of European caves painted and repainted in the Upper Paleolithic period. The Karadjeri custom of impressing a palm print near the entrance of the cave, to assure the right to enter, is also to be compared to the palm prints of the Upper Paleolithic caves in southern Europe.

It was understood among many of the Australoids, that upon death, the spirit of the dead person would enter the cave, there to join and remain with The First Mother until the time of the next birth or incarnation. This belief in reincarnation, among the Australoids of Australia, suggests the possibility of extremely ancient cultural connections to the Australoid groups of India. Though it is most often assumed that the concept of reincarnation arrived in India with the Indo-Aryan invaders of about 2000-1500 B.C., and that this important aspect of Hindu religion originated with them, it may well have been adopted from the indigenous Australoids of India, who comprised a major part of the non-Aryan Goddess worshipping Dravidians.

The migrations of the Polynesian peoples, (a combination of Australoids, Mongolians and possibly the Ainu people now living in northern Japan), to the many widely separated islands of the Pacific, have been linked with periods of great geological upheaval, and the sinking of land masses, as a result of earthquake and volcanic activity throughout the western Pacific area—especially between Indo-China and Australia, where there are a great number of volcanoes, and the ocean waters are relatively shallow. It may have been these vast changes in sea and land distribution that provided the basis for the legends of a sunken Pacific continent—referred to as Lemuria or Gondwanaland. Flood accounts and mythic memories of a most ancient ancestress crossing the seas to found a new tribe, as an explanation of tribal origins in a specific area, or on a particular island, offer interesting sidelights to these theories.

Among the Polynesian Maoris of New Zealand, there is the belief that they originally came from a place in the west known as *Uru* or *Irihia,* which some scholars link to an early Sanskrit name for India, *Yrihia.* In the Maori language *uru* literally means west. Though probably coincidental, *ur* or *ura* was the word for ancient among the Sumerians who lived near the Persian Gulf, and also wrote of an ancient homeland, Dilmun, which some scholars of the Sumerian culture conjecturally link with India. Memories of an ancient paradise, a land in the west most often referred to as Hawaiki, appear in the legends of Polynesians in many areas of the Pacific, the name Hawaii probably based upon ideas about this long lost homeland.

Though we may be tempted to speculate upon a specific location for an original homeland for the Polynesian peoples, the continual waves of their migrations across the Pacific, and the interweaving of their Australoid, Mongolian, and possibly Ainu ancestry, make this a truly complex area of study. Yet we may certainly go as far as noting the similarities between the languages of the Polynesians and the Malayans of Indonesia, the speech of both included in the same language group—Malayo-Polynesian.

The association of caves with ideas about the Goddess or First Mother, among the Polynesians, may be observed in the accounts of the Goddess as Mahuea in New Zealand. Mahuea is said to have given birth to Her Goddess Daughter Hina in a cave. This cave is specifically described as being in a volcanic mountain; Mahuea Herself is described in volcanic imagery. The connection of volcanoes to Goddess reverence, in Polynesia, is found in areas as far apart as New Zealand and Hawaii. Volcanic images of the Goddess do not appear in the accounts from Australia, at least not in the ones I have so far found, but the concept of the sacred cave may be related, as an adaptation in a land that does not have volcanoes. The more parallel concepts of the Goddess as Pele in Hawaii, as Fuji among the Ainu (see Japanese Section), and the volcanic imagery in the beliefs about the Goddess as Chantico and Coatlicue among the people of early Mexico, offer interesting comparative material, as do the accounts of the Goddess as Parvati in India, Her association with a luminous mountain in the Himalayas repeatedly mentioned, while in Her aspect as Kali, She is linked to the peak known as Blood Red Mountain (see Indian Section).

TO WATCH OVER THE PEOPLE OF THE ISLANDS

The rituals and sacred lore, of both the Australoid and Polynesian peoples, offer us some insight into the spiritual contemplations and images of the Goddess as Divine Ancestress among people whose life may seem simple or even childlike to many who perceive through the eyes of urban European-oriented cultures. Yet it is clear that a structure of values, perceptions, and spiritual beliefs—about birth, death, reincarnation, and the universe—have served the spiritual needs of the Oceanic peoples as fully and as well as those of the so called 'developed' cultures. We may even be moved to question the very concept of technological civilization as 'progress', in light of the evidence that many of the Oceanic peoples have survived in virtual peace for so long, a record that many more 'developed' cultures might well respect and study.

PELE

The worship of the Polynesian Pele is as the Goddess whose spirit inhabits the volcanic Mt. Kilauea on the island of Hawaii. The relationship of volcanic imagery to concepts of the Goddess in other areas bordering on the Pacific Ocean may be observed in the descriptions of the Goddess as Mahuea in New Zealand, as the Goddess known as Fuji among the Ainu people of northern Japan, and as the Goddess known as Chantico in Mexico. Earlier Polynesian beliefs associated Pele with the islands of Kuai, Oahu, Molokai, and Maui, many accounts explaining Pele's creation of various salt lakes, rock formations, and craters, on those islands—before She finally settled at Kilauea on Hawaii.

Often said to be seen as a woman shortly before an eruption, Pele was known to fancy handsome young chiefs, and to enjoy joining in the holua sled racing and other sports—Her wrath incurred if any rejected Her company. It was the angry stomping of Her foot that would cause the ground to tremble before a volcanic eruption. Her priestesses wore robes whose sleeves and hems had been burnt ragged by fire, and carried a wand or digging stick, in imitation of the *Paoa* staff that Pele had used when She " . . . first dug the volcanic craters".

Reverence for Pele was discouraged in the early nineteenth century when the missionary Reverend William Ellis of England converted Kaahumanu, the *kuhina-nui* (queen) of Hawaii, to Christianity. It was further discouraged when the converted Chieftainess Kapiolani, of the Puna District of Hawaii, defied the rage of Pele by throwing rocks into the sacred crater, daring Pele to punish her. Yet when Mauna Loa erupted in 1880, sixty-three year old Princess Ruth Keelikolani still knew the ancient chants of the priestesses of Pele. Courageously, she walked up to the edge of a lava flow that was threatening the city of Hilo, reciting the chants and offering gifts of silk cloth and libations of brandy (in memory of the ancient sacred *awa* drink) to the hot lava stream of Pele. The eruptions stopped the next day, before the town of Hilo had been touched. Again in 1955 when the village of Kapoho was threatened, villagers offered food and tobacco as gifts to Pele—and again the lava stream stopped short of the village.

164

For us you are the Goddess spirit
who dwells within the boiling glowing Halemaumau,
lava lake heart of Mount Kilauea,
woman energies of fiery liquid,
your angry mass of molten lava
shooting your hot bubbling cones
of red and black
high into the heavens,
furiously loosing fume and flames,
clouds of smoky steam,
crackling lightning sparks
and thundering forth raging geysers of melted rock
that burst beyond the rim
of your crater cup of being
to crash down upon that which holds you,
your freedom allowing you to cool into pahoehoe,
glassy crystal slivers of your hair,
sparkling satin smooth stone of your body,
as you form the earth about you.

There you sit upon the plain,
central core of earth and ocean,
reaching into the heavens
while guarding the sulphur world below,
always ready to make known your will,
to crack the earth apart when you are not pleased
with what you see going on about you,
to send your lavablood of life
pouring through earth's gaping wounds
to announce your rage and your displeasure
at those who will not listen to your quieter messages—
and then heal
with the black stone of your holy being.

Are you telling us
to look upon your obsidian mirrors
so that we may see ourselves in you?

MAHUEA AND HINA

These five accounts of the Goddess as Mahuea (Mahu Ika, Mahui I'a) and
Her Goddess Daughter Hina are not found as a group in any one area of the
Pacific Islands. The imagery and narrative lore surrounding Mahuea are
primarily from New Zealand. Hina is known on New Zealand as the
daughter of Mahuea, but is a major Goddess figure throughout the
Polynesian islands. Like Borneo Fire Woman, Mahuea is revered as the
one who discovered how to make fire. The volcanic imagery associated
with Her, probably linked to Her role as the originator of control over fire,
presents interesting parallels to the worship of the Goddess as Pele on
Hawaii. The figure of the male Maui is well known in Polynesian lore, but
the seniority of Hina, and the even greater seniority of Mahuea, perhaps
reveal that the accounts of Maui were later additions to the beliefs about
the ancient Goddess who brought fire. One account of Maui, describing
him as the one who first taught the Polynesian people how to make fire,
briefly explains that he gained this knowledge from his ancient
Grandmother, Mahuea, who kept fire in the tips of Her fingernails. The
account of Hina and the moon may be from an entirely separate body of
beliefs. Although the source of this account is Hawaii, its concept and
imagery appear to be quite different from the other accounts of Hina, and
the legend may have been linked to Her name as a result of the name Hina
becoming almost synonymous with the concept of Goddess.

1. Mahuea

To the land of Ngaurohoe, to the land of Ruapehu—whose insides
boil with the molten lava of the innards of the earth; to the land of
Wanganui, to the land of Waitiki—whose waters run to serve the
ocean's constant thirst; to the land of Wanoka, to the land of
Hawea—who catch the mountain waters and keep it in their deep
laps—the ancient Mother Mahuea came. Great Mahuea, Kind
Mahuea, brought the Maori people from the west, from the Uru
Irihia, the ancient homeland, to live upon the two great lands, most
beautiful in all the waters of the great ocean.

When the home of the Maori people was overrun by snakes,
Mother Mahuea took Her digging stick to frighten one away, but
driving it hard into the ground, the stick snapped in half—and from
the splintered ends—a flame burst forth. Thus Mahuea first
discovered fire and gave this gift to the Maori people. Mahuea,
Guardian of Fire, taught Her people how to use its flames for
warmth, taught her people how to use its flames for light, taught
Her people how to use its flames for cooking—and how to bring the
fire back if all its flames have disappeared—by rubbing a digging
stick into a hollow tube of wood upon the ground.

Her flashing eyes could once be seen far across the islands, bright as the fires of Ngaurohoe and Ruapehu. Her teeth were as fine and sharp as the glass splinters of cooled lava. Her hair streamed from Her head, like the hot red melting rivers that sparked down the mountainsides. Her sacred body emanated brilliant fire and dazzling light, while Her gentle presence could be found deep in Her dark volcanic caves, especially where the cool wet rivers flowed along the ancient lava paths.

In just such a hidden cave, its entrance veiled by falling mountain waters that dropped from a high ledge, Mahuea nurtured a child within Her womb. Mahuea felt Her belly move with life wanting to exist. Mahuea gave birth to Her daughter, the Holy Goddess Hina.

2. Mahuea and young Hina

Nursed at the breasts of Mahuea, Hina grew tall and strong and soon walked along with Mahuea through the tall fern of the evermoist forests, learning which trees gave gifts of fruit, learning which roots were good to eat, and which plants were known to heal. To the waters of the nearby river, Mahuea brought young Hina, watching Her small brown body, laughing, kicking, splashing, in the water, until Hina learned to move as easily in the water, as She moved upon the land, soon chasing fish and tying them together to bring them home for supper.

Always watching Mahuea, who worked with the ease of many years, Hina learned to pound the pulp from the bark of the mamake, until it formed the tapa cloth. Though the great boulders, which held the corners of the tapa from blowing as She worked, sometimes fell to earth with the crashing noise of thunder, Hina learned to use the iakuko mallets, and learned the chants that helped to ease the tapa into perfect shape—so that the rolls of tapa that She kept in the heavens soon flashed as brilliant lightning a-cross the skies.

3. Hina as a young woman

Of all the gifts of knowledge that Mahuea passed to Hina, the greatest was the gift of fire, and the making of the imu oven for the cooking of the food and the ceremonial fires, whose flames still beckon to Her holy being. As the imu fires are lit, there are some who still remember the story of days long passed, when the people of Hina found themselves with no food, and great hunger was

167

swimming in the emptiness of their stomachs. In their time of wanting, Hina appeared before them, telling them how to build the imu oven and which stones must be used, asking for the wood of the koa tree to be brought for the making of the fire.

When the sacred oven had been built, the branches of the many armed koa began to burn until—in the intense heat of the imu—Hina's spirit left Her body. Three days and three nights, while the hungry people stoked the fire, Hina's spirit travelled beneath the earth, exploring the maze of caverns of the Underworld until She found the object of Her search, the cavern that contained the fresh spring waters. These She channelled upward through an opening in the earth, so that the precious saltless waters fountained forth, not far from where the imu stood.

Her spirit then returning to Her body, Hina directed the people who had patiently kept the fire blazing, to dig among the ashes of the imu. To their astonishment, they discovered yams and cocoanuts, bananas and fish, foods that their bodies had so longed for, tastily roasted by the fire of the imu, gifts of abundance from the Holy Hina—She who had brought the fresh saltless water so that the food could once more grow.

4. Hina and Maui

On the beach by the Great Sea, Hina gave birth to a son, but She found him to be as unruly and disrespectful to his mother as She had been loving to Hers. After many years of unfilial behaviour, son Maui decided to take his mother's life, thinking that upon Her death, he could add the years of Her life to his own. Some say that he tried to crawl back into Her womb and out Her mouth, to reverse the process of birth, and thus to cause Her death, but that he was crushed between Her thighs as She protected Herself from his murderous plot. Others say that Hina had heard of the plan, even before Her son had taken any action, and had decided to capture Maui's hau, the core of his life essence and being, that which could be obtained in a drop of Maui's blood.

Thus She called upon the butterfly and sent the lovely Kahukurra to steal the hau of Maui, but when Maui saw the winged creature approach upon its mission, he killed it in its graceful flight. When Kahukurra did not return, Hina sent the tiny Tuia gnat, hoping that its smaller body might slip by unnoticed, but even Tuia was seen by Maui's watchful eyes and put to death by Hina's son.

Hearing of all that had happened, Hina summoned Waroa the mosquito, instructing it to fly by night, so that in the darkness it might succeed in returning with the drop of blood. But as it landed upon the shoulder of the sleeping Maui, he awakened from the itch and slapped his hand upon his shoulder, killing Waroa as easily as he had killed the others.

Still Maui planned to murder Hina, to take the remaining years of Her life for his own. Still Hina hoped to capture Maui's hau, but could not find a way until She sent the loyal Manu, golden sandfly whose gauzy wings spread wide enough to carry her body in swift silence. In the darkness of the night, Manu flew to the grass hut of Maui, landed upon his forehead, drew the drop of blood, thus capturing his hau—and quickly delivered it to Hina. Placing a magic spell upon the hau, Hina used Her powers until the callous son could only do as She commanded. So it happened that Hina prevented Her own murder, continuing to live, and to watch over the people of the islands that rose above the vast blue ocean.

5. Hina of the Moon

In Her days of great age, Hina took a husband, thinking that he might help Her with Her work, but though She was willing to stay with him in a small grass hut among the palms of earth, She found that he spent his days doing nothing. He did not fish. He did not hunt. He did not even help to gather fruit, or search for roots, or pound the tapa bark. He said little that was pleasant to hear, and did little that made Hina feel glad that She had married.

In the sadness of a long unpleasant day, Hina's eyes fell upon the glow of a rainbow, as it formed a curving pathway across the sky. Memories of better places, happier ways to live, sent Her thoughts walking along the brilliantly coloured path, hopes leaping ahead even faster than thoughts—along the rainbow road of heaven.

To the brightly shining sun I shall travel, She decided, where I can start my life again. With this goal in mind, Hina set off on the path of the rainbow, hoping to reach the brightly shining sun, but as the day went on and Hina drew ever closer to the sun, She felt the blazing burning heat, saw only the blinding whiteness. Soon thinking that this might be even worse than the life that She was living, Hina made Her way back down the rainbow road, returning to hut and husband.

Though at first relieved, simply to be away from the intense heat of the sun, Hina once again began to feel the discomfort of the misery of Her life, once again began to grow angry at the laziness of Her husband, at the sullenness of his voice. This time, She thought I will travel to the moon, the softly glowing light of heaven, where I will be able to live in peace and comfort.

When the sky had darkened and the moon was clear and whole, it was time for Hina to begin Her journey, but searching for the rainbow road, Hina realized that She could not see it in the darkness of the night and had to feel along each step of the way, trying to remember where the colourful path had been. Slowly, carefully, She began to ascend, testing the invisible path before Her with each movement of Her foot, climbing ever higher, climbing ever closer to the moon.

Higher and yet higher She went, stars greeting Her along the way. Hina soon began to smile with the joy of regained freedom, as the warm night air brushed across Her golden cheeks. Then suddenly She heard the voice of Her husband calling out behind Her, begging Her to stop, shouting that he would change his ways, that he would try to please Her—if only She would return. Hina thought of the many times that She had heard him say such things, and of each time that he had forgotten all that he had promised. This time, more determined than ever to live as She wished—Hina continued to walk.

Turning back to look, hoping to see Her husband retreating from the path, Hina saw him running towards Her, now shouting that he would never let Her leave, drawing closer and closer yet. Though She ran to escape his threat, he was suddenly upon Her, throwing Her down on the slightly curving rainbow road, still invisible in the darkness. Struggling to free Herself of his determined grasp, and from the blows that fell upon Her, She pushed against him, pounding Her fists against his face and chest so hard that he inched back as they battled. But as he jumped back, to avoid Her kicking leg, he fell off the edge of the rainbow road—hurtling into the emptiness of the night time sky.

With tears that sought to wash away the horror of all that had happened, Hina again began to climb, feeling Her way along the rainbow road, until the moon sent out a brighter path, one so soft and light that She hardly felt the aches of Her bruised and beaten body. At last, reaching the glowing silver moon, She made Her home upon it and lives there still—remembered by the women of the islands as Hina of the Moon.

KUNAPIPI

In the area of Arnhemland in northcentral Australia, the reverence for
Kunapipi as The First Mother still exists in the twentieth century. Much of
the lore of this area of Australia recalls a time when The First Mother
arrived from across the sea, settling in Arnhemland and establishing Her
tribe. Those who call upon The Mother as Kunapipi consider themselves to
be Her descendants. It is Her 'womb' that is entered in the sacred cave or the
substitute crescent trench. It is believed that the spirits of the dead remain
with Her until the next rebirth, while the 'twin' or 'double' spirit of each
person stays with Her throughout the time one is alive. The ritual described
here, in which the initiate enters the 'womb', swinging a bullroarer fast
enough to hear the sound of Kunapipi's voice, is enacted only once in a
person's lifetime.

Great Mother Kunapipi,
you who have travelled
far across the vast oceans
to bring your children to this new world
from submerged Gondwanaland
as it sunk into the sea,
hoping that loved ones
had perhaps found their way
to the summits of Java and Sumbawa,
as you brought us
to Arnhem Land in the Arafura Sea,
Mother, it is you we call upon,
in life, as in death.

Dear Kunapipi,
Great Kunapipi,
I do not forget you
as I climb back into your holy womb
to make contact with my spirit soul,
crawling into the crescent vessel
of your protection
dug deep into the soil of your body,
carved into the precious earth beneath me.
I beckon to my spirit soul
which lives within you
until my time of finishing this life
and though I leave your womb

at this initiation time,
though I choose to climb out
from your nurturing warmth,
to live my years of life,
I ask you to care for my spirit soul
until my return
so that after my passing from this life
my two spirits may be reunited in you,
before you send me forth again
to once more live on earth.
Dear Kunapipi,
no matter how far I wander,
how many lives I live—
to you I shall always return.

FIRE WOMAN

This account, from the Sea Dyak culture of southern Borneo, offers us an explanation of how and why the original ancestress of a particular tribe came to found Her tribe on the land on which they live. It is also an explanation of how the making of fire was first introduced, linking this event of human development with woman, as the one who first taught the method of rubbing wood to create fire. It is an account of the discovery of fire that provides an interesting parallel to that of the Goddess as Mahuea in New Zealand—the imagery of the mountain of Fire Woman perhaps to be linked to the volcanic images of Mahuea. The sanctity of the snake, and its connection with rain, may be related to the Rainbow Serpent of Australia.

Between the banks of the Dyak Rivers that flow into the Java Sea, the women and the children made their way through the thick fern mat of the jungle where little sun can enter, searching for a bit of food to appease their empty stomachs. Chancing upon a great snake, enough to feed them all, they pounced upon it with their sticks, until all life had fled from its thick trunk—and dividing it among themselves, they sat upon the damp green ground and began to eat their dinner.

No sooner had they raised their portions of serpent to their mouths, torrential rains began to press upon the highest branches of the upward stretching jungle growth. Great hard drops of water forced openings between the leaves, spearing their way between the branches, falling so hard and fast that the jungle soon submerged beneath the raging, rising waters, drowning all but one woman, who ran towards where the land was higher. Though she carried the weight of an infant in her arms, she made her way to the top of a nearby mountain—and there survived the great flood.

As darkness came, winds that visited the mountains brought such chilling cold that the woman thought to rub her shivering body against the bark of a high growing tree, hoping to dry and warm herself and the infant in her arms. So fast and hard were her movements, against the roughness of the tree, that suddenly sparks leaped forth, landing upon some dry leaves and twigs. Thus the woman saw, before her unbelieving eyes, the unfamiliar light, the unfamiliar glow—of the first fire—its unfamiliar warmth caressing her in the damp loneliness.

In the flickering light of these first flames, the motion of a rabbit caught the woman's eye, reminding her of the hunger that had almost gone from her mind during her flight for survival. Catching the rabbit with her stick, she roasted it over the fire, and ate her fill, until the hunger pains subsided and the milk flowed once again into her breasts. In this way the woman and the infant survived the great flood, as she watched the raging waters pressing close about their mountain sanctuary.

Living for years upon the mountain in the waters, finding the food that would satisfy hunger, learning to make the fire, each day quicker than before, the woman began to understand that the flood had been a punishment, for killing a snake that was holy. Over the many years, the waters grew lower, as the infant that became a young man grew higher, until the time that the flood finally subsided, and the woman and her grown son wandered back to the land she had once known when she was young—only to realize that all the others had disappeared, and the now dry ground was empty.

Thus it was that Fire Woman took her son as her husband, and along the now calm waters of the Dyak they raised children, passing on the gift of fire to the Dyak people they brought forth, but warning them always—that to kill or eat a sacred snake might bring another storm of destruction.

STAR GIRL

This simple but poetic explanation of how stars came to be in the heavens comes from the Australoid people of the Nullarbor Plain of southcentral Australia. Though Star Girl is spoken of as mortal, her act exhibits powers that reveal her nature as someone who was regarded as a quite special being. The idea of the sun and the stars as 'fire in the sky' presents a concept of the bodies of heaven not unlike that of the most advanced scientists of today.

In the days
when only the sun and the moon
lived in the heavens,
some nights would come
when even the moon would disappear
and all was dark,
except for the light of a tribal fire
on the dark open plain.

It was such a night
when Star Girl stood in the darkness,
watching those who sat about the fire,
wishing that the moon
had chosen to arrive that night
to brighten her view
of the earth and the sky
and looking at the blazing flames,
she reached into the fire,
grasping a handful
of still glowing embers
that had fallen from a log,
and threw these pieces of fire
high into the heavens—
where they stayed
to form a trail of light
across the sky
so that none could ever
lose their way again,
even when the moon was too tired
to guide them through the night.

LIA

This thirst provoking account of the heroic Lia comes from the southeastern section of Australia now known as New South Wales. It is an account of the Gippsland Australians, who have been conjecturally linked with Ainu groups of Japan and the East Indies. It appears to have developed around two separate themes. One is to explain the origin of the Murumbidgee River, that flows west from the southeastern coastal mountain range; the other seems to be an explanation of the origins of a people who had once been part of another tribe. Though the area near the river is much more fertile and moist than many other sections of Australia, this story gives some insight into the extreme hardships of survival in the desert areas. The origins of the account are a bit puzzling, in that it would be somewhat unlikely that a group living near the river would be so aware of the difficulties of desert life, whereas a desert group would hardly be likely to develop an explanation of the origins of a river that was not especially familiar to them. The account may be based upon an actual rebellion of the women of a desert tribe, and a subsequent migration to the area of the Murumbidgee, though some readers may prefer to free their imaginations enough to read it as the literal truth.

Looking down from the heavens, seeing only dry cracked land where once there had been grass, seeing only mudholes where once there had been lakes, seeing only ditches and widening gullies, where once there had been river beds, Lia decided to descend to earth to live among the people of the Goanna tribe. How different were their lives from that which the Mother of Life had planned.

Living in the heat of the constantly blazing sun was far from easy, but Lia was determined to help with the work of the Mother— and thinking upon how best this might be done, she soon became the wife of the chief of the Goannas. Why was it, she wondered, that he was never dry, never thirsty? Why was it, she wondered, that all the men of the Goannas seemed freshly washed, comfortable in the intense heat, while the lips of each woman were dry and parched, the skin of each woman covered with the pale dust of the arid desert stretches?

As each day came, Lia stayed with the other women, as they wearily poked their digging sticks in search of roots, all carefully sharing the water of the one water skin, that Lia's husband had provided for them. The men said they had more important work to do, and from early dawn to dusk none could be found near the village. Only in the bright orange glow of the setting sun did the men return, once again bringing the gift of the one precious skin of water, to the dry and thirsty women.

In the dark of the night, Lia lay upon her mat, images of cool, clear, flowing water rippling through her thoughts. Finally, turning to the man who lay beside her, she said, 'How fortunate we are that each day you bring us water. Where do you find it?' Much to her surprise, the man beside her laughed; the chief of the Goannas laughed louder and louder, as if at some secret joke. Then from the side of his mat, he brought out a second water skin and raised it to his mouth, allowing precious water to trickle carelessly down his chin. When he had had his fill, he offered it to Lia, and laughing yet again, he told the heavenly Lia that it was only for men to know the source of the water. Did he not bring a water skin to the village each night? Was it not he who was kind enough to bring water to the women? Lia fell asleep, hot and dry and troubled.

In the morning light, the women walked wearily to the edges of the village, each carrying her digging stick. Each began to poke the dry land as she had always done. Though Lia's head was bent in concentration, as if her eyes saw only what she hoped to discover at the end of her stick, carefully she watched as each man left the village. Carefully she watched, as they walked towards the place where the great grey rocks were so tall that she could see no further.

When the sun was nearly overhead and not a man was left in the village, Lia called to the other women. 'We must find water for ourselves. One skin is not enough for all. The Mother had made water enough for everyone.' Long sleeping anger woke abruptly in each woman. Truly, it was not fair that they should dig all day for supper, in the burning heat of the sun, while the men were cooling themselves, drinking freely, yet bringing so little water home.

Lia pointed to the mountains, in the direction of the tall grey rocks, where the men had gone. 'Tomorrow we will look for roots, but we shall look for water as well. We'll start out alone, each with her digging stick, but we'll meet further down at the foot of the great grey rocks—and from there we will hunt for water!'

The plan went well, and after gathering at the base of the mountains, not far from where the men had disappeared, the women began to climb. They searched every crevice, listened in silence for any hopeful sound, the slightest trickle of moving water, but when the dusk began to settle in, the women were as dry and as thirsty as ever. More exhausted than ever before, they returned to the village, only to be severely berated by the men for returning so late, and with so few roots for supper. And when the men began to notice the telling brown dirt of the mountains, layered over the pale dust that usually covered their feet and ankles, they began such a shouting that even the birds and snakes were frightened away.

It was Lia's husband who made the greatest noise, blustering like the hottest summer winds, roaring as only animals roar, violent, menacing, thundering, about what Lia had done and how she of all women, the wife of the chief, must teach the other women to obey. 'We must leave the village for several days,' he boomed and then threatened painful beatings, even death, to any woman who went near the mountains during the absence of the men. The women cringed in dread, and by the time the men had disappeared in the morning light, each had decided it was safer to obey. One could live with the thirst and the dry parched lips and throat.

Only Lia had not been frightened from her plan. 'Dig the roots if you must', she said to the others. 'I will find water for all of us.' At this show of defiance, two others offered reluctantly to join her. Thus the three women set off for the mountains, but they were hardly to where the grey rocks began, when one felt the terror of a possible fatal beating, and with apologies to Lia, she returned to the village to search for roots. Hardly was the woman out of sight, when the second too grew fearful for her life—and left Lia to climb the mountains by herself.

Alone, Lia began the rugged ascent. Higher she climbed, here balancing herself on a small rock ledge no larger than one foot, there lifting herself up on a small determined sapling. So Lia made her way, until the sun had completed its arc in the heavens, and chancing upon the entrance of a small cavern in the mountain, just as the sun slipped into its crack in the earth, Lia crawled inside—gratefully laying her tired body on the cool stone floor. The feverish heat of the day, the exhaustion of the climb, had left her tongue thick and dry in her mouth. Slowly, she let her eyelids cover her tired eyes, as a mother might cover a sleeping child, and prayed that sleep would come quickly.

Was it an hallucination from the heat, from the fatiguing efforts of the day—or was there truly a tiny person standing near her feet? Raising her tired eyelids upon hearing an unexpected sound, she saw another—and another. The Tukonee, they called themselves, the little people of the cave. More of them poured forth, from the deepest hidden part of the small rock shelter, and as if in a dream, Lia heard them tell her to return to the village in the morning—and to once again bring all the women to the mountains. Together the women must climb to the top of the mountain, high enough to see the sea beyond. There in a place the little ones described, Lia was to drive her digging stick deep into a crevice of the rocks, deep enough to touch the heart of the mountain—and when the mountain's heart was touched, fresh water would be theirs. Then as quickly as the Tukonee appeared, they were gone, and in the dark grey granite silence, Lia slept more soundly than she had since she had come to earth.

So excited was Lia's voice, as she spoke to the women of the village; so certain was Lia's plan, as it was explained in the morning light—that there was no argument when the women began to climb the grey rocks this second time—though anxious prayer passed across blistered lips, and throats hoarse with lack of moisture reduced those desperate prayers to private whispers.

Standing at the place described by the Tukonee, the women watched with a monolithic disbelief, that cracked only slightly with the pressure of deepest hopes—as Lia thrust her digging stick into the jagged crevice of the highest boulder. Suddenly, the entire mountain shook. A thunderous noise enveloped them, a shaking of the very air, as the stick seemed to pull itself from Lia's grasp and to push its own way deeper, far deeper, into the rock—until all disbelief and doubts were washed away by a crashing cascade of crystal clear water.

The fierce flow of the water splashed upon the grey rocks, finding its own pathways along the ridges of the stones, until it formed itself into racing rivulets, that covered themselves with bubbly white foam and swiftly slid into wider brooks, hurrying into broader streams that bounded down the mountainside, meeting on the edge of a wide plateau, to plunge fearlessly through the air and fall upon the dry sands of the desert—where the waters spread into a broad blue band that became the Murumbidgee River.

Dusty faces filled with awe at the sight of so much water. Some kneeled upon the rocks and moistened long cracked lips on the ripples of its surface. Hot throats soon gulped its coolness. Hands splashed grey faces into a rich, dark brown. Wet brown legs, wet brown breasts, wet brown shoulders, soon began to glisten in the sunlight—as the pale dust that had covered them returned to the earth where it belonged.

Playful hands became scoops to toss the wetness upon a sister, upon a daughter, upon a mother whose skin had only known the painfully shrivelling heat of a mercilessly blazing sun. The air soon filled with gleaming droplets. Pale sandy hair regained its rich

178

dusty faces filled with awe

darkness, as the water continued to leap forth from the crevice that Lia had opened—pouring, racing, falling down the mountainside, ever fresh, ever clean, ever cool. It seemed that women laughed who had never laughed before. They embraced in exultation, together felt their jubilant success, as tears of pain and tears of triumph mingled upon their cheeks, and slid into the treasured water. Lia had brought them a miracle.

Wading along the pathways of the down hill streams, ankles hesitant to leave the coolness, the women finally reached the ground below. They rested upon the bank of the new river, as the descending sun touched the blue with orange, the coolness of the water flying through the air—to touch them still. The world of the Goanna women floated like a perfect dream.

Thus the women sat, until the moment that unexpected voices reached their ears. The men had returned to the village—and they were demanding their dinners! But the voices of the men echoed with a distance. They were on the other side of the river! The eyes of the women met in silence. The new river was wide. The smiles of the women met in silence. The new river was very wide. So it happened that on that day the women of the Goannas set off to found a village of their own, leaving the Goanna men to live by themselves for the rest of their lives—on the other side of the Murumbidgee River.

ARUNTA SUN WOMAN

The Arunta (Araunta, Araunda) now living in central Australia, just west of Queensland, are one of the larger and better known groups of the Australoid people. This account of Sun Woman not only reveals the Arunta association of the sun with fire, but also explains some of the ideas about life after death of the Arunta people. As with Akewa of the Toba of Argentina, Sun Sister of the Inuit, Amaterasu of Japan, Allat of the

TO WATCH OVER THE PEOPLE OF THE ISLANDS

Arabians and the Sun Goddess of the Arinna in Anatolia, the image of the
Arunta Sun woman confronts the erroneous stereotype of the sun as a
universally male image.

Sitting out upon the sandy plain,
we watch the fiery Sun Woman
as She returns each morning
to the people of the earth,
carrying Her glowing torch of fire
to bring us warmth
after the night time chill,
to bring us light
after the night time darkness,
rising higher and higher
above the earth,
Her torch growing ever brighter
as She reaches the summit heights of heaven
and as the wooden torch
slowly burns away
She slowly lowers Herself again,
finally sinking in the dimming light—
into the ground.

Beneath the desert sands, She descends,
welcomed there by those
who have passed from earth
as they form a line on either side
creating a path of ancient souls,
so that She might pass by
with honour and respect,
each night receiving from them
a bright new dress of red
and a new log with which to light
Her daytime torch.
Then bidding them farewell
She begins Her morning travels
as She raises Her firebrand high,
floats up on to the earth,
rises upon the sandy plain—
to once again light the day of the Arunta people.

while Amazons danced an armed dance

ncient Anatolia, Asia Minor, the land we today speak of as Turkey, provides us with a body of evidence of Goddess reverence that spreads across some seven thousand years—from the neolithic sites of Hacilar and Catal Huyuk to the time of St. Paul's confrontation with Goddess worship in the city of Ephesus.

It was in the land we know as Turkey that the Goddess worshipping cultures of Hacilar and Catal Huyuk had once flourished, the excavated sites of these most ancient cultures revealing shrines and statues of the Goddess, as She had been revered between about 7000 B.C. until about 5500 B.C. The buildings and artifacts, unearthed at the site of the Catal Huyuk culture, may help us to better understand religious and social customs that began to grow not long after the initial development of agriculture in the Near and Middle East. The people of the culture of Catal Huyuk, burials suggesting a surprising majority of women, were short, somewhat stocky, and doliocephalic (narrow headed). Although this culture existed some eighty-five centuries ago (i.e. some *sixty centuries* before the rise of Classical Greece), murals of priestesses wearing vulture masks and wings; evidence of the dead being buried carefully beneath the homes, and hearths set in open courtyards of closely clustered houses built of mud brick—each give us some idea of the life style of these Goddess worshipping people who lived so long ago.

ANCIENT MIRRORS of WOMANHOOD

At about 5000 B.C., sites of the Goddess worshipping Halafian culture sprung up near the headwaters of the Tigris and Euphrates Rivers in Anatolia, spreading south into northern Mesopotamia. Although there are some similarities, no direct connections between the Halafians, and the earlier cultures of Catal Huyuk and Hacilar, have yet been made with certainty. One of the most significant factors of the Halafian culture was the use of the symbol of the double axe, in conjunction with statues of the Goddess (at the Halafian site of Arpachiyah in northern Mesopotamia). This Goddess symbol, later used repeatedly on the island of Crete, and often portrayed as a weapon of the Amazons in Anatolia, thus first appeared at about 5000 B.C.—at a site that was later known as a sacred centre of the Goddess as the Semitic Ishtar.

Little is known about the cultures of Anatolia directly after the Halafian period. This may be the result of the people of these earlier cultures leaving Anatolia, or a possible period of nomadic migration that would have left few remains behind. This lack of evidence may also be a matter of chance discovery of sites, many perhaps still lying deep beneath the earth, waiting to tell their stories, as Hacilar and Catal Huyuk were just some fifty years ago. Whatever the reason, so far there has been little evidence of settled and developed sites in Anatolia from about 4500 to about 2700 B.C.

Once we reach the middle of the third millenium B.C., we are again heir to a wealth of Goddess images, from sites such as Alaca Huyuk, Boghazkoy, Yazilikaya, Beycesultan, Kultepe, Tahurpa, Gavurkales, Fraktin, Arslan Kaya, Yarre, Magnesia, Erythrae, Kohnus, Pessinus, Samuha, Hurma, Kyme, Priene, Pitane, Gryneium, Toprakkale, Kios, Bandirma—and of course the well known Goddess site of Ephesus. The numerous marble Goddess figures from the Aegean Cycladic Islands (found both on Crete and in western Anatolia), and those of the larger island of Rhodes, just off the southwestern tip of the mainland, add to our body of information about the nature of Goddess reverence in Anatolia.

Probably earlier, but at least by 2000 B.C., tribes speaking an Indo-European language entered the area of central Anatolia, migrating southward from the Russian steppes and the Caucasus regions. Riding in swift, horse drawn, war chariots, these tribes eventually conquered the inhabitants of central Anatolia, and established themselves as the ruling class of royalty and aristocracy. From these Indo-European invaders, who then adopted a method of writing from the neighboring Semites, we learn that the

184

indigenous population of central Anatolia had spoken a non-Indo-European, non-Semitic, language, known as *Hattili.* They had referred to themselves as the people of the Land of Hatti.

Through a misunderstanding of the limited evidence available at the time, early scholars of Anatolian archaeology dubbed both the invaders, and the invaded, as Hittites—and thus the name still stands. (The Hittite records reveal that the conquerors spoke of their own language as *Nesili* or *Nasili.)* Although the term Hittite is still used to refer to the entire culture, after the conquest in Anatolia, it most often indicates the invaders, who assumed the roles of royalty, government, army and clergy. Thus, when referring to the indigenous population only, the term Hattian is now used.

The Sun Goddess of Arinna, known as Wurusemu and Arinitti to the Hittites, was a deity originally worshipped by the Hattians; Her Hattian shrines were eventually appropriated by Hittite clergy. Evidence of the relationship of beliefs about the Sun Goddess to the precept of the divine right to rule, alongside the extremely important position of the High Priestess/Queen, raises the possibility that the invading Hittites may have adopted older Hattian customs to gain legitimization and social acceptance of their control over the Hattian peoples—control they had initially gained by well documented martial force.

From texts of rituals, found in the city of Tahurpa, we learn that several former High Priestesses of the Sun goddess had incorporated the name Nikkal into their own names. Since the name Nikkal was the northern version of the Goddess name Ningal (Great Lady), (best known from Sumer and generally associated with the moon), there is the possibility that the original Hattian shrines at Tahurpa and Arinna may once have been linked to the widespread reverence for the Goddess as Nikkal/Ningal. The site of the most sacred centre of the worship of the Anatolian Sun Goddess, the city of Arinna, has not yet been located. Hopefully, its eventual discovery and excavation may clarify the actual origins of the great Anatolian Sun Goddess, who was invoked as Mistress of Heaven and Earth.

Other names of the Goddess that appear throughout the inscriptions and texts of Anatolia, names such as Hepa, Hebat, Kubebe, Kupapa, Lilwani, and Ma—were used among various groups that were to the east, west, and south, of the centrally located Hittites. Some of these names, especially Hepa and Hebat, were used by Hurrian groups—people who did not speak an Indo-European language, but, like the Hattians, were ruled by people who did. The Hittites also knew of the worship of the Goddess as the Semitic Ishtar, and incorporated legends, customs and images of Ishtar into Hittite religious records.

The later appearing Goddess name of Kybele (Cybele) is often associated with Phrygian groups, who entered Anatolia from the north some time between 1200 and 1000 B.C. Though the Phrygians appear to have revered the Goddess, and may even have introduced the name Kybele, similarities of ritual and legend (especially of the son/lover, whose death was enacted annually, and the presence of eunuch attendants—known as Galli) reveal that the worship of Kybele was linked to legends, rituals, and customs, that had long been known in the worship of the Goddess as Ishtar and Inanna. What is perhaps most interesting, in the exploration of the reverence for the Goddess as Kybele, is that these legends, rituals, and customs, so closely associated with Goddess worship in Mesopotamia, were imported into Rome in 204 B.C. The sacred black stone of Kybele, long kept in the city of Pessinus in Anatolia, was brought to Rome at that time, and a great temple, built to house it, was completed in 191 B.C. The discovery of several tablets, found in Rome in 1608 A.D., by workmen repairing St. Peter's Church, raises the possibility that the Kybele temple was not far from, possibly beneath, where the Basilica of St. Peter's stands today.

Anatolia is also especially interesting in that accounts of Amazons were often linked to various Anatolian towns and cities, particularly those of the western coastal areas of the provinces of Lydia, Lycia and Caria. Diodorus Siculus traced the long and complicated path of a large group of Amazons from Libya into Anatolia, citing a mass migration, and a series of conquests, led by Amazon sister/queens, Myrina and Mitylene. Whether the use of the name Libya by Diodorus refers to the lands we now know as Libya, or to Africa in general, as the writings of Herodotus suggest (see African Section Introduction), this report of a Libyan origin for the Amazons of Anatolia certainly calls for further examination.

The temple at the city of Ephesus (in the province of Lydia), spoken of by Greeks as a shrine of Artemis, and later by the

Romans as a shrine of Diana—was described by both Pindar and Callimachus as a holy site first founded by Amazons. This shrine in turn links the Amazons to the island of Crete; an inscription found at Ephesus dedicated to the Goddess as—The Cretan Lady of Ephesus. Many writers of Classical Greece, including Herodotus and Pausanius, claimed that these areas of western Anatolia that were linked to Amazon accounts, had been settled by people of Crete. The two seemingly contradictory origins of the Amazons, Libya and Crete, are not necessarily in conflict, for the excavations under the guidance of Sir Arthur Evans, on the island of Crete, provided a good deal of evidence of links between Libya and Crete, as early as 3000 B.C. Still, we would do well to keep in mind that the double axe symbol appeared in association with Goddess imagery in northern Mesopotamia at about 5000 B.C. (at the Halafian site of Arpachiyah). Discoveries of *tholos* buildings (circular buildings with long rectangular corridors leading to them), on the Messara Plain of Crete, may indicate that people of the Halafian culture had migrated to Crete, bringing both the tholos design, and the double axe symbol, with them. Whether from Libya, or Halafian Mesopotamia, or both, Pindar wrote that Amazon steeds rode across the plains of Xanthos in Lydia, while the legend of Bellerophon describes him battling with Amazons in Lycia.

There is also some confusion concerning the name of the Goddess, as She was worshipped by the Anatolian Amazons. Though the name generally given in Classical accounts is simply the title, The Mother of Deities, various contemporary scholars have sought to link The Mother of Deities with Kybele, or with Artemis. After a great deal of study on this, I suspect that the name most often used may have been Lato, the Mother of Artemis. The name Artemis is certainly linked with the Anatolian Ephesus shrine, but all statues of the Goddess at that site were of a matronly image of woman. Lato, whose name appears to be derived from the most ancient Lat, Elath, or Allat, of Canaan, is known in Greek accounts, but is most closely associated with Anatolia and Crete. One of the most important Goddess festivals of western Anatolia was the *Latoia,* probably related to the Cretan festival, the *Hellotia.* And although Classical Greek accounts state that Lato gave birth to Artemis on the island of Delos, Ephesians claimed that Artemis was born in a cavern at the foot of a mountain near Ephesus. The Anatolian town of Lata Kaya, (Latakia, Laodicea of the New

Testament) claimed to possess the most ancient statue of The Mother of Deities in existence. A great temple for Lato was built high on the mountains of Crete, not far from the town known as Lato even today, while Cretan Goddess names such as Eilythia, Eleuthera, and Eleuthia, appear to be derived from the names: Lato, Lat and Elath.

The Amazons were not only closely linked to the western Anatolian provinces of Lydia, Lycia, and Caria, but also to several large Aegean islands just off the mainland. Samothrace was described by Diodorus as the island most sacred to the Amazons, one that they had designated as the site of their holiest rituals for The Mother of Deities. These rituals may have been the origin of those later described as The Mysteries of Demeter and Kore (Kore literally meaning Daughter, most often named as Persephone) as they were celebrated on the island of Samothrace—rituals perhaps once performed for The Mother and The Daughter, as Lato and Artemis. The major town on the island of Lemnos, an island mentioned in Greek accounts as one on which Jason found an all female population, was known as Myrina—the name Diodorus gave as one of the Amazon sister/queens. The major town on the nearby island of Lesbos is still known by the name of Myrina's sister—Mitylene. The island of Samos also has a major town named Mitylene. Samos lies just across the waters from the Anatolian city of Priene—a city that Diodorus included among those he listed as having been founded by Amazons. Hellenic Greeks described this Anatolian island of Samos as the *birthplace* of the Goddess known as Hera, though they portrayed Hera as the ever jealous wife of Zeus.

Settlements of Celtic peoples in Anatolia, in the third century B.C., resulted in the area of central Anatolia, including the eastern parts of Lydia, then being known as Galatia. It would be difficult to ascertain the degree of influence that Anatolian reverence for the Goddess may have had upon the Celts, but Strabo's account that Celtic representatives attended a religious council in the sacred centre of Kybele, the city of Pessinus, does suggest this as a topic deserving further exploration.

As a result of the enormous amount of often extremely fragmented bits of information, covering thousands of years: archaeological artifacts; written records from Classical Greece and Rome; connections between areas such as Libya, Crete, Canaan,

Mesopotamia, and the islands of the Aegean—it would be impossible to fully describe or discuss Goddess reverence in Anatolia in a book such as this. But perhaps the following accounts of some of the evidence about the reverence for the Goddess in Anatolia, may help to provide us with at least a partial view of the multi-faceted nature of the Goddess, as She was known and worshipped throughout the many millenia.

GREAT GRANDMOTHER OF ANATOLIA

This piece is based upon the many statues and shrines of the Goddess that were discovered in excavations of the very early neolithic sites of Catal Huyuk (about 6500 to 5500 B.C.), and Hacilar (about 7000 to 5500 B.C.) Since writing had not yet been developed at the time these cultures existed, our knowledge of Goddess reverence from these periods is based solely upon the architecture and artifacts discovered. Murals of priestesses dressed as vultures, found upon the walls of the shrines of Catal Huyuk, invite comparison with the worship of Nekhebt, the later pre-dynastic Vulture Goddess of Upper Egypt. Some insight, into the symbolic importance of the vulture, may be gained from an examination of the still existent rituals of the Parsees of India. The Parsees place the bodies of their dead on decks in trees, to allow the vultures to clean the bones, so that they may be buried with respect and care. The horns, set in the altars of Catal Huyuk, also suggest comparison with later Egyptian symbolism, as manifested in the importance of the Holy Heifer of Heaven—as well as the horns of consecration, so familiar at Cretan sites (see Egyptian Section).

Mother with no name,
may I simply call you Great Grandmother,
you whose images were left lying
deep beneath the Anatolian earth
for some eight thousand years.
You are the ancient one
who sat upon the lioness throne
in the days when the planting of the seeds
was still a new idea
and small houses made of earthen brick,
entered through the roof by ladder,
were occupied by those who built
your many sacred shrines,
placing your images safe within them.

Deep beneath the earth at Catal Huyuk,
deep beneath the earth at Hacilar,
villages for which you had once cared
lay dark and silent waiting
to once again see the light of day,
obsidian mirrors void of reflections,
jewellry of copper, shell and marble
adorning ancient bones
that had been painted with red ochre,
and placed beneath the floors
of the homes where those who died
had once breathed and laughed and cried,
their spirits protected and protecting
those they had brought into this world—
embraced by your ever guiding presence.

Wall paintings of your priestesses,
dressed in wide vulture wing,
left visions of ancient ritual
of those who had trusted the sacred bird,
perhaps to prepare the dead for final burial.
Pairs of sacred horns
rise as upraised arms from your altars,
said to be those of wild bull or auroch,
yet resembling the long curved horns of heifers
that still roam upon the lands that you once knew.

Mother with no name,
Great Grandmother of Anatolia,
your silent mysteries are many,
as are the myriad shadows
of your eight thousand years
as they flicker across the obsidian mirrors
that had lain so long beneath your earth
and now cast reflections of reflections of reflections
of your most ancient Mother essence
on the many layered mirrored hallways
of the obsidian infinity of our minds.

SUN GODDESS OF ARINNA

The ancient Anatolian site of Arinna, the most sacred centre of the Sun Goddess, is known to us from the texts of Boghazkoy (the site of ancient Hattusas), and Tahurpa—but Arinna itself has not yet been located. The prayer included here is from tablets found at Boghazkoy, while the ritual, of the High Priestesses of the Sun Goddess, is from a text of the Nuntari-yashas Festival of Tahurpa. It is clear, from the evidence of many Hittite tablets, that the right to rule was regarded as being given by the Sun Goddess of Arinna. This ancient precept, of receiving divine right to rule from the Goddess, was also known and practiced in Babylon and Sumer, and was probably the origins of the later Christian idea that divine right to rule was provided by Jehovah—a precept that long remained the foundation of royalty in Europe, and still functions in England today.

Though She shines above us as bright as the Anatolian day, Her holiest city of Arinna, Her most sacred shrine of days long past, still lies dark beneath the earth, silently waiting to be found. Just "one day's walk from Hattusas" the ancient tablets say, but they do not tell us in which direction, or we might go to find the many secrets that She keeps in Arinna—far from the light of Her holy being.

As if to tantalize, a tablet written in Her honour, left in Hattusas, tells us that She was all, reciting from its markings in baked clay:

Thou Sun Goddess of Arinna
art most highly honoured.
Thy name is highest among names,
Thy divinity greater than all other deities.
Compared to Thee there is no other deity
as honoured or exalted
for it is Thee who is sovereign over all,
controlling all rulership
both in heaven and upon earth,
settling boundary disputes,
dispensing Thy mercy,
feeling compassion for all
who call upon Thy name.
Thou art the source of all warmth,
parent of the people of every land,
Thy worship most reverently remembered,
Thy righteousness and justice ever present,

even as Thou allottest the other deities their worship,
their rituals, their holy days, their sacrifices,
for they protect the gates of heaven,
respectfully standing to each side
as Thou passeth through each day
in all Thy shining, omnipotent glory.

Some called upon Her as Wurusemu, while others said Her name was Arinitti, and at the city of Tahurpa they remembered Her sacred daughters Hulla and Mezulla, and the youngest Goddess, She who had not yet grown Her breasts of womanhood, Granddaughter Zintuhi. At the yearly Nuntariyashas Festival, Her Tawawannas priestess performed Her rites, remembering with honour and respect the women who had served before her. Sacred images of those women stood upon the altar, golden discs haloing the heads of those who had once performed Her rites, each a High Priestess of the Sun Goddess at Her Tahurpa altar, each a queen of the Land of Hatti—women who had once guided the land, carrying out Her rules and wishes. Thus Her Tawawannas priestess dedicated a perfect lamb to each, calling upon each ancient High Priestess name, paying respect and honour to each who had joined the Sun Goddess in Her home in the heavens—then known as Sun Goddess themselves: Sun Goddess Walanni, Sun Goddess Nikalmati, Sun Goddess Asmun Nikal, Sun Goddess Dudu Hepa, Sun Goddess Henti, and Sun Goddess Tawawannas, said to be a most ancient High Priestess of the shrine at Tahurpa and a long remembered Queen of the Land of Hatti.

HEPAT

At Anatolian sites in the southeast, some quite close to the Euphrates as it runs through northern Syria, the Goddess was known as Hepat, Hepa, Hebat, Hebatu, Kubebe, and Kupapa. The prayer from Boghazkoy (ancient Hattusas) included here, written at about 1300 B.C., by Queen Pudu Hepat of Hattusas, reveals the queen's opinion that Hepat was the same deity as the Sun Goddess of Arinna. As a former worshipper of the Goddess as Hepat, there may have been some poltical intent in pointing out the connection, but it could hardly have been done if the reverence for the Goddess in each area had been for quite different images or attributes. The records of Hattusas reveal that Pudu Hepat took an important part in state and governmental affairs throughout her life.

Long revered at Aleppo and Samuha, shrines where Ishtar was sometimes said to live, Mother Hepat stands upon Her lioness on the great rock carvings of the mountain pass at Yazilikaya. Her tall cylindrical crown and long straight robes that touch Her shoes declare Her divine dignity, as the double circle symbol of deity grows from the blossoming flower that She holds in Her extended hand. There She has stood for many thousands of years, Her priestesses standing in close attendance behind the mighty Anatolian Mother.

When the princess of the city of Comana of the Taurus Mountains came to live as queen in Hittite Hattusas, young Pudu Hepat spoke her prayers, and then left them carved in stone for all to see, thus explaining that the holy Hepat glowed with the brilliance of Arinna's sovereign Queen of Heaven and Earth:

Sun Goddess of Arinna,
Mistress of the lands of Hatti,
Sovereign Queen of Heaven and Earth,
I, Pudu Hepat, have always been Thy servant,
a heifer of Thy stable since my childhood,
a strong cornerstone on which Thou can depend,
for Thou art the highest,
the most exalted of deities
and though all other deities bow down to Thee,
no mortal appeals to Thee in vain.
Sun Goddess of Arinna,
Queen and Ruler of all lands,
in the city of Hattusas
Thou art called upon as Sun Goddess of Arinna,
yet in the far country, that from which I come,
that which Thou created as The Land of Cedars,
I called upon Thee there as Hepat,
Mother of Deities.

HANNA HANNA

Hanna Hanna was the name of the Divine Ancestress, as known by a Hattian group called the Gulsas. This Hattian account also includes mention of other deities, such as Kamrusepa who presided over magic and healing, and the sisters Istustaya and Papaya who spun the threads of the future (perhaps the source of the Greek image of The Fates). The relationship, of the The Bee to Hanna Hanna, raises questions about possible links between this Hattian imagery and the title of the priestesses who served the Goddess as Kybele, Artemis, and Demeter—each known as Mellissae—Bees. The symbolic association of the Goddess, as Queen Bee, may well be the source of this imagery, as well as the symbolism intended in the depictions of Artemis surrounded by bees—on gold jewellry discovered at Camirus on the island of Rhodes. The symbolism of the evergreen tree, to invoke new growth and abundance, may offer some insight into the Winter Solstice tree later used in Europe, eventually incorporated into Christianity as the Christmas tree.

$\mathbf{H}$oly Grandmother who brought life, Hanna Hanna, Goddess of all, guided Istustaya and Papaya who spin the thread of destiny for those who dwell on earth, as they sit by the spindle of fate, as they sit by the waterbowls of reflection, forming all future events. Hanna Hanna guided the gentle Kamrusepa, She who had the knowledge of the healing and thus could free those who were bound by the demons of illness. Grandmother Hanna Hanna, oldest and wisest of all, guided each of Her divine children as they carried out Her wishes.

To Her grandson, Hanna Hanna assigned the work of bringing the rains, of stirring up the storms, so that the fields of barley and emmer, so that the fields of peas and beans, so that the orchards of pomegranate and olive which grew on both sides of the Marassan-tiya River, might provide Her people with ease and abundance. Thus Zaskhapuna gained the office of he who makes storms, so that his angry outbursts might be harnessed into watering the crops. Then trusting that each chore would be done, by one or another of Her great and holy family, Hanna Hanna rested in Her home, as a grandmother might well deserve to do.

But there came a time when all was not well. Hot steam fogged the window openings. Homes filled with the smoke of logs that would not burn in the hearth. Though seeded with barley and emmer, the fields lay barren; even the trees of the mountains dried and died. No new saplings took their place. Wells and brooks no longer offered water. Thirsty cows and ewes rejected their own young, refusing to bring forth calf or lamb even when their bellies had seemed filled with life. But none of this was noticed by Zaskhapuna until he found that his own throat was dry, and then realizing that something was wrong, he laid the blame on Telipinu; he laid the blame on his own son.

Zaskhapuna complained, 'I appointed my son to do my work so that I might relax and feast in heaven. I gave him the lightning and the thunder. I gave him the clouds and the vessels of rainwater, but now he is not even to be found.' So it was that swift Eagle was sent out, the sharp eyed bird sent to find the youth to bring him back to do the work of his father. Eagle flew over the highest of mountains. Eagle swooped over the lowest of valleys, gliding slowly to see what could be seen. Even over the broad sea, Eagle hunted, but when Eagle returned to Zaskhapuna, no trace of the lad had been found and the world remained dry and thirsty.

Zaskhapuna went to his father. 'Is this my fault', he asked, 'that even the seeds in the field have perished in the drought? My son, your grandson, has not done the work. Whose fault is this?' Zaskhapuna challenged, hoping for a word of solace, a confirmation of his own innocence in the matter. But the weight of responsibility was laid firmly in his hands. For when his father heard what had happened, he replied, 'It is your fault. You alone must carry the blame for passing the work on to your son, when it was yours to do. If great damage has been done, it is your life that shall be taken.' So saying Zaskhapuna's father ordered Zaskhapuna to search for Telipinu, suggesting that his life might still be spared—if Telipinu could be found in time.

In despair for his very life, Zaskhapuna then went to the highest heaven, the place where Hanna Hanna lived, went to seek the advice of The Grandmother, She who possessed wisdom beyond wisdom—She who could solve problems that Her children did not even understand. Standing before Her, Zaskhapuna began to weep. Through his tears he spoke, hoping for the sympathy that his own father had not given. 'I left Telipinu to do my work', he explained, 'and he disappeared from view. But when I went to my father and told him of the problem, he claimed that it was my fault and that my life will be taken, if Telipinu is not soon found. What shall I do, Grandmother Hanna Hanna? I beg for your help.' And with these words, the man of violent, stormy temper once again lost his voice with weeping.

Hanna Hanna rose from Her resting place and looked at the frightened Zaskhapuna, knowing that he was old enough to have a grown son of his own; still She looked upon him as a child. Thus She reassured him that he need not fear, that She would handle the matter, that She would find the hiding place of Telipinu and return him to his post. Whether Zaskhapuna had done right or wrong, Hanna Hanna would help.

Even at these patiently forgiving words of reassurance, Zaskhapuna's mind was filled with doubts. 'How can you find him when I have already sent the swift and sharp eyed Eagle, the bird that goes everywhere and sees all, for Eagle says that Telipinu is nowhere to be found?' With grandmotherly calm, Hanna Hanna explained that She would send the Bee, dispatch Her sacred messenger, and that Bee would find the lad that Eagle could not find. 'But Eagle is strong', cried Zaskhapuna, 'Eagle's eyes are clear. A bee is weak. Its wings are small. How could it accomplish what even Eagle could not do?' Now irritated at his doubts, Hanna Hanna ordered Zaskhapuna to be silent, to hold his tongue so that Her thoughts would be free to arrange the search for the missing Telipinu.

Thus Hanna Hanna sent the sacred Bee, and it was not long before Bee caught sight of Telipinu fast asleep beneath a tree in a forest near the town of Lihzina. Following the instructions of Hanna Hanna, Bee stung the sleeping lad upon his fingers, sent its burning sting into his toes, so that Telipinu awoke in a frenzy. As he hopped about the forest in discomfort, Bee flew back to fetch Eagle, leading the large bird to the grove where Telipinu had been hiding. Following the sacred Bee, Eagle carried Telipinu back to Hanna Hanna.

Kamrusepa had been summoned to the temple. She who did the healing work of Hanna Hanna stood over the confused youth, soothing his still burning skin with seeds of grape and fig stirred into a bowl of cream and honey. Kamrusepa calmed the moaning Telipinu and called for the torches to be lit, saying that all confusion should now pass, saying that all angers should now be forgotten. And standing by the torches, Kamrusepa spoke these words:

The seven doors of heaven have been unbolted.
The seven doors to the Otherworld are open.
Behind each door is a cauldron of bronze.
Upon each cauldron is a handle of iron.

197

Lifted from each cauldron is the lid of aburu metal.
Let all anger and confusion fall into the cauldrons.
Let it not return.

So chanted Kamrusepa softly and with the last of Her words,
She ordered that the torches be extinguished. Anger and confusion
were safely in the cauldrons, forever deposited in the Otherworld,
from which there was no escape. So it was that despair was raised to
joy, as a feast of twelve rams appeared upon the table of the temple.
A tall evergreen was set in place in the courtyard of the holiest of
shrines. Upon the tree was hung the fleece of the ram; inside the
fleece was sewn the fat of meat; inside the fleece were sewn the seeds
of wheat; inside the fleece were sewn the seeds of grape; inside the
fleece were sewn the prayers for abundance, for days of health and
vigour. So it came to pass that Hanna Hanna presided at the table
of Her family of deities, once again knowing peace and satisfaction.

KYBELE

The numerous and varied associations of the Goddess as Kybele (Cybele),
with earlier Goddess names and images of Anatolia, suggest many possi-
bilities in considering the origins of the worship of Kybele. Her hat and
robe are not unlike those shown in carvings of Hepat, while the name
Kybele may be related to the southeastern Anatolian worship of Kubebe.
The sacred stories and rituals, most closely associated with Kybele, reveal
close connections with the Goddess in Mesopotamia as Ishtar and Inanna
(see Sumerian and Semitic Sections). This is most evident in the rituals
concerned with the death of Attis and the attendant eunuchs. Her title, as
Mother of Mt. Ida, may reveal some links with Crete, or may simply refer
to the Mt. Ida near Troy. The worship of the Goddess as Kybele, at times
geographically overlapped with the worship of Lato, and the title Mother
of Deities, may indicate some connection between the worship of Kybele
and Lato. Yet we should keep in mind that Kybele was never represented as
having a daughter, but most closely connected with the dying son, Attis.
    According to the accounts of Lucretius, the import of the sacred stone,
the worship, and the rituals, of Kybele into Rome, occurred shortly after
the Metaurus battle of the Roman war with Carthage, and was done to

carry out a decree of the prophetic Sibyls [There may well be a link between the name Kybele (softened to Cybele—as Kyprus became Cyprus) and the title of the oracular priestesses known as Sibyls.] The great Roman Spring Festival for Kybele, the Megalesia, was celebrated at least as late as 50 A.D., its title eventually changed to the Hilarion, the predecessor of the rituals we know as Easter. Inscriptions, believed to be from the Roman temple of Kybele, were unearthed when workers were repairing the Basilica of St. Peter's in 1608 A.D., suggesting the proximity of the great Kybele temple, that housed the sacred black stone, to the area now known as the Vatican.

Across the lands of Anatolia, at Pessinus and Priene, at Kohnus and Kios, at Malatya and Bandirma, at Carchemish and Yarre, at Aizanoi and Marrash, at Gavurkales and at Fraktin, and at the two Comanas, statues of the Magna Mater were called upon as Kybele. Mother of Deities, She sat upon Her throne, sacred cymbal in Her hand, flanked by lions in faithful attendance—Her great and guiding spirit watching over all.

Kybele was the Mother Lioness, riding proudly astride a lion's back or sitting upon Her lioness throne, while Her priestesses rode in splendid chariot, drawn by lions in the holy day procession. Yet was She not also the Queen Bee, mightier than any other, Her Bee Priestesses known as Mellissae, while the honey of the bee was used in sacred ritual, and bees especially protected by law in the land of Anatolia. Upon Her perfect head She wore the high cylindrical crown of Hepat, or the turret crown of city walls, revealing Her as the protector of all who dwelled within. Still, She was called upon as Mother of Mount Ida, sacred mountain name, known so well upon the islands of Crete and Cyprus, while the Anatolian Ida rose high into the heavens, close by ancient Troy, its peak visible from the offshore isle of Lesbos.

Eunuchs gathered about Her by the thousands, anxious to shed their maleness to wear the robes of Kybele's clergy, Galli trying to gain the image of Kybele's son lover, thus imitating the castrated body of Attis to declare their dedication to The Mother. Priestesses took lovers from among the strangers who came to pray from field or far off town, their children honoured more than those that had come from contract marriage—for did Strabo not write that an unwed mother in Anatolia was she who was closest to Kybele?

Various were the legends of Her son and lover Attis, youthful shepherd who played upon his flute as he cared for the grazing sheep. Although some tell the tale of Nana who ate the fruit of the pomegranate, and in this way gave birth to Attis; others say that he was the child of Kybele. And stories abound of how he died, tending his flock in the meadow, pierced through by a wild boar, or attacked by the monster Agdistus who tried to force itself upon him, and in the revulsion that Attis felt, Attis tore the genitals from his own body. Still others say that Attis, in fear of being unfaithful to the Mighty Mother, cut the maleness from his own body, thus bleeding to death beneath an evergreen tree, as violets sprang from the ground where his blood had spilled. Yet all agree that Kybele had found his lifeless body and wrapped it in the woollen mourning bands, taking the emasculated body, and the tree upon whose roots the lad had fallen, to the mountain cave in which She lived. Planting the tree by the entrance to the cave, burying his body in the earth beneath, each year at the time of his tragic death She performed the rituals of mourning at the site of burial—each year as the spring time came lamenting the dead shepherd youth.

It was this ancient Anatolian ritual that found its way to Rome. After twelve long years of the Roman war with Carthage, Sibyl priestesses, who gave the oracles of prophetic wisdom and decree, announced that the sacred stone of Kybele—the small black meteorite mentioned in the Sibylline Books, the holy heaven rock of Goddess then housed in the shrine of Anatolian Pessinus—must be brought to Rome, and a temple built to house its sacred essence, in honour of the mighty Kybele.

Thus the ship, carrying this sacred icon, made its way from the western coast of Anatolia to the mouth of the River Tiber. When it grounded there upon the rocks, and none could loose it to continue on its journey, though many sailors tried, the woman Claudia Quinta gently pulled upon its ropes, which she tied to the girdle about her waist, and easily brought it back upon the waters—to pass the rope to relay groups of women, who, each in turn, pulled the ship, carrying the sacred stone, to Rome.

On the fourth day of April, two hundred and four years before the time of Christ, Kybele's stone was placed in the Temple of Victory, on the ancient Palatine of Rome. That summer brought not only the most bountiful of harvests, but the final retreat of the enemy. On the tenth day of April, thirteen years later to the month, the great new temple had been built, and dedicated to Kybele as Matris Magnae Idaea, Great Mother of Mount Ida—as the marble walls glistened in the sunlight of springtime in Rome.

Each year following, as spring began in Rome, it was the time of the sacred Megalesia, the celebration of the Vernal Equinox, when the silver image of Kybele was carried in a chariot, drawn by lions through the city, followed by those who had come with Her from Pessinus. It was these followers who taught the Romans to cut down the sacred pine, and to wrap it in the mourning bands, hanging an effigy of Attis upon its branches, in memory of the time that Kybele had found the youthful shepherd when he lay dead beneath a tree in Anatolia. So it was that these sacramental symbols of tree, and image of Attis, were carried in solemn springtime procession to the temple of Kybele in Rome.

Around the temple doors stood those who lamented for the dying Attis, forbidden to eat of the pomegranate, while eunuch attendants wore pomegranates wound about their heads, or carried them in their hands. Male initiates joined in sacred dancing, cutting themselves in sympathetic sorrow. It was at this time that many dedicated themselves to the service of Kybele, by removing their organs of maleness—in imitation of Attis, the son lover of the Mother of Deities. Three days of sacred dancing passed; three days of solemn lamentation passed—as the blood of castrations seeped deep into the ground, some say, for penitence and for the sins of those who had offended the Goddess law. At the end of the third day, a light shone forth from deep within the temple tomb, where the effigy of Attis had been buried, and Kybele's son lover rose from the dead to great feasting and celebration—as those who worshipped Kybele cried out:

"Be of good cheer, neophytes, for Attis has been saved and so shall we in turn be saved."

The newly dedicated followers, those who had eaten no bread in deference to the memory of the broken body of Attis, those who had smeared their blood as sacrifice upon the altars and the trees, then carried the silver statue of Kybele in joyous parade about the city, until the long procession stopped at the banks of the River Tiber. There they bathed the image of Kybele, even bathing the chariot wagon in which She had been carried, adorning both with violets, before returning sacred image and wagon to the Roman temple of Mother Kybele—until spring would come again.

The worship of the Anatolian Mother, who some came to call upon as Kybele Rhea, thus honouring the name of the mother of Zeus, continued until a fire destroyed the temple. But when the temple was once again restored, Augustus, Emperor of Rome, ignoring those who condemned the rituals, joined in the Megalesia, declaring its importance in the city of Rome. And Roman Emperor Claudius, some fifty years after the birth of Christ, also joined in the rituals of the Megalesia, to lament the dead son Attis whose image hung upon the tree, and to pay honour to the mighty Anatolian Mother of Deities, Ma Kybele, Ma Rhea of Rome.

LATO

The information about the Goddess as Lato (Leto), most often regarded as a Goddess image of Greece, is not plentiful among the Greek records, but emerges more clearly in the evidence from Crete and Anatolia. Lato's name, generally believed to be derived from Lat (Elat, Allat)—a title that literally meant Goddess in Syria, Canaan, and Arabia—suggests that the name of Lato may have been carried to Crete from the Levantine coast, thus reaching the western areas of Anatolia by way of Crete. It was probably in this area of Anatolia that Hellenic Greeks first found the name of Lato, long remembering that She was the Mother of Artemis (see Greek Section). Later known by the Romans as Latona, Lato may be the source of the name of the area of Italy known as Latium, tradition often mentioning Troy of northwestern Anatolia as the origins of early settlers of Rome. Thus it may be, that from the ancient Lat of Canaan, the name of the language known as Latin was derived.

How shall we know Lato best, for Her name appears in many ancient lands, in Canaan, Arabia, Sinai, Egypt, Malta and Crete, but on the western coast of Anatolia, where Amazons once rode their noble steeds, echoes of Her image ride with the warrior women. Although Hellenic Greeks pretended that Lato was but a passing fancy of Olympian Zeus, still they spoke of Lato as the mother of the moon and the sun, and said that Her daughter Artemis, Holy One of the Anatolian Ephesus shrine that Amazons had founded, roamed free and independent in the forests—as Amazons were said to do.

How shall we know Lato best? As Ilat, Allat or Allatu, Great Mother of Arabia, who was known as the sun that gives the light of day? As the Great Goddess whose massive images lie upon the island of Malta, island that was once known as Ma Lata? As Lat, Elat, or Elath—of Ugarit, Sidon and Tyre, Holy Mother of the Sea, Goddess of northern Canaanite lands who was called upon as Mother of Deities—in the Levantine lands that came to be known as Latakia?

As Ba'Alat Ashtart of Canaan's Byblos temple, where Egyptian Isis travelled to find the body of Osiris, close by the lake at Aphaca where the Goddess was said to have arrived as a fiery falling star? As Ba'Alat of Serabit El Khadim, revered upon the sands of Sinai, remembered there in prayers inscribed to Ba'Alat as—The Ancient Serpent Lady? Perhaps even as primeval Cobra Goddess Ua Zit, predynastic Goddess of the marshes of ancient Buto, living there among the waz reeds and the lotus—on the ever floating island, where the Egyptian shrine of prophetic wisdom was later known as the holy place of Lato? As ancient Serpent Mother whose priestesses, entwined with serpents, called upon Her in the caverns of Crete, where double axes made of gold were kept as votive relics of The Mother? As Eilythia, Holy One of childbirth and destiny, who received offerings of honey at Cretan Knossos, and was honoured with small but sacred gifts at the Cretan coastal cave of Amnissos, where they say Odysseus once harboured—while Cretan people long remembered ancient Hellotia rites?

High upon Cretan hills, set between two rising swells of green, ruins of Lato's temple still mark the site where inscriptions to Her as Eilythia were left within the sacred precinct, as silent reminder of the Mother's many natures. Oaths were sworn upon Her name, invocations of The Mistress of Destiny, while some say that it was Eilythia/Lato who made the decisions for the future and gave them to the Triple Fates, just as Goddess Themis was said to do—while the village nearby the temple ruins bears the name of Lato to this day.

Greek Hesiod wrote that Lato was a Titaness, a daughter of Phoebe, the one who is said to have given the Goddess shrine of Delphi to Apollo, Hellenic Greeks pretending that the murder of Delphi's serpent by Apollo had been done to protect his mother Lato. But once the gruesome murder had been enacted, it was not to Lato that Apollo gave the shrine—but kept it for his own from that time on. Hellenic Greeks also claimed that it was on the rocky isle of Delos that Lato had pressed fleet footed Artemis from Her womb, saying that Artemis could be seen in the moon, but adding that a twin, a second born, had been the sun Apollo—though Arabian Allat had long brightened the day.

As if to further confuse memories of ancient times, and to erase the awesome omnipotence of ancient Lat, Elat, or Elath, Hellenic Greeks claimed that Eilythia had served as midwife to Lato, while at the same time claiming that newborn Artemis had aided in Apollo's birth. And, in the middle of the muddle they had made, Hellenic Greeks then said that Artemis *was* Eilythia, while some vaguely hinted at memories that Apollo had come from the land of the northern Hyperborean winds.

But Ephesians of Anatolia claimed that Mother Lato had felt the pangs of labour in the cavern at the foot of a great mountain, not far from the site of sacred Ephesus, and that it was there that Lato brought forth Her fleet footed Daughter Artemis. Thus the shrine of Ephesus had been built close by this most sacred site. Long known as the holy place of Artemis, and as a shrine first founded by Amazons, Ephesus was said to have been built around a holy tree, a xoanan, while Callimachus wrote that the image first revered was that of the Mother of Deities, thus singing of Ephesus:

A long time ago,
the warrior Amazons
set up an image
of The Mother of Deities
under the shade of a great tree
and there Queen Hippolyta offered sacrifice,
while Amazons danced an armed dance,
the shield dance of the sacred rattles,
beating time upon the ground in unison,
as syrinx flutes sang their songs.

Although they later spoke of Ephesus as the holy place of Artemis, they called upon Her as Mother, and Queen Bee; Mellissae Bee Priestesses serving at Her altar, images of golden bees held in deepest sanctity, while Megabyzi eunuchs stood by in attendance.

Not far from holy Ephesus stood the ancient shrine of Beycesultan, its double altars adorned with sacred horns, mirroring those known so well on Crete, altars perhaps dedicated to the worship of the Mother and the Daughter—while at nearby Anatolian Latakia, and at sacred Anatolian Hierapolis, priestesses took the name of Lato. It was in Latakia and Hierapolis that the great Latoia Festival was celebrated, as Cretan people had celebrated the Hellotia. But Anatolian Latakians claimed that *they* possessed the most ancient of ancient statues of The Mother of Deities!

Was it chance, or was it ancient memory, that laid the foundations of the Goddess shrine at Latakia not far from the most ancient site at Hacilar? Though probably buried deep beneath the earth, for thousands of years before the builders of Latakia arrived, there in the ruins at Hacilar lay the statues of the Mother and the Daughter, woman with braided bun, maiden with pigtails. Had one been found by the priestesses of Latakia, or were all the statues of Hacilar seeing only the darkness of millenia of settled earth, through their obsidian eyes? Yet Lato and Artemis were known not far from that most ancient site, where the Mother and the Daughter had been known some eight thousand years ago.

Even closer by the Ephesian shrine, yet another temple was built for the daughter of Lato, at the town of Magnesia. And upon the outer walls of the Magnesia temple were carved images of Amazons in battle, images that perhaps revealed the nature of Lato and Her Daughter Artemis—just as images ordered carved by Artemisia, Queen of Halicarnassos on the Lycian coast, were massive stone reflections of the valiant women warriors, those who may once have honoured Lato as the Mother of fleet footed Artemis, as Mother of Deities. And is it Lato's name that is remembered in that which is hidden—latere; in that which is worshipping—latreia; in that which lets life come forth—latus; in that which signifies that life returns to death—lethe; in that which is revered beyond all other reverence—laud; in that which means The Sacred Mother Lord—The Lady?

One of the seven wonders of the world, the site of Ephesus, where prayer to The Cretan Lady of Ephesus was to The Bearer of Light, was spoken of in Roman times as the holy place of Diana, She who was the Protector of Animals, glowing in the moonlight, as Artemis, daughter of Lato, had been known.

Yet it was this most sanctified of places, the holy site of Ephesus, the shrine first founded by Amazons, that Paul chose to visit when Romans ruled, causing silversmith Demetrius to cry:

The sanctuary of the great goddess Diana
will cease to command respect
and then it will not be long
before she who is worshipped by all Asia
and the civilized world
will be brought down
from her divine pre-eminence. (Acts 19:27)

Thus Ephesians shouted at Paul's approaching steps, 'Great is Diana of the Ephesians!' But all that they had feared, finally came to pass, as the ancient shrine at Ephesus was all but forgotten, and people learned to call upon a father and a son, forgetting the ancient Mother and Daughter who had been called upon for so long, in the land of Anatolia.

HECATE

Though known in Greece, the Goddess as Hecate is most familar to us from the western Anatolian coastal areas, and the island of Samothrace, both areas associated with Amazons. The worship of Hecate was known as far north as Colchis, on the eastern end of the Black Sea, the area in which Euripedes placed Medea as a princess and priestess of Hecate. Apollonius mentioned Colchis as an area in which Amazons venerated a sacred black stone. Though the connections are not certain, the Goddess as Heqit (Hekat) was worshipped in Egypt, known to Egyptians as a Goddess that was from Nubia and the northern Sudan. The appearance of Hecate's altars in Colchis is especially interesting, in that Herodotus described the Colchians as having originally come from Egypt. As a Goddess of witches and magic, the name of Hecate is associated with the 'dark side of the moon', in a sense a mirror image of Artemis, especially as Artemis Lycia, Artemis of the Light. At times Hecate is associated with the Greek Persephone, as Queen of the Dead, perhaps explaining why both names were linked with the sacred island of Samothrace.

Mother of the Heka, the magical power of the Word, She who holds the moon's magnetic reins on ancient magic spells, was known first in the Nubian tongue. Sacred Goddess Heqit, Ancient Goddess Hekat, Oldest of the Old, amphibian being that swims in the water, yet walks upon the dry land, was the magical essence of

even as the wind was sleeping

Isis, She whom all of Egypt called upon, summoning Her from the land of Africa to do Her wondrous works—for the emanations of the Heh Ka, the mighty energies of a million hearts, are contained within Her. Holy Enchantress, Mother who brings birth and rebirth, forever renews the cycle of existence—as the frog brings forth the tadpole, as the tadpole turns to frog, so Hekat guides the transformations, giving power to the spoken word of sacred incantation.

Those who knew Her powers and Her secrets carried them to Lycia, and Lydia, and Caria, even as far as the land of Colchis on the Black Sea's eastern coast, where mighty sorceror Medea—she who may have given her name to the Median lands of Persia, for some say she taught her magic to the Persian Magi—once kneeled before Hecate's altar at Her Colchis shrine. And though far from the land of the Nile, Herodotus explained that it was in Colchis that Egyptians dwelled. And there remembering Egyptian ways, the amulets of leather, of papyrus, of stone and wood, marked with the words of power; figures moulded from the wax of honeycomb; power filled potions of date wine and honey, they carefully recited incantations—protecting, defending, even weakening, the one whose secret name they spoke.

And was it not on the coast of Colchis that Amazons had venerated the sacred black stone, at a temple on a small coastal island, or so Apollonius said. And on the holy island of Samothrace, sacred to the Amazons, Hecate's name was called upon in Her Zerynthian Cave, where dogs were most sacred to Her. Was this in ancient memory of the Dog Star, the one spoken of as Sept in Egypt, the one spoken of as Sirius in Greece, the one that was sacred to Isis when She was called upon by Her true Egyptian name of Au Sept? Or was Hecate but another name for Artemis, called upon when the moon was gone—for Samothracian Mysteries were wound about the Daughter's descent into death, and Her ever recurring return to life.

Those who later called upon the magic of Hecate, spoke Her name in the woods of Thessaly and Greece, as magician and wizard, sorcerer and witch, followed Her ancient knowledge. There they used the sacred cauldron at the threefold crossroads, in the darkness of a moonless night, adding wine or milk or blood in which to stir the sacred herbs, only those that had grown by moonlight, adding sacred stones from the East, using the olive or the willow twig to stir the contents of the bubbling, boiling cauldron—as those who called upon Hecate circled thrice about Her altar, laying flaming twigs upon it.

Even as the wind was sleeping, as were all the others of the village, the magic women of Hecate addressed themselves to each planet of the sky, to each watching star in the heavens that grew brighter as they spoke, listening to the hounds that bayed their knowledge of Her holy presence. And when the chariot of Hecate descended to take them to unknown regions, it was drawn by winged serpents who carried them across the vast heavens of night, as they called upon the Holy One who comes and goes as Artemis, as Diana, as Cynthia, as Selene—as Hecate, The Hidden One, Mighty Queen of Witches, Mother of the ancient Heka magic.

ANAHITA

The adoption of the Goddess into later Iranian beliefs was probably the result of influence from Anatolia, and to some extent from Iraq (Mesopotamia). This particular account is based upon a hymn from an Iranian Yast (Hymnal) that may have been written as late as the fourth century A.D. The combination of Anahita's role, as one who watches over the universe, along with the statement that the male Ahura Mazda assigned this task to Her, is probably the result of foreign concepts of Goddess reverence being incorporated into the male-oriented religious structure of the Indo-Iranians. Tribes of Indo-European speaking peoples are believed to have entered Iran, from the Kirghiz Steppes area of Russia, possibly as early as the fourth millenium B.C. Linguistic connections reveal that the Iranians were related to the Indo-Aryans who conquered the towns of the Indus Valley of India at about 1500 B.C. To a lesser extent, the Iranians were also linguistically related to the Indo-European speaking people who conquered the Hattians and Hurrians of Anatolia.

To the followers of holy Anait, whose worship was renowned across the northern stretches of Anatolia, and in Armenian lands, Medes and Achaemenids spread their empires, thus bringing the worship of the Goddess back with them into the land of Iran. Calling upon Her as Aredevi Sura Anahita, or as Nana whose name was sometimes given as the mother of Attis—even as Creator Nana had been known in ancient Sumer—Iranians claimed that it was Ahura Mazda who assigned to Anahita the task of watching over the universe.

Yet do they not say that it is Anahita who is the Cosmic Ocean in which the stars do float, and Anahita who provides the rain, sending waters from heaven to the springs and rivers, protecting the flocks in the pastures, causing them to bear their young—as it is Anahita who fills the womb with life? How glorious She is as She rides across the heavens, Her chariot drawn by four white steeds named wind and rain and clouds and sleet, or as She rides on the back of a gliding eagle, or even upon a lion. Yet the wings of the eagle grow from Her own shoulders, as the eight pointed crown sits upon Her head, as golden as the eight petalled star of Ishtar—one hundred small stars shining upon it.

Thus in Sardis and in Susa, in Kangawar and Ecbatana, revelations of Anahita's holiness were inscribed to the Mother of Wisdom, Protector of Humanity, while at Istakhr, famed Persepolis, the eternal flame burned within Her shrine, and the words beneath Her image read:

I AM THE CONSCIENCE OF THINE OWN SELF.

RITUALS AND COMMEMORATIONS YOU MAY WANT TO REMEMBER (from Vol. I)

The ritual for menarche—see Mu Olokukurtilisop/Native Americans of Mexico, Central and South America.

The ritual for the joining of the twin spirits within the Goddess—see Kunapipi/Oceanic Section

The rituals for the grain and corn, growing and harvesting—see Chicomecoatl/Native Americans of Mexico, Central and South America.

The commemoration and thanksgiving for water on the 21st day of the third moon of the Chinese lunar calendar. See Golden Lotus/Chinese Section.

February 1st (or 2nd)—Imbolc, the Day of Bridget—especially concerned with the birth of lambs. See Celtic Section.

Vernal Equinox—Spring Festival. See Kybele/Anatolian Section; possibly Ashtart/Semitic Section (this last is listed as the first day of Nisan, later celebrated on April 1st.)

April 4—The arrival of the sacred black stone in Rome. See Kybele/Anatolian Section.

May 1st—Celtic Beltane, probably originating from reverence for the Goddess as Beltis, Belit and Ba'Alat. See Ashtart/Semitic Section. Celebrated in honour of the Goddess as Ostara in Germany.

Summer Solstice—See Danu/Celtic Section, and Iamanja/African Section.

August 1st (or 2nd)—Lugnasadh, see Tailltiu in Celtic Section introduction.

Autumnal Equinox—possibly the original Day of the Sheepfolds listed as the 28th day of the month of Tammuz. Tammuz is known as late June and early July on the Hebrew lunar calendar, but also as the month of September in Turkey. This may have been the origin of the Days of Judgement and Atonement still honoured by Hebrew people as the Hebrew New Year. In the Babylonian tablets it was the day to present a golden star and a vulva of lapis lazuli to the Goddess. See Ishtar/Semitic Section. The death of Tiamat recited; see Tiamat/Semitic Section.

November 1st—Samhain, the Celtic New Year, the day of the emergence of all souls. The day that Gwion was said to have been fished out of the waters and reborn as Taliesin after stealing the knowledge of the Goddess Cerridwen. See Cerridwen/Celtic Section.

December 12—The holy day of the Goddess at Tepeyac. See Coatlicue/Native Americans of Mexico, Central and South America.

Winter Solstice—The raising of the evergreen and the prayers for new growth and fertility. See Hanna Hanna/Anatolian Section.

Have you ever wondered why nearly all of the deities regarded as ruling the astrological signs are male? Have you ever wondered why all the named deities are the deities of Classical Greece? Archaeological evidence suggests that the concept of the astral bodies of our solar system affecting character, personality and life's events, probably originated in Babylonia. Egyptian records reveal concern with astrological ideas at about the same time, or shortly afterwards. The list below contains suggestions for a revision of the deities associated with astrological signs. Drawn from various cultures, rather than relying solely on Greek precepts, each image of Goddess, as the ruler of a particular sign, is in keeping with the aspects generally attributed to it, but provides us with a woman view of astrological influences. Reading the full accounts of each of these images of Goddess, the reader may find that these Goddess images offer more insight into each sign than the Greek deities generally designated today.

ARIES	The Morrigan—Celtic (Vol. I)
TAURUS	Hathor/Isis—Egyptian (Vol. II)
GEMINI	Devi (in Her aspects of Parvati and Kali)—India (Vol. II)
CANCER	Ix Chel—Native Americans of Mexico (Vol. I)
LEO	The Sun Goddess of Arinna—Anatolia (Vol. I)
VIRGO	Nu Kwa—Chinese (Vol. I)
LIBRA	Ishtar—Semitic (Vol. I)
SCORPIO	Pele—Oceanic (Vol. I)
SAGITTARIUS	Artemis—Greek (Vol. II)
CAPRICORN	Pakulpota—Native Americans of North America (Vol. II)
AQUARIUS	Mawu—African (Vol. I)
PISCES	Nammu/Nina—Sumerian (Vol. II)

Printed by Capital City Press
Montpelier, Vermont

745

Mistress of the Irkalla   Volume II   Sumer

Volume II of ANCIENT MIRRORS of WOMAN—
HOOD includes our Goddess and Heroine Heritage
from: the Native Americans of North America, Scandinavia, Egypt, India, Japan, Sumer, Greece, The Aegean
and the full bibliography for both volumes.

If you would like to order Volume II, write for information
on availability and prices to: New Sibylline Books, Inc.,
Box 266—Village Station, New York, N.Y. 10014